THE EXPLANATION OF THE HOLY GOSPEL ACCORDING TO MATTHEW

by Blessed Theophylact,
Archbishop of Ochrid and Bulgaria

Translated from the original Greek
by Fr. Christopher Stade

Volume 1 in the series:
Blessed Theophylact's Explanation of the New Testament

Chrysostom Press
St. Herman of Alaska Brotherhood
2020

St. Herman of Alaska Brotherhood
P.O. Box 70
Platina, California, U.S.A.

website: www.sainthermanmonastery.com
email: stherman@stherman.com

Library of Congress Catalog Card No. 93-174571

Softbound: ISBN 0-9635183-1-3

1st printing 1992
2nd printing 1993
3rd printing 1994
4th printing 1997
5th printing 2000
6th printing 2006
7th printing 2008
8th printing 2020

Contents

Contents

Introduction

For nine hundred years one of the most beloved and widely read Scriptural commentaries among the Orthodox people of Byzantium, Serbia, Bulgaria, Russia, and Greece has been Bl. Theophylact's *Explanation* of the Holy Gospel and Epistles. The comprehensiveness, the patristic authority, and, at the same time, the simplicity of this great work makes it of value to any Christian seeking to understand the meaning of the Gospel preaching.

Here is what Bishop Ignaty Brianchaninov, a renowned spiritual writer and monastic guide of nineteenth century Russia, has to say about this work:

"While reading the evangelists, the novice should also read *The Herald*,[1] that is, the explanation of the Gospel by Blessed Theophylact, Archbishop of Bulgaria. The reading of *The Herald* is indispensable. It is an aid to the right understanding of the Gospel and consequently to the most exact practice of it. Moreover, the rules of the Church require that Scripture should be understood as the holy Fathers explain it, and not at all arbitrarily. By being guided in our understanding of the Gospel by the explanation of the holy Fathers, we keep the tradition of the Holy Church."[2]

Bl. Theophylact's *Explanation* of the New Testament has not been previously translated into any western European language, although he has been known to western scholars of Byzantium since the time of Erasmus. More attention has been given by historians in recent years to his *Letters* which provide an insight into life in the Byzantine empire at the time of the First Crusade. In fact, Bl. Theophylact lived and wrote at a turning point of the history of both the Empire and the whole Christian Church.

He was himself a true son of Byzantium, a product of the highly developed cultural and religious civilization emanating from the "queen of cities", Constantinople. Born on the Greek island of Euboia some time between 1050 and 1060, Theophylact went to Constantinople to study under the finest teachers of literature and rhetoric of his time. He was ordained and served as a hierodeacon assisting the patriarch at Agia

---

[1] *The Herald* [in Russian, *Blagoviestnik*] is the name given to the Slavonic and Russian translations of Bl. Theophylact's commentary.

[2] *The Arena*, Archimandrite Lazarus, tr., Holy Trinity Monastery, Jordanville, N.Y., 1983, p. 21.

Sophia, and soon gained renown as a preacher of the Gospel and a master of rhetoric. The Emperor Alexius I Comnenus made him the tutor of his future son-in-law and heir presumptive.

About the year 1090 Theophylact was sent to the Macedonian city of Ochrid to be enthroned as Archbishop of Bulgaria. Ochrid was the capital city of the Bulgarian kingdom that had been conquered by the Byzantines some sixty years earlier. In this demanding position in a conquered territory on the outskirts of the Empire, Bl. Theophylact conscientiously and energetically carried out his archpastoral duties over the course of the next twenty years or so. Although a Byzantine by upbringing and outlook, he was a true father and archpastor of the Bulgarian Church, defending its interests and protecting its independence and prerogatives. He acted vigorously to protect his flock from the propaganda of the heretical Paulicians and Bogomils by ordaining dedicated and educated priests. He endured many slanderous accusations that were made against him both within the diocese and in Constantinople, but he won the respect and love of the faithful who saw his tireless labors on their behalf. The exact year of his repose is not known, but the latest date that can be ascertained from his letters is 1108. The Serbian Orthodox Church, whose jurisdiction in later years came to include Ochrid and Macedonia, commemorates Bl. Theophylact on December 31.[3]

It is during this period of his life as Archbishop of Bulgaria that he wrote his *Explanation* of the New Testament, at the request of the princess Maria, who was the mother of the imperial boy he had earlier tutored, and who had now become the abbess of a convent. His *Letters* also date to this time, as well as two other writings for which he is well known: *The Life of St. Clement of Ochrid* and a treatise entitled *The Errors of the Latins in Ecclesiastical Matters*. These works highlight two developments of enormous consequence for the history of the Church. The first is the spread of Orthodox Christianity into the Slavic lands; for St. Clement of Ochrid was a disciple of Sts. Cyril and Methodius, and he brought to fruition in Bulgaria the labors begun by his mentors in carrying the Orthodox faith to the Slavs in their own languages. The second is the tragic schism which occurred between the eastern and

---

[3] *The Prologue From Ochrid*, Bp. Nikolai Velimirovic, Lazarica Press, Birmingham, England, 1985, vol. 4, p. 393.

western halves of the Church. Bl. Theophylact wrote his treatise, *The Errors of the Latins*, only some fifty years after the exchange of anathemas between Rome and Constantinople. While firmly defending the Orthodox doctrinal position rejecting the *Filioque*, Bl. Theophylact writes with a tone of moderation rare for his time, urging from both sides a spirit of conciliation concerning matters of local custom.[4]

The contents of Bl. Theophylact's *Explanation* are based entirely on the works of the great Fathers of the early Church, and above all, St. John Chrysostom. Bl. Theophylact employs to perfection the commentary form introduced by St. Photius the Great and known as "links" or "series" (in Greek, *seirai*; in Latin, *catenae*).[5] The inspiration behind this form of commentary is the Orthodox desire, and indeed, commandment, to guard and transmit to future generations the living apostolic tradition of the early Church. Therefore, later commentators and Fathers such as St. Photius and Bl. Theophylact, for each passage of Scripture under consideration, would gather together the explanations and interpretations of the early Fathers. The result is not simply the interpretation of one person, but an expression of the consensus of the mind of the Church, in short, what the Church has believed and taught "at all times and in all places."

But Bl. Theophylact's *Explanation* does not at all read like a list of quotations. What is truly remarkable is that, although the work is wholly derivative from the tradition of the fathers, in it the reader hears but a single voice speaking clearly as a teacher to a disciple.

Mindful of the need for the wealth of Orthodox Scriptural commentary to be accessible in English, we offer this translation of Bl. Theophylact's *Explanation of the Holy Gospel According to St. Matthew*. It is the first volume in a series of what will be, with God's help, a translation of the complete commentaries of Bl. Theophylact on the New Testament, except for the Book of Revelation which he did not include in his own work.

---

[4] The above biographical and bibliographical information is taken from: *Theophylact of Ochrid*, chapter 2 of *Six Byzantine Portraits*, Dimitri Obolensky, Clarendon Press, Oxford, 1988, pp. 34-82; also, the introduction of the Russian translation of Bl. Theophylact's commentary on the Holy Gospel entitled *Blagoviestnik, Tolkovanie na Svyatiya Evangeliya*, Blazh. Feofilakta, Archiep. Bolgarskago, Knigoizdatelstvo P.P. Soikina, S.—Peterburg, [n.d.], reprinted, 1988, by the Australian Diocese of the Russian Orthodox Church Outside of Russia.

[5] *Ekklēsiastikē Istoria*, Arch. Basileios Stephanides, Astir, Athens, 1978, pp. 467-4.

The translation has been made from the original Greek text of Migne, vol. 123 in the series *Patrologia Graeca*, with comparisons made to Slavonic, Russian, and modern Greek translations. The English text of the Gospel itself is for the most part that of the King James Version. Revisions to the King James text have been made according to three criteria. First, a few changes were required in order to agree with the text of the Gospel used by Theophylact himself as printed by Migne, where that differs from the Greek text followed by the translators of the KJV. Second, for the purposes of greater clarity, a few archaic Elizabethan usages have been rendered into more modern English. Third, a few words have been retranslated to reflect Orthodox interpretation and usage. For example, in Chapter 26 of St. Matthew, the New Testament Greek word *Pascha* has been rendered as "Pascha", and not "Passover".

Quotations from the Old Testament used by Bl. Theophylact in his *Explanation* are taken from Sir Lancelot Brenton's translation of the Septuagint.[6] But quotations from the Psalms are taken from the *Psalter* translated by Holy Transfiguration Monastery.[7] For the sake of easier recognition, we have elected to use the form of Hebrew names most familiar to English readers rather than the Greek and Slavonic forms, e.g. Isaiah instead of Esaias, Jeremiah instead of Ieremias, Elijah instead of Elias. In references to the Old Testament we have followed the Septuagint arrangement and numbering of books and chapters. An Old Testament reference within parentheses indicates the arrangements of books as in the King James Version.

Because we intended this work primarily for pious and thoughtful reading of the Holy Scriptures, and only secondarily for academic use, we have kept to an absolute minimum the number of Greek words employed, and indeed footnotes. The Greek words appear in English transcription rather than in Greek script so as to be more recognizable to the general reader, and they are in a form of transcription we deemed most useful to our readers, i.e. no rough breathings, but a primarily alphabetic, rather than phonetic, transcription. Except for a few "scholia" (comments added to the original manuscript by medieval copyists) identified as such, the

---

[6] *The Septuagint with Apocrypha: Greek and English*, Sir Lancelot C.L. Brenton, Samuel Bagster and Sons, London, 1851, reprinted, Zondervan Publishing House, Grand Rapids, Michigan, (1988).

[7] *The Psalter According to the Seventy*, Holy Transfiguration Monastery, Boston, MA, 1987.

footnotes are all the product of the translator and editors of this work. In a few places we have omitted a line or two of Bl. Theophylact's explanation where he defines the meaning of a New Testament Greek word (already clearly translated here into English) in terms of eleventh century Greek. Square brackets within the text of the *Explanation* indicate a clarifying word or phrase added by the translator; text within parentheses is always Bl. Theophylact himself.

Many people have contributed in vital ways to this translation project. The Rt. Rev. Bishop Hilarion, Deputy Secretary of the Synod of Bishops of the Russian Orthodox Church Outside of Russia, first gave guidance and a blessing to choose the work of Bl. Theophylact as a subject for translation. Hieromonk Kallistos, pastor of St. John Chrysostom Church in House Springs, Missouri, has done more than can be expressed in words to open doors for this project, and to give his continuing support. Hieromonk Ioanniky of the Prophet Elias Skete on the Holy Mountain of Athos went over the entire manuscript in great detail, providing extensive comments and revisions on all aspects from theology to punctuation. We pray that God will continue to strengthen and protect him in his monastic struggle. The typesetting of the text was undertaken by Galina and Matthew Hanover as a labor of love. Last, but by no means least, is the "brotherhood" of the Chrysostom Press itself, which has given constant and unflagging aid in bringing this work to completion. Editing, proofing, printing, encouragement and support was always near at hand, thanks most of all to Dr. John Johnstone, Dismas Kriegel, James Smith, and Michael Orlando.

If, despite the efforts of these many individuals, there remain errors and flaws in this translation, there is only myself to blame. Having dared to engage in the task of rendering the Holy Gospel and its Orthodox interpretation from one language and culture into another, I beg God's forgiveness for sin, ignorance, and negligence on my part, and I beg of you, the reader, your prayers and forbearance. Comments, corrections, and inquiries will be gratefully received at:

St. John Chrysostom
Russian Orthodox Church
P.O. Box 536
House Springs, Missouri 63051

Fr. Christopher Stade
June 11/24, 1992
Holy Apostles Bartholomew
and Barnabas

The Life of the Evangelist Matthew According to Sophronius[1]

Matthew, also known as Levi, tax collector turned apostle, was the first to compose the Gospel of Christ, in Judea in the Hebrew language for those of the circumcision who believed. It is unknown by whom it was later translated into Greek. The Hebrew text is preserved to this day in the library of Caesarea that was most diligently assembled by the Martyr Pamphilus. The Nazarenes of Berroia in Syria, who use this text, gave me permission to copy it. From this one is easily convinced that where the evangelist makes use of the testimony of the Old Testament Scriptures, either himself, or in the person of our Lord and Saviour Jesus Christ, he does not follow the authority of the Seventy,[2] but of the Hebrew text. It is from the latter that these two passages come: ''Out of Egypt have I called My Son''[3] and ''He shall be called a Nazarene.''[4]

---

[1] This brief *Life* is traditionally included in the introductory sections of the liturgical Gospels of the Orthodox Church in Greek and Church Slavonic; hence it is included also with the commentaries on the Gospels by Bl. Theophylact. St. Sophronius I was Patriarch of Jerusalem (634-638) and as a patristic writer is also known as Sophronius the Sophist. His extant writings, including liturgical hymns, poetry, accounts of lives and miracles of the saints, and dogmatic works, have been published in Migne's *Patrologia Graeca*, vol. 87, columns 3147-4012. He is also co-author, with John Moschus, of the *Lemonarium*, a classical collection of accounts of the ancient desert fathers.

[2] The authoritative version of the Old Testament used by the Church from apostolic times is that of the Seventy, better known as the Septuagint. This translation of the Hebrew scriptures into Greek was made during the second century before Christ by the most competent Jewish scholars and rabbis of the time. The great majority of the quotations from the Old Testament in the writings of the New Testament are taken directly from the Septuagint, with a few exceptions such as the two noted here. Down to the present day, the Septuagint serves as an essential witness to the pre-Christian Hebrew text and understanding of the Old Testament not only for the Church but for other Biblical scholarship as well.

[3] Mt. 2:15

[4] Mt. 2:23

Preface by Blessed Theophylact

Those divine men who lived before the law were not taught by writings and books, but they had a pure mind and so were enlightened by the radiance of the Holy Spirit. Thus they knew the will of God, and He Himself conversed with them mouth to mouth. Such were Noah, Abraham, Job, and Moses. But when men grew weak and became unworthy to be enlightened and instructed by the Holy Spirit, God Who loves mankind gave the Scriptures so that at least by these means they might be made mindful of the will of God. So also did Christ converse in person with the apostles, and He sent the grace of the Spirit to be their teacher. But after these events heresies would arise and our morals would be corrupted. Therefore it was His good pleasure that the Gospels be written down in order to teach us the truth, so that we would not be drawn away by the falsehood of these heresies, and our morals would not altogether be corrupted. He gave us four Gospels, perhaps because we learn from them the four universal virtues: courage, prudence, righteousness, and self-control. We learn courage when the Lord says, "Fear not them which kill the body, but are not able to kill the soul;"[1] we learn prudence when He exhorts, "Be ye wise therefore as serpents;"[2] we learn righteousness when He teaches, "Therefore all things whatsoever ye would that men should do to you, do ye even so to them;"[3] and we learn self-control when He declares, "Whosoever looketh on a woman to lust after her hath committed adultery with her already in his heart."[4] For another reason are there four Gospels: because these are pillars of the world. As the world is divided into four parts, east, west, north, and south, it was right that there also be four pillars. And for another reason are there four Gospels: because these contain four elements: teachings, commandments, warnings, and promises. To those who believe the teachings and observe the commandments, God promises the good things that are to come. But those who do not believe the teachings and do not keep the commandments, He threatens with the punishments that are to come.

---

[1] Mt. 10.28

[2] Mt. 10:16

[3] Mt. 7:12

[4] Mt. 5:28

It is called "Gospel" because it announces to us things that are good,[5] namely, remission of sins, being counted as righteous, ascent into the heavens, and adoption as sons by God. It also announces that we can receive these things easily. For we ourselves have not labored to obtain these good things, nor have we received them as a result of our own accomplishments, but by God's grace and love for man we have been deemed worthy of such good things.

The Gospel according to St. Matthew.

There are four evangelists; two of them, Matthew and John, were of the company of the twelve, and two, Mark and Luke, were of the seventy. Mark was also a follower and disciple of Peter, and Luke, of Paul. Matthew, then, first wrote the Gospel, in the Hebrew language for the Jews who believed, eight years after Christ's Ascension. Some say that John translated it from the Hebrew language into Greek. Mark wrote his Gospel ten years after the Ascension, instructed by Peter. Luke wrote his Gospel fifteen years after the Ascension, and John the most wise Theologian, thirty two years after the Ascension.

It is said that after the death of the first three evangelists, the three Gospels were brought to John while he yet lived that he might see them and judge if they had been composed according to the truth. When John saw them he fully accepted the grace of the truth in them; and whatever the other evangelists had omitted, he himself completed, and whatever they had touched on briefly, he elaborated in his own Gospel. This was the beginning of theology. Since the other evangelists had not mentioned the existence of God the Word from before the ages, John himself spoke the word of God, that is, theology, concerning this, so that no one would think that God the Word was a mere man, that is, without divinity. For Matthew speaks only of the existence of Christ in the flesh, as he was writing for the Jews for whom it sufficed to learn that Christ was begotten from Abraham and David. A Jew who believes is content to know that Christ is from David.

---

[5] The Greek word for "Gospel," *euangelion*, from which we derive the word "evangelist", consists of two parts, *eu*, "good," and *angelein*, "to announce, proclaim," meaning, therefore, "the proclamation of good things."

You might ask, ''Was not one evangelist enough?'' Listen, then: one was enough, but four were allowed to write so that the truth might be revealed all the more. When you see these four evangelists, not convening in one place, nor sitting down together, but each one in a different place writing about the same things as if with one mouth, do you not marvel at the truth of the Gospel and say that they spoke by the Holy Spirit? And do not say to me that they do not agree in all points. Look at those things in which they do not agree. Does one evangelist say that Christ was born, and another, that He was not? Or one, that He rose, and another, that He did not? Indeed not! For in the things that are crucial and essential, they speak with one voice. Therefore, if they did not diverge in the essential points, why do you marvel if they appear to vary in minor details? It is precisely because they did not agree in every detail that we can see that they present the truth. For if they had agreed in every point it would cause the suspicion that they had sat down and deliberated together to write the Gospels. Instead, what one evangelist has omitted, another has written down, and it is for this reason that they seem to be at variance on some points. This having been said, let us now turn to the text.

THE EXPLANATION

by

BLESSED THEOPHYLACT

of

THE HOLY GOSPEL
ACCORDING TO
ST. MATTHEW

ІС
ХС
О
Ѡ
Н
ГДЬ ВСЕДЕР
ЖИТЕЛЬ

CHAPTER ONE

Concerning the genealogy of Christ.

1. The book of the generation. Why did he not say "vision" or "word" as did the prophets who prefaced their writing in this manner: "The vision which Isaiah saw,"[1] and "The word which came to Isaiah."[2] Do you wish to know why? Because the prophets were speaking to hard-hearted and disobedient people, and therefore they would say, "This is a divine vision," or "This is the word of God," so that the people would be frightened and not disdain what was said. But Matthew was addressing believers who were obedient and of a good disposition, and for this reason he did not begin in the manner of the prophets. I will also add that what the prophets saw, they saw noetically, that is, with their minds, envisioning these things by the Holy Spirit; and this is why they called them "visions". But Matthew did not see Christ noetically, nor did he envision Him in his mind, but he was with Him tangibly and listened to Him with his senses and saw Him in the flesh. Therefore he did not say, "The vision which I saw," but "The book of generation." **Of Jesus.** The name "Jesus" is not Greek but Hebrew, meaning "Saviour", for *Iao* is the Hebrew word for "salvation".[3] **Christ.** The Hebrew kings and priests were called "christs" [i.e. "anointed ones"], because they were anointed with the holy oil poured out from a horn held over the head. The Lord, therefore, is called Christ, both as King because He ruled over sin, and as Priest because He offered Himself as a sacrifice for us. He Himself was pre-eminently anointed with the true oil, the Holy Spirit; for who else possessed the Spirit as did the Lord? In the saints, the grace of the Holy Spirit was at work, but in Christ it was not the grace of the Spirit at work, but rather Christ being of one essence with the Spirit worked the miracles. **The Son of David.** Since Matthew had said "Jesus", he added "the Son of David", so that you would not think he

---

[1] Is. 1:1

[2] Is. 2:1

[3] *Iao* is a Greek transliteration of the Hebrew word.

was speaking of the other Jesus [i.e. Joshua];[4] for there was another renowned Jesus, who became commander after Moses, but he was called "son of Nave",[5] and not "son of David". For he preceded David by many generations and was not of the tribe of Judah, from which David was descended, but of another. **The son of Abraham.** Why did he place David before Abraham? He did so because to the Jews David had greater renown, both because he was more recent than Abraham and because he was more illustrious on account of his kingdom. For of the kings, David was the first to please God, and he received the promise from God that the Christ would arise from his seed. For this reason all men called Christ "the Son of David". And indeed David was also a symbolic type of Christ; for just as David ruled after Saul, that outcast from God who was rejected, so too Christ came in the flesh to reign over us after Adam had been deprived of the kingship and the dominion which he had over all things, both animals and demons.

2. Abraham begat Isaac. Matthew begins the genealogy with Abraham because he was the father of the Hebrews, and because he first received the promises that in his seed all the nations would be blessed.[6] Therefore it is fitting that he should give the genealogy of Christ beginning with Abraham, for the seed of Abraham is Christ by Whom all we nations have been blessed who were formerly cursed. "Abraham" means "father of the nations", and "Isaac", "joy" or "laughter". The evangelist makes no mention of the illegitimate children of Abraham, Ishmael and the others, because the Jews were not descended from them, but from Isaac. **And Isaac begat Jacob, and Jacob begat Judah and his brethren.** You see that he mentioned Judah and his brothers because the twelve tribes were from them.

3. And Judah begat Pharez and Zarah of Tamar. Tamar was the

---

[4] In Greek and in Hebrew "Jesus" and "Joshua" are the same name: *Iēsous* in Greek, *Yeshua'* in Hebrew. There are two forms of the same name in English due to the fact that "Joshua" was taken from the Hebrew, not the Greek (Septuagint), text of the Old Testament, while "Jesus", of course, was taken from the Greek of the New Testament.

[5] i.e. son of Nun

[6] Gen. 22:18

daughter-in-law of Judah, the wife of his son Er.[7] When Er died childless, Judah married her to another of his sons, Onan. But when he, too, was cut down from among the living on account of his wickedness, Judah did not marry her to any other of his sons. But she desired to have a child of the seed of Abraham, and so she put off the garments of a widow, dressed as a harlot, came together with her father-in-law, and from him conceived twin boys. As she was giving birth to them, the first child reached its hand out from her womb, as if it would be born first, and at once the mid-wife marked the extended hand of the child with a scarlet thread so as to distinguish the firstborn. But the child drew its hand back into the womb and the other one was born first, followed by the one who had reached out its hand. So the one who was born first was named "Pharez" which means "interruption", for it had interrupted the natural order; and the child which withdrew its hand was named "Zarah". This account indicates a certain mystery. For just as Zarah first showed his hand and then withdrew it, so, too, the life in Christ appeared in those holy ones who lived before the law and circumcision. For all these were not counted as righteous by the observances of the law and the commandments, but by living the evangelic life of the Gospel. Consider Abraham who left his father and his home for God's sake and even denied the order of nature by his willingness to sacrifice Isaac. Consider Job, and Melchizedek. But when the law came, this manner of life receded. Just as in the story, Pharez was born and then Zarah came forth again, so too, when the law had been given, the evangelic life later shone forth again, marked with the scarlet thread, that is, sealed with the blood of Christ. The reason why the evangelist mentioned these two children, therefore, is that their birth revealed something mysterious. But there is another reason why he mentions Tamar, who does not appear to be praiseworthy on account of her physical relations with her father-in-law; and that was to show that Christ Who accepted all things for our sake, accepted even to have such forbearers as these. It was moreover for this very reason that He was born from them, that He might sanctify them; for He came not to call the righteous, but the sinners.

3-5. And Pharez begat Hezron; and Hezron begat Ram; and Ram

---

[7] Gen. 38:6-30

begat Amminadab; and Amminadab begat Nahshon; and Nahshon begat Salma; and Salma begat Boaz of Rahab. Some believe Rachab to be that Rahab the harlot who received the spies of Jesus son of Nave [i.e. Joshua son of Nun].[8] She saved them, and was herself saved as well. He mentions her to show that just as she was a harlot, so, too, was the congregation of the nations, for they went whoring in their practices. But all those who accepted the spies of Jesus, that is, the apostles, and were convinced by their words, were saved from among the nations. **And Boaz begat Obed of Ruth.** Ruth was a foreigner but nevertheless she was married to Boaz.[9] So, too, the Church is from among the Gentiles. For like Ruth, these Gentiles had been foreigners and outside the covenants, yet they forsook their people, their idols, and their father, the devil. And as Ruth was wed to Boaz of the seed of Abraham, so too was the Church taken as bride by the Son of God.

5-6. And Obed begat Jesse; and Jesse begat David the king; and David the king begat Solomon of Uriah's wife. Again, he mentions Uriah's wife[10] to show that no one should be ashamed of his forefathers but rather should strive by his own virtue to make even them illustrious. He also mentions Uriah's wife to show that all are acceptable to God, even those born of adultery, if only they have virtue.

7-11. And Solomon begat Rehoboam; and Rehoboam begat Abia; and Abia begat Asa; and Asa begat Jehoshaphat; and Jehoshaphat begat Joram; and Joram begat Ahaziah; and Ahaziah begat Jotham; and Jotham begat Ahaz; and Ahaz begat Hezekiah; and Hezekiah begat Manasseh; and Manasseh begat Amon; and Amon begat Josiah; and Josiah begat Jeconiah and his brethren, about the time of the deportation to Babylon. The "deportation to Babylon" means the captivity which they later endured when they were all led away into Babylon. For the Babylonians campaigned against them on another occasion, causing less affliction. But on this occasion, the Babylonians carried them all away from their homeland.

---

[8] Joshua 2:1-21; 6:21-25. See also footnote above on p. 14.

[9] Ruth 4:13-17

[10] II Kings (II Samuel) 11:2-27; 12:24

12-16. After the deportation to Babylon, Jeconiah begat Salathiel; and Salathiel begat Zerubbabel; and Zerubbabel begat Abiud; and Abiud begat Eliakim; and Eliakim begat Azor; and Azor begat Sadok; and Sadok begat Achim; and Achim begat Eliud; and Eliud begat Eleazar; and Eleazar begat Matthan; and Matthan begat Jacob; and Jacob begat Joseph the husband of Mary, of whom was born Jesus, Who is called Christ. Why does he give the genealogy of Joseph and not of Mary, the Theotokos?[11] What participation did Joseph have in that seedless birth giving? Surely Joseph was not the true father of Jesus, so that Matthew could give Christ's genealogy through Joseph? Listen then: Joseph truly had no share in the birth of Christ; and therefore the genealogy of the Theotokos ought to have been given. But as it was not lawful to reckon ancestry through the mother, he did not give the genealogy of the Virgin. And yet, by giving the genealogy of Joseph, Matthew gave her genealogy as well. For it was the law that a woman was not to be taken as wife by a man who was of a different tribe and who was not of her father's lineage.[12] This being the law, it is obvious that Joseph's genealogy includes that of the Theotokos, for she was of the same tribe and the same lineage. If she were not, she could not have been betrothed to him. So the evangelist both kept the law which forbade the reckoning of ancestry through the mother, and at the same time provided the genealogy of the Theotokos by giving the genealogy of Joseph. He calls Joseph "the husband of Mary", according to the common practice. For we are accustomed to call the man who is betrothed the "husband" of her who is betrothed, even before the marriage has taken place.[13]

17. So all the generations from Abraham to David are fourteen generations; and from David until the deportation to Babylon are

---

[11] "Theotokos" means literally "She who gave birth to God." It is a name for Mary that the Holy Church has expressly commanded its children to use (by a decree of the Third Ecumenical Council in the year 431 A.D.). For the name expresses the most profound mystery of theology, and the awe and reverence in which Christians hold the Most Holy Virgin.

[12] Num. 36:8-9

[13] Both in New Testament language, and to this day in Greece, the common word for "husband", *anēr*, [*andra*, accusative case] is simply the word for "man". It is easy to see, therefore, how it was also used for "betrothed", just as in informal contemporary English, "her man" can refer to a wide variety of relationships.

fourteen generations; and from the deportation to Babylon unto Christ are fourteen generations. He divides the generations into three [different] conditions [of leadership], to show the Jews that although they were ruled by judges, as they were until David, and by kings, as they were until the deportation, and by priests, as they were until Christ, yet it did not benefit them at all in acquiring virtue; but they were in need of the true Judge and King and Priest, Who is Christ. For when the line of their rulers had failed, then Christ came, in accordance with the prophecy of Jacob.[14] How can there be fourteen generations from the deportation to Babylon until Christ when only thirteen persons are mentioned? If the reckoning of ancestry through the mother could be given, we would list Mary as well, and thus complete the number. But since it cannot, how can this be resolved? Some say that he counted the deportation itself as a person [i.e. as a generation].

18. Now the birth of Christ took place in this manner: when His mother Mary had been betrothed to Joseph. Why did God permit her to be betrothed, and thus give men any cause at all for suspicion that Joseph had come together with her? So that she would have a protector in hardships; for Joseph took care of her during the flight to Egypt and preserved her. She was betrothed for another reason: to escape the notice of the devil. For the devil had heard that the Virgin would conceive,[15] and was keeping the Virgin under his surveillance. So that the deceiver might be deceived, Joseph betrothed the Ever-virgin, outwardly appearing to be her spouse, but not so in actual deed. **Before they came together, she was found to be with child of the Holy Spirit.** "Come together" here means "physical relations". For she had conceived before there were any physical relations. Therefore the evangelist is amazed at the extraordinary event and cries out, "she was found."[16]

---

[14] Genesis 49:10 reads: "A ruler shall not fail from Judah, nor a prince from his loins, until there come the things stored up for Him; and He is the Expectation of the Nations." When Herod the Great, a non-Jew and usurper, assumed the title "King of Judea", the line of Judah had indeed for the first time "failed", thus heralding the coming of the Christ in fulfillment of Jacob's prophecy.

[15] Is. 7:14

[16] The amazement in the voice of the evangelist is not so apparent in English. But in Greek the single word for "she was found", *eurethē*, is simply another form of the verb immortalized by Archimedes, and preserved intact in English as "Eureka!" meaning literally, "I have found [it]!"

19. Then Joseph her husband, being a righteous man, and not willing to make her a public example, was minded to divorce her secretly. The law decreed that the adulteress be pilloried, that is, exposed and punished publicly. How, then, was Joseph righteous since he intended to cover up her sin and thus to transgress the law? The answer is, first, that he was righteous for intending to do this very thing. He did not wish to be harsh, but in his great goodness took compassion on her, showing himself to be above the law, and already living in a manner superior to the decrees of the law. Secondly, since he himself knew that she had conceived of the Holy Spirit, he did not wish to pillory and abuse her who had conceived not by adultery but of the Holy Spirit. Behold what the evangelist says: "She was found to be with child." Found by whom? By Joseph; that is, he discerned that she had conceived of the Holy Spirit. Therefore he "was minded to divorce her secretly," for he no longer dared to take as a wife her who had been deemed worthy of such grace.

20. But while he pondered these things, behold, the angel of the Lord appeared unto him in a dream, saying. When the righteous one was uncertain, then the angel appeared in order to show him what to do. The angel appeared to him in a dream, because Joseph had great faith. With the shepherds the angel conversed openly, as they were rough country men; but the angel spoke to Joseph, who was righteous and believing, in his sleep. How could Joseph not believe, when the angel spoke to him of matters that were in his mind and that he had not revealed to anyone? For it says, "while he pondered," but did not speak of, these things, the angel appeared to him. It was right that he believed the angel to be of God, for it is the attribute of God to know the things that are unspoken. **Joseph son of David.** The angel called him "son of David" to remind him that the prophets had foretold that the Christ would come from the seed of David.[17] It is as if the angel were saying to him, "Do not doubt, but remember David who received the promise concerning Christ." **Fear not to take unto thee.** Here he shows that Joseph was afraid to keep her, lest he spurn God by harboring an adulteress. Or, in another sense, "Fear not," that is, "Though you fear to touch her who has conceived of the Holy Spirit, do not fear to take her

---

[17] II Kings (II Samuel) 7:12-16; Ps. 88:35-37

unto thee, that is, to keep her within your house.'' For in his thoughts and deliberations he had already divorced her. **Mary thy wife.** This means, you perhaps think that she is an adulteress. But I say to you that she is your wife, that is, she has not been corrupted by anyone, but she is your own betrothed. **For that which is conceived in her is of the Holy Spirit.** Not only is she acquitted of any unlawful union, but she has conceived in some divine and wondrous manner. Therefore you ought rather to rejoice because of this.

21. And she shall bear a son. So that no one could ask, ''How can I believe you that she has conceived of the Holy Spirit?'' the angel speaks of the future, saying that she shall bear a son. ''For if I tell the truth in this matter, it is clear that what I said concerning her conception of the Holy Spirit is also true.'' The angel did not say, ''She shall bear you a son,'' but simply, ''She shall bear a son.'' For Mary did not bring forth for Joseph's sake, but for the whole world; nor did this grace concern him alone, but it was poured out on all. **And thou shalt call His name Jesus.** ''Thou shalt call,'' as though you were His father, and as the protector of the Virgin. For you must not think, Joseph, that because the conception is of the Holy Spirit that you can leave the Virgin helpless, but rather you will serve her in all things. **For He shall save His people from their sins.** Here he interprets the name ''Jesus'', showing that it means ''Saviour''. The angel says that Jesus will save His people, not only the Jewish people, but also the Gentiles who are eager to believe and to become His people. From whom will He save them? Perhaps from enemies? No, but from their sins. Hence it is clear that it is God Who will be born, for it is the attribute of God alone to forgive sins.

22. Now all this was done, that it might be fulfilled what had been spoken by the Lord through the prophet, saying. Do not think that only now in these recent times did God resolve to do these things, but from before, even from the beginning. For you know the prophets, Joseph, as the student of the law which you are. Remember what was spoken by the law. He did not say, ''what Isaiah had spoken,'' but, ''what the Lord had spoken.'' For it was not man who spoke, but God, through the mouth of the prophet, and therefore the oracle is trustworthy.

23. Behold, the Virgin shall be with child. The Jews say that it is not written in the prophecy ''virgin'' but ''young woman''. To which it may be answered that ''young woman'' and ''virgin'' mean the same thing in Scripture, for in Scripture ''young woman'' refers to one who is still a virgin. Furthermore, if it was not a virgin that gave birth, how would it be a sign, something extraordinary? Listen to Isaiah who says, ''For this reason the Lord Himself shall give you a sign,'' and immediately he adds, ''Behold, the Virgin.''[18] So if it were not a virgin that would give birth, it would not be a sign. The Jews, then, alter the text of Scripture in their malice, putting ''young woman'' instead of ''virgin''.[19] But whether the text reads ''young woman'' or ''virgin'', it should be understood in either case that it is a virgin who will give birth so that the event may be a miraculous sign. **And shall bring forth a son, and they shall call His name Emmanuel, which being interpreted is, God with us.** The Jews say, ''How then is it that He was not called Emmanuel but Jesus Christ?'' One may answer, ''The prophet did not say 'You shall call,' but 'They shall call.''' That is, the events and deeds of His life will show that He is God and that He keeps company with us. For Holy Scripture gives names that are derived from the events of one's life; for example, ''Call his name Plunder Swiftly.''[20] Yet where does it record that anyone was ever called by such a name? But since error was despoiled and taken captive at the moment of the Lord's birth, Scripture gives this as His name, which He acquires from the event.

24. Then Joseph awoke from sleep and did as the angel of the Lord had bidden him. Behold a wakeful, vigilant soul who immediately obeyed. **And took unto him his wife.** The evangelist continually calls her ''the wife of Joseph'' to allay evil suspicion and to show that she was not anyone else's wife but his.

25. And knew her not until she had brought forth. That is, he never came together with her at all. ''Until'' here does not mean that before the

---

[18] Is. 7:14

[19] Note: the Hebrew text of Isaiah found among the Dead Sea Scrolls at Qumran in 1947 does confirm the accuracy of the Septuagint reading of ''virgin''.

[20] Is. 8:3

birth he did not know her and afterwards he did, but that he absolutely never knew her. Scripture employs this expression. For example, the raven "returned not unto the ark until the water had dried off from the earth."[21] But neither did it return after the water had dried off. Again, "I am with you until the end of the world."[22] So after the end He will no longer be with the saints? But how can that be? For at that time more than ever will He be with them. So must you understand here "until she brought forth" to mean, neither before the birth nor after the birth did he know her. How could he have touched the Holy Virgin having once understood the ineffable birth giving? **Her firstborn son.** The evangelist does not call Him "her firstborn son" in the sense that she later gave birth to a second son, but simply that He was the first and only child that she bore. For Christ is both the "firstborn" by having been born first, and the "only begotten",[23] in that He had no brother. **And he called His name Jesus.** And here, too, he shows Joseph's ready obedience to do everything that the angel had told him to do.

---

[21] Gen. 8:7

[22] Mt. 28:20

[23] The attribute "only begotten" here refers to the single birth giving of the Holy Virgin, and not, as in the Creed, to the relationship of God the Son to God the Father.

CHAPTER TWO

Concerning the Magi
and the slaying of the children.

1. Now when Jesus was born in Bethlehem of Judea. Being interpreted, "Bethlehem" means "house of bread" and "Judea" means "confession". May we also now become a house of the spiritual bread by means of our confession. **In the days of Herod.** He mentions Herod so that you, O reader, might learn that the line of rulers and kings of the tribe of Judah had failed, and so by necessity Christ came. For Herod was not a Judean, but an Idumean, the son of Antipater by an Arab woman. So when the line of the rulers had failed, then came the Expectation of the Gentiles, as Jacob had prophesied.[1] **The king.** There was another Herod, the Tetrarch, and so the evangelist adds the title "king".[2] **Behold, there came Magi from the east to Jerusalem.** Why did the Magi come? For the condemnation of the Jews. For if the idolatrous Magi believed, what defense could the Jews give? The Magi also came so that the glory of Christ might shine forth all the more through the witness of the Magi who before had been subject to the demons and were enemies of God. "From the east." This, too, is for the condemnation of the Jews; for the Magi came from such a great distance to worship Him, while the Jews, who had Christ there in their midst, persecuted Him.

2. Saying, Where is He that is born King of the Jews? For we have seen His star in the east and are come to worship Him. It is said that these Magi were descendants of Balaam the soothsayer; and that when they discovered Balaam's oracle, "A star shall arise out of Jacob,"[3] they understood the mystery concerning Christ, and so they came desiring to

---

[1] Gen. 49:10. See footnote on Mt. 1:17, above, on p. 18.

[2] King Herod the Great was the son of Antipater who founded the Idumean dynasty. King Herod ruled over Galilee and Judea from 40 B.C. until the birth of Christ. He divided his kingdom among his sons Archelaus, (Mt. 2:22), Herod Antipas, and Philip. Herod Antipas was Tetrarch of Galilee and Peraea and is the Herod who slew John the Baptist (Mt. 14:1-12). In the Acts of the Apostles there is mention of later members of this Idumean dynasty: Herod Agrippa I (Acts 12) and Herod Agrippa II (Acts 25 and 26).

[3] Num. 24:17

see Him that had been born. "For we have seen His star in the east." When you hear "star", do not think that it was a star such as we see, but a divine and angelic power that appeared in the form of a star. The Magi were astrologers, and so the Lord used what was familiar to them to draw them to Himself. In the same manner, the Lord astonished Peter the fisherman by the multitude of fish which he caught by the name of Christ. That the star was an angelic power is apparent from the fact that it shone even by day, and that it moved as they moved, and stood still as they rested; also, that it moved from Persia in the north to Jerusalem in the south. For a star never moves from north to south. "And are come to worship Him." These Magi are seen to possess great virtue. For if they came to worship Christ in a strange land, how much more would they preach Him with great boldness in Persia?

3. When Herod the king had heard these things, he was troubled, and all Jerusalem with him. Herod was troubled because he was a foreigner and feared for his kingdom; for he knew that he was unworthy of it. But why were the Jews troubled? They ought instead to have rejoiced that they would have a king to whom the kings of Persia paid homage. But evil is indeed a senseless thing.

4. And when he had gathered all the chief priests and scribes of the people together, he inquired of them where the Christ was to be born. The scribes were the teachers of the people, like those whom we call "scholars". God ordained in His providence that these men be asked, so that they would confess the truth, and by this confession be condemned. For those who crucified Him had first confessed Him.

5. And they said unto him, In Bethlehem of Judea; for thus it is written by the prophet. By which prophet? By Micah,[4] who said:

6. And thou Bethlehem, in the land of Judah, art not the least among the princes of Judah. Since Bethlehem was small, it was despised, but now it is greatly renowned for Christ Who came forth from it. For all people from the ends of the earth come to venerate this holy

---

[4] Micah 5:2

Bethlehem. **For out of thee shall come a Governor.** Rightly did he say, "out of thee shall come" and not "in thee shall remain." For Christ did not remain in Bethlehem, but came out from, that is, left it after His birth, and spent most of His years in Nazareth. The Jews say that this prophecy concerns Zerubbabel, but they plainly are lying; for Zerubbabel[5] was not born in Bethlehem, but in Babylon. Consider his name: "Zeru" means "seed" or "birth", and "babel" means "Babylon", therefore, "he that was born in Babylon." But even the prophecy refutes them where it says, "His goings forth are from the beginning, and in the days of the age."[6] Of whom else are the goings forth both from the beginning and in the days of this age if not of Christ, Who had two goings forth, that is, a double genesis? The first, His begetting, was from the beginning from the Father, and the second, His Nativity according to the flesh, was in the days of this age, and took its beginning from the Theotokos and occurred in time. Let the Jews say, therefore, that Zerubbabel was from the beginning; but they have no grounds on which to make this claim. **Who shall shepherd My people Israel.** The prophecy said, "shall shepherd", not "tyrannize" or "devour" them. For the other kings were not shepherds but wolves. But Christ is a shepherd, as He Himself says, "I am the good shepherd."[7] "My people Israel" means those who believed, whether Jew or Gentile. "Israel" means "seeing God", so all those who see God are Israelites, even those who are Gentiles.

7. Then Herod summoned the Magi secretly. He summoned them secretly on account of the Jews, for he suspected that perhaps the Jews would highly esteem the Child and devise means to save Him as their future liberator. Therefore Herod meets with the Magi secretly. **And carefully ascertained from them what time the star had appeared.** That is, he learned the exact time. The star had appeared to the Magi before the Lord was born. Since their journey would take a long time, the star appeared well before His birth so that they could worship Him while He was still in swaddling clothes. Some say that the star appeared

---

[5] See Haggai and Mt. 1:12.

[6] Micah 5:2

[7] Jn. 10:11

simultaneously with Christ's birth, and that the Magi came two years later and found the Lord neither in swaddling clothes nor in the manger, but in the house with His mother when He was two years old. But you, O reader, consider the former interpretation to be better.[8]

8. And he sent them to Bethlehem, and said, Go and search diligently for the Child. He did not say, "search for the king" but "search for the Child", for he could not endure even to utter Christ's name. From this it is clear that he was in a rage against Christ.

8-9. And when ye have found Him, bring me word again, that I may come and worship Him also. And when they had heard the king, they departed. The Magi were guileless and thought that Herod, too, spoke without guile. **And lo, the star which they saw in the east went before them.** The star was hidden for a time by God's providence so that they would inquire of the Jews, and Herod would be troubled, and thus the truth would be made all the more apparent. But when they had departed from Jerusalem, it again appeared and guided them; from which it is clear that the star was a divine power. **Until it came and stood over where the young Child was.** This, too, was extraordinary. For the star descended from the heights and came closer to the earth to show them the place. For if it had appeared to them from the heights, how would they have been able to know the particular spot where Christ was? For the stars are visible over a great area. So it is that you may see the moon over your house, while it appears to me that it is over my house alone; and, in short, to each one the moon, or a star, appears to stand over them alone. Neither could this star have pointed out where Christ was if it had not descended and all but stood over the head of the Child.

10. When they saw the star, they rejoiced with exceeding great joy. They rejoiced that they had not been led astray but had found what they were seeking.

11. And when they were come into the house, they saw the young

---

[8] In supporting the former view Bl. Theophylact follows St. John Chrysostom. Saints Epiphanios and Jerome, among others, suggest the latter.

Child with Mary His mother. At the time of His birth, the Virgin laid the Child in the manger as they could not find a house then. But later it is most likely that they found a house, and it is there that the Magi found them. Joseph and Mary had gone up to Bethlehem to be enrolled there, as Luke says,[9] and as there was a great number of people assembled there for the census, they did not have a house for a time, and so He was born in the cave. Later a house was found and there the Magi saw the Lord. **And they fell down and worshipped Him.** Behold, what enlightened souls! They saw a pauper, and worshipped. For they had been informed that He was God, and therefore they also offered Him gifts, as to God and man. Listen, then: **And when they had opened their treasures, they offered Him gifts: gold and frankincense and myrrh.** Gold they offered to Him as to a king, for we pay tribute of gold to the king to whom we are subject. They offered frankincense as to God, for we burn incense to God. They offered myrrh since He would taste of death. For the Jews would prepare the dead for burial with myrrh to preserve the body from corruption. Myrrh, which is dry, desiccates the body and prevents worms from breeding. Do you see the faith of the Magi? They had been taught by the prophecy of Balaam alone that the Lord was both God and King and would be born for our sake. Listen to the prophecy: "He reclined and rested as a lion, and as a young lion; may they be blessed that call Thee blessed."[10] Behold the kingship in the lion, and death in the reclining. Behold the divinity; for only the divine nature has the power to bless.

12. And being warned by God in a dream not to return to Herod, they departed into their own country another way. Consider the sequence of events. First God guided them to faith by means of the star. Then they came to Jerusalem and He taught them through the prophet Micah that Christ was to be born in Bethlehem. And finally, they were warned by means of the angel. They obeyed the warning, that is, the divine speech. Therefore, having received the warning, that is, having accepted the revelation from God, they deceived Herod. They were not afraid of pursuit, but were bold in the power of Him that had been born.

---

[9] Lk. 2

[10] Num. 24:9

Thus they were true witnesses and confessors.

13. And when they had departed, behold, the angel of the Lord appeareth to Joseph in a dream, saying, Arise, and take the young Child and His mother. Do you see now the reason why God permitted the Virgin to be betrothed? It is revealed to you here: that Joseph might care for her and watch over her. The angel did not say, "take thy wife," but "take the mother of the Child." For once his suspicion had been allayed, and the righteous man had understood from the miracles attendant at His birth that everything was of the Holy Spirit, the angel no longer calls her Joseph's "wife". **And flee into Egypt.** Even the Lord flees, to confirm that He was truly man. For if He had fallen into the hands of Herod and had not been slain, it would have seemed that He had been made flesh only in appearance. He flees into Egypt to sanctify even that place. For there were two lands that were the workshops of every iniquity: Babylon and Egypt. By means of the Magi He accepted the adoration of Babylon, and Egypt He sanctified by His own presence. **And be thou there until I bring thee word.** Remain there until you receive God's command. So we, too, should do nothing apart from the will of God. **For Herod will seek the young Child to destroy Him.** Behold the foolishness of a man who labors to prevail against the will of God. For if it is not of God, what do you fear? But if it is of God, how can you destroy the Child?

14-15. And he arose and took the young Child and His mother by night, and departed into Egypt; and was there until the death of Herod: that it might be fulfilled which was spoken by the Lord through the prophet, saying, Out of Egypt have I called My Son."[11] The Jews say that this was said of the people whom Moses led out of Egypt. We reply, is it anything remarkable that something which was spoken of the people in type as a foreshadowing, was realized by Christ in truth? Furthermore, who is the Son of God? The Hebrew people who worshipped the idols and carvings of Beelphegor, or He Who truly is the Son of God?

---

[11] Hosea 11:1

16. Then Herod, when he saw that he had been tricked by the Magi, was exceedingly wroth, and sent forth, and slew all the children that were in Bethlehem. As God used Moses to trick Pharaoh, so, too, He used the Magi to trick Herod. For both Herod and Pharaoh were child slayers: Pharaoh slew the male children of the Hebrews in Egypt, and Herod slew the male children of the Hebrews in Bethlehem. Herod vents his wrath against the Magi upon those who had wronged him in nothing. Why were the children allowed to be slaughtered? So that Herod's wickedness might be revealed. But perhaps you will ask me, "Why did the children suffer wrong to show Herod's wickedness?" Listen then. They were not wronged but were made worthy of crowns. For anyone who suffers some evil here, suffers either so that his sins might be absolved, or so that his crowns might be multiplied. So it is with these children; for their suffering they will receive a greater crown in heaven. **And in all the region thereof, from two years old and under, according to the time which he had carefully ascertained of the Magi.**

17. Then was fulfilled that which was spoken by Jeremiah the prophet, saying. Lest anyone think that the slaying of the children took place against the will of God, the evangelist shows that God both knew of it beforehand and foretold it.

18. In Rama was there a voice heard. Rama is a place in Palestine of high elevation, for the name itself means "high". This place fell by lot to the inheritance of the tribe of Benjamin, who was the son of Rachel, and Rachel was buried in Bethlehem. By "Rachel", therefore, the prophet Jeremiah means "Bethlehem", for Rachel was buried in Bethlehem.[12] He is saying that weeping and lamentation will be heard from on high. Listen to what the prophet says: **Lamentation, and weeping, and great mourning, Rachel weeping for her children,** that is, Bethlehem weeping for its children, **and would not be comforted, because they are not.** In this life they are no more, but their souls are immortal.

---

[12] Gen. 35:19

19. But when Herod was dead. Herod came to a bitter end. For with fever, torment of the bowels, itching, swelling of the feet, rotting of the private parts, breeding of worms, difficulty in breathing, trembling and spasms in every member, he cast off his evil soul.

19-20. Behold, the angel of the Lord appeareth in a dream to Joseph in Egypt, saying, Arise, and take the young Child and His mother, and go into the land of Israel. He did not say "flee" but "go", for there was no longer any need for fear. **For they are dead which sought the young Child's soul.** Where is Apollinarius, who said that the Lord did not have the soul of a man?[13] For here he is reproved.

21-22. And he arose, and took the young Child and His mother, and came into the land of Israel. But when he heard that Archelaus was reigning in Judea in place of his father Herod, he was afraid to go thither. Herod left three sons: Philip, Antipas, and Archelaus. He had directed Archelaus to be king, and the other two, tetrarchs. Joseph was afraid to go into the land of Israel, that is, Judea, because Archelaus was similar to Herod, his father. Antipas was the young Herod who slew the Forerunner. **And being warned by God in a dream, he withdrew to the district of Galilee.** Galilee was not of the land of Israel, but of the Gentiles, and for this reason the Jews considered the Galileans an abomination.

23. And he came and dwelt in a city called Nazareth. How is it that Luke says that after the Lord was born, He completed the forty days, was held in the arms of Simeon, and then went down to Nazareth?[14] But here Matthew says that after the return from Egypt He went to Nazareth? Learn, therefore, that Luke spoke those things on which Matthew was silent. I will give an example: after the birth, He completed the forty

---

[13] This false teaching of Apollinarius was condemned as heresy at the Second Ecumenical Council held at Constantinople in 381 A.D. The Greek word in the Gospel here translated as "soul" is *psychē*. It means literally "the breath of life" and can be variously translated into English as "soul" or "life", depending on the context. The same is true of the Latin word *anima*, from which we derive the word "animate". See also the commentary on Mt. 6:25 on p. 61 and on Mt. 22:37 on p. 193.

[14] Lk. 2:22-40

days, and then went down to Nazareth. This is what Luke says. Matthew speaks of what took place afterwards, that He fled into Egypt, and then returned from Egypt to Nazareth. They do not contradict each other. One of them, Luke, speaks of the descent from Bethlehem to Nazareth, while the other, Matthew, speaks of the return from Egypt to Nazareth, which took place later. **That it might be fulfilled which was spoken by the prophets, He shall be called a Nazarene.** Which prophet said this? It is not to be found now. For many books have been lost, because of both the carelessness of the Hebrews and the frequent captivities. But perhaps this was an unwritten prophecy among the Jews. "Nazarene" means "sanctified" and as the Christ is holy, it is right that He is called "a Nazarene". For by many prophets the Lord was called "The Holy One of Israel".[15]

---

[15] Ps. 88:18, Is. 1:4, etc.

CHAPTER THREE

John was the first to preach the kingdom of heaven.

1. In those days. Not when the Lord was a child and was living in Nazareth, but rather the evangelist makes this simple statement, ''at that time, before the present generation.'' **Came John the Baptist.** John was sent by God to reprove the Jews and to persuade them to come to a consciousness of their own sins and so to accept the Christ. For if one is not conscious of his sins, he cannot come to repentance. This is why John was sent.

1-2. Preaching in the wilderness of Judea, and saying, Repent ye. The Jews were arrogant, and so he urges them to repent. **For the kingdom of heaven is at hand.** The kingdom of heaven means the first and second comings of Christ, and also the virtuous life. For when we walk on earth as if we lived in heaven, not living according to the passions, then we possess the kingdom of heaven.

3. For this is he that was spoken of by the prophet Isaiah, saying, The voice of one crying in the wilderness, Prepare ye the way of the Lord, make His paths straight.[1] ''The way'', that is, the highway, means the Gospel. The ''paths'' are the ordinances of the law, which are well-trodden and ancient. He is saying, therefore, ''Prepare yourselves for the evangelic life, the life that is lived according to the Gospel, and make the commandments of the law straight, that is, make them spiritual.'' For the Spirit is straight and right.[2] So then, when you see a Jew who understands the content of the law in a fleshly manner, you may say, ''This man has not made straight the paths,'' that is, he does not understand the law spiritually.

---

[1] Is. 40:3

[2] ''Straight'' and ''right'' have been given as two different meanings in English of the same word in Greek, *euthys*. Compare Ps. 50:10 ''And renew a right spirit within me.'' Here the adjective translated by ''right'', *euthes*, is the same adjective that occurs in Isaiah ''make His paths straight (*eutheias*).'' The English word ''rectitude'', derived from the Latin word for ''straight'', *rectus*, also combines the two meanings of ''straight'' and ''right''.

4. Now this John wore a garment of camel's hair. Even by his appearance John called them to repentance, for he wore the garb of mourning. It is said that the camel is somewhere between a clean and unclean animal: it is clean in that it chews its cud, but it is unclean in that its hoof is not cloven.[3] Another reason, then, that John wore camel's hair is that he was leading to God both the Jewish people, who appeared clean, and the Gentiles, who were unclean, and he was a mediator between the Old and the New Testaments. **And a leather belt about his loins.** All the saints appear in Scripture girt about the waist with a belt, for they labored continuously; but the careless and the gluttonous are not girt, but let their robes flow to the ground, like the Saracens of today. Or, the saints are girt because they have mortified the desires of the flesh, for leather is a part of a dead animal. **And his food was locusts and wild honey.** Some say that "locusts" refer to a type of herb; others say that the word refers to the fruit of wild pod-bearing trees.[4] Wild honey is produced by wild bees, and is to be found in trees and rocks.

5-6. Then went out to him Jerusalem, and all Judea, and all the region round about Jordan. And they were baptized by him in the Jordan, confessing their sins. They were baptized, but the baptism of John did not have the power to forgive sins; for John was only preaching repentance and bringing them towards the forgiveness of sins, that is, he was guiding them to the baptism of Christ, from which there is remission of sins.

7. But when he saw many of the Pharisees. "Pharisee" means "one who is set apart", for they appeared to be set apart by their life and knowledge, and to be superior to others. **And Sadducees.** These believed neither in the resurrection, nor in angels, nor in the spirit. Their name

---

[3] Levit. 11:1-8

[4] The Greek word in the text translated as "locusts" is *akrides* (singular *akris*). The Greek word, as does the English, has more meanings than that of the insect. As Theophylact mentions here, there is patristic evidence that *akrides* refer to some kind of sprouts of plants or herbs. Furthermore, there is an ancient Palestinian tradition that St. John the Baptist ate the pods of a type of carob tree native to the Middle East, and still found there to this day. These pods are large and tough, somewhat resembling a locust in shape, and sweet to the taste. These pods are traditionally known as "St. John's bread", in German "Johannisbrot". The carob tree is related to the locust tree, and its pods are known as "locust beans".

means "the righteous ones", for *sedek* means "righteousness". Either they called themselves "the righteous", or they were so named after a certain leader of heresy, Sadok. **Coming to him for baptism, he said unto them.** They did not come with sincerity, as did the others, and for this reason he upbraids them. **O brood of vipers! Who hath warned you to flee from the wrath to come?** He speaks to them bitterly, knowing their perversity, but he also praises them by saying, "Who hath warned you?" For he marvels how it has come about that their wicked generation should repent. He calls them a "brood of vipers" because in the same way that vipers are said to eat their way out of their mother's womb, so these murdered their fathers, that is, their teachers and prophets. "The wrath to come" means gehenna.

8. Bring forth therefore fruits worthy of repentance. Do you see what he is saying? One must not only flee from wickedness, but also bring forth fruits of virtue. For it is written, "Turn away from evil and do good."[5]

9. And think not to say within yourselves, We have Abraham as our father. This was to their destruction, that they put their trust in their noble lineage. **For I say unto you, that God is able of these stones to raise up children unto Abraham.** The "stones" mean the Gentiles, many of whom believed; but John is also saying simply that God is able to make children for Abraham out of stones. For the womb of Sarah was a stone on account of her sterility, but she gave birth nevertheless.[6] When also did the Lord raise up children unto Abraham from stones? At His crucifixion, when many believed upon seeing the stones which were sundered.[7]

10. And now also the axe is laid unto the root of the trees. The axe means the judgement of Christ, and the trees stand for each one of us. Therefore he who has not believed, and thus is rooted only in himself, is now and henceforward being cut down and cast into gehenna. **Therefore**

---

[5] Ps. 33:14

[6] Gen. 18:11-12; 21:1-2

[7] Mt. 27:51

every tree, even though descended from Abraham, **which bringeth not forth good fruit.** He did not say, "which hath not brought forth," but "which bringeth not forth," for one must continually be bringing forth fruit. For if you gave alms yesterday but today you are greedy and grasping, you are not pleasing to God. **Is hewn down and cast into the fire.** The fire, that is, of gehenna.

11. I indeed baptize you with water unto repentance; but He that cometh after me is mightier than I. He had told them to bring forth fruit; now he shows them what fruit to bring forth: to believe in Him that is coming after John. After him came Christ. For just as Christ came after John in birth, by only six months, so it was also in His public manifestation. First the Forerunner was made manifest, and then came Christ, after the testimony of the Forerunner. **Whose sandals I am not worthy to bear.** I am not even the least of His servants, he says, who carries His sandals. By "sandals" understand the Lord's two descents, the one from heaven to earth, and the other from earth to hades. For the sandals, being leather, represent flesh and mortification. The Forerunner, then, is not able to carry these two descents, that is, not able to understand how they occurred. **He shall baptize you with the Holy Spirit.** That is, He shall flood you with the gifts and the grace of the Holy Spirit. For my baptism, John says, provides neither spiritual grace nor forgiveness of sins, but He will forgive you and give you the Spirit in abundance.

12. His winnowing fan is in His hand. Do not think, if you are baptized by Him and then remain an unrepentant sinner, that He will forgive you. For He also has a winnowing fan, that is, judgement and examination. **He will clean His threshing floor,** namely, the Church, which holds many who are baptized, just as the threshing floor holds all the crop. But some of those who are baptized are chaff, those who are light-minded and moved about by the evil spirits, while others are the wheat, who bring benefit to others and nourish them with teachings and deeds. **And gather the wheat into His granary, but He will burn up the chaff with unquenchable fire.** That fire is unquenchable. Therefore Origen is babbling nonsense when he says that there will be an end to hell.[8]

13-14. Then cometh Jesus from Galilee to Jordan unto John, to be baptized of him. But John forbade Him. Jesus is pure, yet He is baptized in order to wash us, and to show us that if we intend to be baptized we must first be cleansed. Otherwise we might stain our baptism, being easily sullied afterwards because of our evil habits. John forbade Him so that those who saw the baptism would not think that Christ was being baptized unto repentance like one of the multitude. **Saying, It is I that needeth to be baptized of Thee.** The Forerunner was in need of cleansing by the Lord; for as he was descended from Adam, he too carried with him the stain of disobedience. But when Christ took flesh, He cleansed all mankind. **And comest Thou to me?** John did not dare to say, "Art Thou baptized by me?" but "Comest Thou to me?" such reverence did he have for the Lord.

15. And Jesus answering said unto him, Let it be so now. Permit it now, He says. For there will be a time for us to have the glory that is befitting, even if we do not appear in such glory now. **For thus it becometh us to fulfill all righteousness.** "Righteousness" means the law. Human nature was accursed, Jesus says, because it was not able to fulfill the law. Therefore I have fulfilled all the other requirements of the law. One thing remains for Me to do, that I be baptized. When I have fulfilled this, I shall have delivered human nature from the curse. And this is befitting for Me to do.

15-16. Then he permitted Him; and Jesus, when He was baptized. He was baptized at the age of thirty; for by this age one has experienced all the sins. In the first ten years, there is great foolishness; in the second, during adolescence, the great flame of desire and anger; and in the years of adulthood, great avarice. Jesus waited for this age, therefore, so that He could fulfill the law in all the ages of a man, and sanctify us. **Went up straightway out of the water.** The Manichean heretics say that He

---

[8] Here Bl. Theophylact is referring to Origen's teaching of *apokatastasis*, i.e. "restoration", which was condemned by the Fifth Ecumenical Council in Constantinople in 553. According to this false teaching, the punishment of the demons and the impious in hell will one day come to an end, and "all will be restored."

left His body in the Jordan and thereafter displayed another, illusory, body. But their mouths are shut by this, for it says, "Jesus went up"; it was not another who went up, but He Who went down into the water. **And lo, the heavens were opened unto Him.** Adam had closed the heavens, but through Christ they are opened, so that you may learn, O reader, that when you are baptized, you, too, open the heavens.

16-17. And he saw the Spirit of God descending like a dove, and lighting upon Him; and, lo, a voice from heaven, saying. The Spirit came down to bear witness that He Who is baptized is greater than he who baptizes. For the Jews held John in high regard, but they did not esteem Christ so highly. They all saw the Spirit descending upon Jesus so that they would not think that the voice which said, "This is My beloved Son," was referring to John; but by seeing the Spirit they might believe that this voice spoke concerning Jesus. It was like a dove because of the dove's innocence and meekness, and because the dove is very clean, not remaining in any place where there is foul odor. So it is with the Holy Spirit. But also, as in the time of Noah a dove announced the deliverance from the flood by bearing an olive twig, so too, here, the Holy Spirit reveals the deliverance from sins. There, the twig of olive; here, the mercy of God.[9] **This is My beloved Son, in Whom I am well pleased.** That is, in Whom I am content, and He is pleasing to Me.

[9] The parallelism of the two events is much more striking in Greek where the words for "olive" and "mercy", *elaias* and *eleos*, are very similar to the ear, though unrelated in etymology. These two words are frequently drawn into association with one another. See, for example, the commentary on Mt. 6:17-18 on p. 59 and on Mt. 25:1-5 on p. 214.

CHAPTER FOUR

Concerning the temptation of Christ.
Concerning the calling of
Peter, Andrew, and the sons of Zebedee.

1. Then was Jesus led up by the Spirit into the wilderness. Teaching us that it is especially after our baptism that we should expect temptations, He is led up by the Holy Spirit; for He did nothing apart from the Holy Spirit. He is led into the wilderness to show us that the devil tempts us when he sees us alone and without help from others. Therefore we must not put our trust in ourselves without any counsel from others. **To be tempted by the devil.** The devil is called "the slanderer"[1] because he slandered God to Adam, saying, "God envies you." And even now among us the devil slanders virtue.

2. And when He had fasted. He fasted to show us that fasting is a great weapon against temptations, just as the love of delicacies was the beginning of all sin. **Forty days and forty nights.** He fasts as long as Moses and Elijah did, for if He had fasted longer, it would have seemed that He had taken flesh in appearance only. **Afterwards He hungered.** He hungered only when He permitted His nature to do so, to give the devil an opportunity through hunger to approach Him and engage Him in combat, so that Christ could throw him down and vanquish him and grant us the victory.

3. And when the tempter came to Him, he said, If thou be the Son of God, command that these stones be made bread. That prowler, the devil, had heard the voice from heaven, and then he saw the Lord hunger, and he was in doubt, wondering how the Son of God could hunger. Therefore he tempts Him, to find out. He flatters Christ, meaning to snare Him by saying, "If thou be the Son of God." You might ask, "What sin was it to make bread out of stones?" Listen, then: it is a sin even to

---

[1] The Greek word for "devil", *diabolos*, comes from the verb *diaballein*, "to slander". See Gen. 3:5-6.

listen to anything that the devil says. Consider this as well; the devil did not say, "Command that this stone be made bread," but "these stones", wishing to cast Christ into gluttony. For one loaf would certainly suffice a man who is hungry. For these reasons, then, Christ did not listen to him.

4. But He answered and said, It is written, Man shall not live by bread alone, but by every word that proceedeth out of the mouth of God. This testimony is from the Old Testament, from the words of Moses.[2] The Hebrews, too, had been fed by manna, not by real bread; by the word of God the manna fulfilled every need of the Hebrews, and it became whatever food each one might desire to eat. For the manna provided to each Jew the taste he desired, whether of fish, eggs, or cheese.[3]

5-6. Then the devil taketh Him up into the Holy City, and setteth Him on a pinnacle of the temple, and saith unto Him, If Thou be the Son of God, cast Thyself down: for it is written, He shall give His angels charge concerning thee, and in their hands they shall bear thee up, lest at any time thou dash thy foot against a stone. "If Thou be the Son of God." As if he were saying, "I do not believe the voice from heaven; but if Thou art the Son of God, show me." Yet, O foul one, though He is the Son of God, would He have thrown Himself over the precipice? That is the mark of your own savagery, to hurl over the precipice those who are demonized; but it is the mark of God to save. But the words "In their hands they shall bear thee up" were not written of Christ, but of the saints who are in need of angelic help.[4] Christ, being God, does not need such help.

7. Jesus said unto him, It is written again, Thou shalt not tempt the Lord thy God. Christ calmly repels the devil, teaching us to defeat the demons with meekness.

---

[2] Deut. 8:3

[3] Wisdom of Solomon 16:20

[4] Ps. 90:11-12

8-9. Again, the devil taketh Him up onto an exceeding high mountain, and showeth Him all the kingdoms of the world, and the glory of them; and saith unto Him, All these things will I give Thee, if Thou wilt fall down and worship me. Some think that the high mountain is the passion of avarice into which the enemy strives to lead Jesus. But those who think this do not reason well. The devil appeared to Him visibly, for the Lord did not entertain any evil thoughts—far from it! The devil, therefore, visibly showed Him all the kingdoms, presenting them before His eyes in an image, and said, "All these things will I give Thee." In his pride, he considers the world to be his own. Even now the devil makes this offer to the greedy, with the result that those who worship him do possess these things.

10. Then saith Jesus unto him, Get thee behind Me, Satan. For it is written, Thou shalt worship the Lord thy God, and Him only shalt thou serve. The Lord became angry with him when He saw him appropriating what was God's and saying, "All these things will I give Thee," as if they were his own. Learn how much the Scriptures benefit; for with them the Lord shut the mouth of the enemy.

11. Then the devil leaveth Him, and, behold, angels came and ministered unto Him. The Lord conquered the three temptations of gluttony, vainglory, and avarice. These are the chief passions, and by conquering them, how much more so does He conquer the others. Wherefore Luke says that the devil "ended every temptation",[5] having ended these chief temptations. Whereupon angels serve Him to show that the angels will serve us as well after our victory over temptation. For everything that Christ did and revealed was for our sake, since the angels are always serving Him as God.

12-13. Now when Jesus had heard that John had been handed over, He departed into Galilee; and leaving Nazareth, He came and dwelt in Capernaum, which is upon the sea coast, in the borders of Zabulon and Nephthalim. Jesus departs, teaching us not to throw ourselves into dangers. He departs into Galilee, which means "rolling

---

[5] Lk. 4:13

down'', for the Gentiles had rolled down into sin.[6] He dwells in Capernaum, which means ''house of comfort and consolation'', because Christ came down from heaven to make the Gentiles the house of the Comforter. ''Zabulon'' means ''nocturnal'' and ''Nephthalim'', ''a broadening''. The life of the Gentiles, therefore, was both dark and broad, for they were walking not the narrow way, but the way leading to destruction.[7]

14-16. That it might be fulfilled which was spoken by Isaiah the prophet, saying, The land of Zabulon, and the land of Nephthalim, by the way of the sea, beyond Jordan, Galilee of the Gentiles; the people which sat in darkness saw a great light; and on them which sat in the region and shadow of death light hath dawned. ''By the way of the sea'' means ''which is situated along the road of the sea''. The ''great light'' is the Gospel, for the law, too, was a light, but a small one. ''The shadow of death'' is sin, for sin is the likeness and silhouette of death. Just as death overpowers the body, so too does sin overpower the soul. The light has dawned on us, for we were not seeking it, but it appeared to us as if it were pursuing us.

17. From that time Jesus began to preach and to say. From the time John was arrested, Jesus began to preach. For Jesus waited for John to first bear witness to Him and to prepare the way for Him, in the same manner in which servants make preparations for their masters. Being equal to the Father, the Lord also had John as a prophet, just as God the Father had the prophets who were before John; yet in truth these were the prophets of both the Father and the Son. **Repent: for the kingdom of heaven is at hand.** The kingdom of heaven is Christ and it is also the life of virtue. For when someone lives as an angel on earth, is he not heavenly? So the kingdom of heaven is within each one of us when we live as angels.

18-19. As He was walking by the Sea of Galilee, He saw two brethren, Simon called Peter, and Andrew his brother, casting a net

---

[6] Galilee was known as ''Galilee of the Gentiles'' (Is. 9:1) because Gentiles made up the majority of its population.

[7] Mt. 7:13

into the sea: for they were fishermen; and He saith unto them. These two had been disciples of John, and while John was still living they had approached Christ. But when they saw John arrested, they returned again to their fishing, and so Christ comes, fishing for them, and says:

19-20. Come follow Me and I will make you fishers of men. And they straightway left their nets, and followed Him. Behold obedient men, who followed Him immediately. From this it is clear that this is the second time that He called them. For they had been taught by Christ on a previous occasion,[8] then left Him, and when they saw Him again followed Him readily.

21. And going on from thence, He saw two other brethren, James the son of Zebedee, and John his brother, in a boat with Zebedee their father. It is the greatest of virtues to care for one's father in his old age, and for the father to be supported by the just labors of his sons. **Mending their nets.** They were poor and as they were unable to buy new nets, they were stitching together their old ones.

22. And they immediately left the boat and their father, and followed Him. It appears that Zebedee did not believe and it is for this reason that they left him. Do you see when it becomes necessary to leave one's father? When the father becomes an impediment to virtue and reverence for God. When James and John saw the first two follow Christ, they rightly followed Christ as well, imitating their good example.

23. And Jesus went about all Galilee, teaching in their synagogues, and preaching the Gospel of the kingdom. Jesus enters the synagogues of the Hebrews to show that He is not opposed to the law. **And healing every disease and every infirmity among the people.** He begins with miracles, to give credibility to what He teaches. By "disease" is meant chronic illness, and by "infirmity", a temporary bodily disorder.

24. And His fame went throughout all Syria: and they brought unto Him all sick people that were afflicted with various diseases and

---

[8] Jn. 1:35-42

torments, and lunatics, and paralytics, and He healed them. Christ did not ask for faith from any of the sick that were brought to Him, for the very fact that they were brought from a distance was a sign of faith. "Lunatics" means those who were possessed by demons. For the devil wanted to instill in men the belief that the heavenly bodies cause evil, and so would wait until the moon was full and then would set upon men. The devil does this so that the moon would appear to be the cause of suffering, and thus God's creation would be slandered, as it was by the heretical Manichees in their delusion.

25. And there followed Him great multitudes of people from Galilee, and from Decapolis, and from Jerusalem, and from Judea, and from beyond the Jordan.

CHAPTER FIVE

On the beatitudes.
On not quarreling with one's neighbor.
On not committing adultery.
On not divorcing one's wife.
On not swearing at all.
On enduring insults and resisting the evil one.
On loving one's enemies.

1. And seeing the multitudes, He went up onto the mountain. He teaches us not to do anything ostentatiously. For when He is about to teach, He goes up onto the mountain, thus instructing us also when we would teach, to depart from the bustle in the city. **And when He had sat down, His disciples came to Him.** The multitude comes for the miracles, but the disciples come for the teachings. So when He has finished the miracles and healed their bodies, then He heals their souls as well, that we may learn that He is the Creator of both souls and bodies.

2. And He opened His mouth. Why does the evangelist say, "He opened His mouth"? It would appear that this is superfluous; but it is not. For He also taught without opening His mouth. How did He do this? By His life and His miracles. But now He opens His mouth and teaches. **And taught them, saying**. He taught not only His disciples, but the multitude as well. He begins with the beatitudes, "Blessed are they", just as David began the Psalms with the beatitude, "Blessed is the man."[1]

3. Blessed are the poor in spirit, for theirs is the kingdom of heaven. First He lays down humility as a foundation. Since Adam fell through pride, Christ raises us up by humility; for Adam had aspired to become God. The "poor in spirit" are those whose pride is crushed and who are contrite in soul.

4. Blessed are they that mourn, for they shall be comforted.

---

[1] Ps. 1:1

''Blessed are they that mourn'' for their sins, not for things of this life. Christ said, ''They that mourn,'' that is, they that are mourning incessantly and not just one time; and not only for our own sins, but for those of our neighbor. ''They shall be comforted'' both in this life, for he who mourns for his sin rejoices spiritually, and even more so in the next life.

5. Blessed are the meek, for they shall inherit the earth. Some say that the ''earth'' is the spiritual earth, that is, heaven. But understand it to mean this earth as well. Since the meek are thought to be those who are despised and deprived of wealth, Christ says that it is the meek, rather, who possess everything. The meek are not those who never get angry at all, for such people are unfeeling and apathetic. Rather, the meek are those who possess the capacity for anger but control it, and become angry only when it is necessary.

6. Blessed are they who hunger and thirst after righteousness, for they shall be filled. Since He is about to speak about almsgiving, He first shows that one must pursue righteousness, and not give alms from what has been acquired by theft and extortion. And one must avidly practice righteousness, for this is what it means to ''hunger and thirst''. Since it is the greedy who are thought to be well off and satisfied, Jesus says that it is rather the righteous who shall be filled, even here in this life, for what is theirs they possess with surety.

7. Blessed are the merciful, for they shall obtain mercy. Not only with money does one show mercy in almsgiving,[2] but also with words. And should you have nothing at all to give, show mercy with tears of compassion. ''They shall obtain mercy'' even here in this life from men; for if he who showed mercy yesterday should be in want today, he will obtain mercy from all. And in the next life, how much more shall he obtain mercy from God?

8. Blessed are the pure in heart, for they shall see God. There are many who are not rapacious and greedy, but are generous in almsgiving,

---

[2] The Greek word for ''almsgiving'', *eleēmosynē*, has the literal meaning of ''mercifulness''. To show mercy and to give alms are two differing human attributes in English. In Greek they are expressed by the same verb, *eleein*.

yet they fornicate and commit other uncleanliness. Christ commands, therefore, that along with the other virtues we should also be pure, that is, chaste and temperate, not only in the body, but in the heart as well. Without holiness, namely, chastity, no one will see the Lord. Just as a mirror will reflect images only if it is clean, so also only a pure soul admits the vision of God and the understanding of the Scriptures.

9. Blessed are the peacemakers, for they shall be called sons of God. "The peacemakers" are not only those who are themselves peaceable with all, but also those who reconcile others who are at odds. "The peacemakers" are also those who by their teaching convert the enemies of God. Just as the Only-begotten Son reconciled us to God when we were His enemies, so too are the "peacemakers" "sons of God".

10. Blessed are they that are persecuted for righteousness' sake, for theirs is the kingdom of heaven. It is not only the martyrs who are persecuted; many others are persecuted as well, for helping those who have been wronged, and simply for every virtue which they possess. For "righteousness" means every virtue. Thieves and murderers are also persecuted, but they are not blessed.

11. Blessed are ye, when men shall revile you and persecute you. He addresses the apostles directly, showing that it is especially the mark of a teacher to be reviled. **And shall say all manner of evil against you falsely, for My sake.** It is not simply he that is reviled who is blessed, but when he is reviled for Christ's sake, and falsely. If these two conditions are lacking, he is a wretch, as he has been a cause of temptation to many.

12. Rejoice and be exceeding glad, for great is your reward in heaven. Of the others whom He has said are blessed, He does not speak of a great reward. But here He does, to show that to patiently endure reviling is a great and most difficult thing; so difficult that there have been many who have even hanged themselves to escape this trial. Even Job, who patiently endured his other trials, was troubled when his friends reviled him by saying that he was suffering for his sins. **For so persecuted they the prophets which were before you.** So that the apostles would not think that they would be persecuted for teaching something contrary to God, He exhorts them by saying, "Even the prophets before you were persecuted for the sake of virtue, and so you have the example of their sufferings to give you courage."

13. Ye are the salt of the earth. The prophets were sent to one race only, but you are the salt of the whole earth. By your teachings and reproofs you act as an astringent upon the slack and the indolent, so that they will not breed the worms that never die. So do not desist from your astringent reproofs, even if you are reviled or persecuted. Therefore He says: **But if the salt has lost its savour, wherewith shall it be salted? It is thenceforth good for nothing, but to be cast out, and to be trodden under foot by men.** For if the teacher has become insipid, that is, if he does not give astringent reproofs, but has become soft and lax, "wherewith shall it be salted?" that is, how can this be corrected? So from then on he is cast out from the rank of teacher and is trodden under foot, that is, despised.

14. Ye are the light of the world. First He calls them salt and then light. He who reproves what is done in secret is light, "for whatsoever doth make manifest is light."[3] The apostles did not enlighten one nation only, but the world. **A city that is set on a hill cannot be hid.** He teaches them to struggle and to be strict in living a virtuous life, for they will be in view of all. Do not imagine, He says, that you will be hidden away in some corner, for you will be most visible. See to it, then, that you live blamelessly, lest you become a stumbling block for others.

15. Neither do men light a lamp, and put it under a bushel, but on a lamp stand; and it giveth light unto all that are in the house. Christ says, "It is I Who have kindled the light in you, but it is for you to labor zealously so that you do not extinguish that grace; in this way, the brightness of your life will shine upon others." He says, therefore:

16. Let your light so shine before men, that they may see your good works, and glorify your Father Who is in heaven. He did not

---

[3] Eph. 5:13

say, "You must display your virtue," for that is not good; but rather He said only, "Let it shine," so that even your enemies will marvel and glorify not you, but your Father. If we practice virtue, we must practice it for the glory of God, and not for our own glory.

17. Think not that I am come to abolish the law, or the prophets: I am not come to abolish, but to fulfill. He was about to introduce new laws, yet He did not want them to think that He was opposed to God. Therefore He says, anticipating the suspicion that many would have, "I have not come to abolish the law, but rather to fulfill it." How did He fulfill it? First, He did everything which the prophets had foretold concerning Him, which is why the evangelist often says, "So that what was spoken by the prophet might be fulfilled." He also fulfilled every commandment of the law. "For He did no sin, neither was any guile found in His mouth."[4] And He fulfilled and completed the law in yet another way: whatever the law had sketched in outline, Christ fully painted in. The law said, "Do not murder"; but Christ said, "Neither be angry without a cause." So too the painter does not destroy the sketch, but rather completes it.

18. For amen, I say unto you. The "amen" is an assurance, meaning, "Yes, truly I say unto you." **Till heaven and earth pass away, one jot or one tittle shall in no wise pass from the law, till all be accomplished.** He indicates here that the world passes away and undergoes a change in form. He is saying, therefore, that while the universe subsists, not the least letter of the law will pass away. Some say that the "jot" [i.e. the Greek letter iota] and the "tittle" [i.e. accent mark] signify the ten commandments of the law;[5] others say that they indicate the Cross, for the iota is the upright beam of the Cross, and the accent, the transverse beam. Christ is saying, therefore, that everything that was spoken concerning the Cross will be fulfilled.

19. Whosoever therefore shall disregard one of these least commandments, and shall teach men so, he shall be called least in the

---

[4] I Peter 2:22

[5] In the Greek system of numerals, an iota followed by an accent indicates the number 10.

kingdom of heaven. The "least commandments" are those which He Himself is about to give, not those of the law of Moses. He calls them "least" out of humility, to instruct you, O reader, to have moderate thoughts of yourself as you give your teachings. He who "shall be called least in the kingdom of heaven" means he who will be last in the resurrection and who will be cast into gehenna. For such a one shall not enter the kingdom of heaven, far from it! By "kingdom" understand the resurrection. **But whosoever shall do and teach them, the same shall be called great in the kingdom of heaven.** First Christ says, "whosoever shall do", and then, "and shall teach"; for how can I guide another along a road that I have not myself travelled? By the same token, if I practice the commandments, but do not teach them, my reward is not so great. There can even be condemnation, if I do not teach because of spite or sloth.

20. For I say unto you, That except your righteousness shall exceed the righteousness of the scribes and Pharisees, ye shall in no case enter into the kingdom of heaven. "Righteousness" means all the virtues, as in "Job was a righteous man, holy and blameless."[6] Tremble then, O man, when you have understood how much is required of us. Then He teaches us how we can exceed the righteousness of the scribes and Pharisees, and He enumerates the virtues.

21. Ye have heard that it was said to men of old, Thou shalt not murder; and whosoever shall murder shall be liable to judgement. Christ does not mention by whom this was said. For if He had said, "My Father said to the men of old, but I say to you," it would have appeared that He was giving laws in opposition to the Father. Again, if He had said, "I said to the men of old," this would have been hard to accept. Therefore He speaks indefinitely, "It was said to the men of old."[7] He shows that the law has become antiquated by saying, "It was said to the men of old." Therefore, since the law has become old and antiquated and near the point of obliteration, it is necessary to leave it and to run to the new commandments.

---

[6] Job 1:1

[7] Ex. 20:15; Deut. 5:17

22. But I say unto you, That whosoever is angry with His brother without good cause shall be liable to judgement. The prophets, about to prophesy, would say, "Thus saith the Lord," but Christ says, "I say", showing the authority of His divinity. For the prophets were servants; but He is the Son and possesses all that the Father has. He who "is angry with his brother without good cause" is condemned; but if anyone should get angry for good reason, either by way of chastisement or out of spiritual zeal, he is not condemned. For even Paul spoke words of anger to Elymas the Magician and to the high priest, not "without good cause", but out of zeal.[8] But when we get angry over money or opinions, then it is "without good cause". **And whosoever shall say to his brother, Raca, shall be liable to the council.** "The council" means the court of the Hebrews. "Raca" means something like "Hey, you!" as when we say to someone whom we scorn, "Hey you, get out of here!" The Lord exhorts us in these matters because He desires to teach us to be strict even in small things and to give honor to one another. Some say that "Raca" is a Syriac word for "despicable" or "scum". Therefore, whoever insults his brother as "despicable" will be liable to the council of the holy apostles when they sit to judge the twelve tribes. **But whosoever shall say, Thou fool, shall be liable to the gehenna of fire.** There are many who say and believe that this is too grievous and severe a judgement. But it is not. For is he who would deny the existence of his brother's faculties of reason and thought, those characteristics by which we differ from the beasts, is such a man not deserving of gehenna? For he who reviles and insults, dissolves love; and when love is dissolved, all the virtues are destroyed along with it, just as when love is present it unites to itself all the virtues. Therefore, he who hurls insults, destroys all the virtues by tearing love to shreds, and rightly does he deserve the fire of hell.

23-24. Therefore if thou bring thy gift to the altar, and there rememberest that thy brother have aught against thee, leave there thy gift before the altar, and go thy way; first be reconciled to thy brother, and then come and offer thy gift. God disregards His own honor solely that we might love one another. He said, "If thy brother

---

[8] Acts 13:6-12 and 23:2-3.

have aught against thee,'' and added nothing more. Whether rightly or wrongly your brother has anything against you, be reconciled. And Jesus did not say, ''If thou hast aught against him,'' but, ''If he hath aught against thee'' hasten to make him your friend. He commands you to leave the gift so that you will be compelled to be reconciled. For when you intend to make an offering, you must first be reconciled. At the same time the Lord shows that love is the true sacrifice.

25-26. Agree with thine adversary quickly, while thou art on the way with him, lest thy adversary deliver thee to the judge, and the judge deliver thee to the officer, and thou be cast into prison. Verily I say unto thee, Thou shalt by no means come out thence, till thou hast paid the uttermost farthing. Some believe the ''adversary'' to mean the devil, and ''the way'' to mean our life. The Lord is thus exhorting us: while you are still in this life, give back to the devil what belongs to him and be done with him, so that later he will not be able to accuse you of some sin, as if you had something that belonged to him. For then you will be handed over for punishment so that you make an accounting for even the smallest transgressions. For a farthing equals two mites.[9] You, O reader, understand that this passage also refers to human adversaries and that the Lord is exhorting us not to become entangled in lawsuits, lest we be distracted from doing the works of God. Even if you have been wronged, He says, do not enter the court but settle the dispute while still on the way, lest you suffer something worse on account of your adversary's power.

27-28. Ye have heard that it was said, Thou shalt not commit adultery. But I say unto you, That whosoever looketh on a woman to lust after her hath committed adultery with her already in his heart. That is, if one stands gazing and examining, kindling desire by looking, and looking again to desire even more, he has already brought the evil to readiness in his heart. If he did not add to it the deed itself, what of it? He was not able. If he had been able, he would immediately have perpetrated the evil. But nevertheless understand that if we have lusted, and then were prevented from committing the deed, clearly we were

[9] Lk. 12:6, 21:2

protected by grace. And if a woman has adorned herself in order to attract others, yet does not succeed in attracting, she is guilty of having mixed the poison into the cup, though no one drank.

29-30. And if thy right eye causeth thee to sin,[10] pluck it out and cast it from thee: for it is profitable for thee that one of thy members should perish, and not that thy whole body should be cast into gehenna. And if thy right hand causeth thee to sin, cut it off, and cast it from thee: for it is profitable for thee that one of thy members should perish, and not that thy whole body should be cast into gehenna. When you hear "eye" and "hand" do not imagine that the Lord is speaking of parts of the body, for He would not in that case have specified "right eye" and "right hand". He is speaking instead of those who appear to be friends, but who are in fact harming us. Take, for example, a young man who has friends living in debauchery, and who is harmed by their bad influence. Cut these off from you, the Lord says, and perhaps you will also save them, when they come to their senses. And if you cannot save them, you will at least save yourself. But if you continue in your affection for them, both you and they will be destroyed.

31. It hath been said, Whosoever shall put away his wife, let him give her a writing of divorcement. Moses commanded that if a man hated his wife, he should be separated from her lest anything worse occur.[11] For if he hated her, he might kill her. Moses also commanded that the husband give the divorced woman a writing of divorcement. By this writing she could no longer return to him, thus preventing the confusion that would result if she did so and he was now living with another woman.

32. But I say unto you, That whosoever shall put away his wife, saving for the cause of fornication, causeth her to commit adultery:

---

[10] The Greek verb *skandalizein*, here rendered as "cause to sin", derives from the noun *skandalon* which may mean in the New Testament: trap, snare, hindrance, obstacle, stumbling block, occasion of sin, or scandal. It may also, depending on the context, mean "offense", as the King James Version consistently translates it. See *The Arena*, Archimandrite Lazarus, tr., Holy Trinity Monastery, Jordanville, N.Y., p. 57.

[11] Deut. 24:3

and whosoever shall marry her that is divorced committeth adultery. Christ does not abolish the Mosaic decrees but corrects them by making the husband fearful of hating his wife without cause. If he divorces her with good cause, that is, if she has committed adultery, he is not condemned. But if there has been no fornication, he is condemned, for by divorcing her he compels her to commit adultery. And he that takes her is also an adulterer, for if he had not taken her she would have returned and submitted to her husband. For a Christian must be a peacemaker, both towards others and even more so towards his own wife.

33. Again, ye have heard that it hath been said, Thou shalt not swear falsely, but shalt perform unto the Lord thine oaths. That is, when you take an oath, speak the truth.

34-35. But I say unto you, Swear not at all; neither by heaven, for it is God's throne; nor by the earth, for it is the footstool of His feet; neither by Jerusalem, for it is the city of the great king. Since the Jews had heard God say, "Heaven is My throne, and earth is My footstool,"[12] they would swear by such things. In prohibiting them from swearing by these things, the Lord does not say, "Do not swear by them because heaven is good and great, and earth is useful." Instead He says, "Do not swear by them because the one is the throne of God and the other is His footstool," so that idolatry would not occur. For they might make gods out of those elements by which they swore, which indeed had happened before.

36. Neither shalt thou swear by thy head, because thou canst not make one hair white or black. God alone swears by Himself as He is not subject to anyone or anything. Since we do not have authority over ourselves, how can we swear by our own head? It is the property of another. But if you think your head is your own, then change one hair of it if you can.

37. But let your speech be, Yea, yea; Nay, nay. Lest you ask, "How then will people believe what I say?" He says, "They will believe you

---

[12] Is. 66:1

if you always tell the truth and never swear at all.'' For no one is disbelieved more than he who is eager to swear that he speaks the truth. **What is more than this, is of the evil one.** The Lord says that swearing, which is more than ''Yea'' and ''Nay'', is of the devil. But, you will ask, is the law of Moses, which bids us to swear, also evil? Learn, then, that at that time it was not evil to swear. But after Christ, it is evil. And so it is with circumcision and, in short, with all the Judaic practices. So also, to nurse at the breast is proper for infants, but shameful for adults.

38. Ye have heard that it hath been said, An eye for an eye, and a tooth for a tooth. Condescending to human perversity, the law permitted retaliation so that men would not harm each other, out of fear of suffering the same themselves.[13]

39. But I say unto you, that ye resist not the evil one: but whosoever shall smite thee on thy right cheek, turn to him the other also. ''The evil one'' here means the devil, who works through man. We ought not, then, to resist the devil? Yes, we should, but not by striking back at our neighbor, but through patient endurance. For fire is not extinguished by fire but by water. Do not think that the Lord is speaking only of a blow on the cheek, but of any and every other kind of affliction.

40. And if any man will sue thee at the law, and take away thy tunic, let him have thy cloak also. If he drags you into court and harasses you, give him your cloak as well, and not only what he asks for. The ''tunic'' is what we would call the inner garment, and the ''cloak'' is the outer garment. But the names are sometimes used one for the other.

41. And whosoever shall compel thee to go a mile, go with him two. ''Why should I speak of cloaks and tunics?'' the Lord is saying. Give even your body to him who wrongfully compels you, and do more than he wants you to do.

42. Give to him that asketh thee, and from him that would borrow of thee turn thou not away. Give to him whether he be friend, enemy,

---

[13] Ex. 21:24

or infidel, and whether he asks for money or any other kind of help. The loan here means one without interest, the simple giving of the use of the money. For even under the law they would lend without charging interest.

43-44. Ye have heard that it hath been said, Thou shalt love thy neighbour and hate thine enemy. But I say unto you, Love your enemies. Here the Lord has reached the very pinnacle of the virtues. For what is greater than to love one's enemies? But it is not impossible to accomplish. For Moses and Paul loved the Jews who were raging against them more than they loved themselves, and all the saints have loved their enemies. **Bless them that curse you, do good to them that hate you, and pray for them which despitefully use you, and persecute you.** We bless them because we must consider them our benefactors. For anyone who persecutes us and puts us to the test, lightens the punishment that we will suffer for our own sins. We will also bless them when God gives us the great crown of the contest. For hear what He says:

45. That ye may be the sons of your Father Who is in heaven. For He maketh His sun to rise on the evil and on the good, and sendeth rain on the righteous and on the unrighteous. Do you see how good a gift is given to you by him who hates and abuses you, if only you will endure it with patience? By rain and sun, understand knowledge and teaching, for God enlightens and teaches all.[14]

46. For if ye love them which love you, what reward have ye? Do not even the publicans do the same? Let us tremble with fear since we are not the equal of the publicans, but hate even those who love us.

47-48. And if ye salute your friends only, what do ye more than others? Do not even the publicans so? Be ye therefore perfect, even as your Father Who is in heaven is perfect. To love some men, that is, one's own friends, and to hate others, is imperfection. Perfection is to love every one.

---

[14] A scholion in the text of the Slavonic version adds: "He that receives the teaching lives in the light, but he that closes his eyes in the sunlight remains in the darkness."

CHAPTER SIX

On almsgiving, prayer, and fasting.
On disdaining the things of this world.

1. Take heed that ye give not your alms before men, to be seen by them: otherwise ye have no reward of your Father Who is in heaven. Having led them up to the greatest of the virtues, which is love, now He drives away vainglory, which follows after the achievement of the virtues. See what He says, "Take heed", as if speaking of some terrible wild beast. Take heed that it not tear you limb from limb. If you give alms "before men" but your motive is not "to be seen by them", you are not condemned. But if your motive is vainglory, then even if you give alms from within your inner chamber, you are condemned. For it is the intent that God either punishes or crowns.

2. Therefore when thou givest thine alms, do not sound a trumpet before thee, as the hypocrites do in the synagogues and in the streets, that they may be praised by men. The hypocrites did not actually have trumpets; the Lord is here deriding their thoughts, for they wanted their almsgiving to be trumpeted. "Hypocrites" are those who differ in appearance from what they really are. These men, therefore, appear to be merciful and generous, but are in fact the opposite. **Verily I say unto you, They have received their reward.** Having been praised by men, that is the only reward they will receive.

3. But when thou givest alms, let not thy left hand know what thy right hand doeth. Using hyperbole of language, the Lord said, "If it is possible, do not even be aware yourself that you are giving alms." Or, in another sense as well, the left hand represents vainglory and the right hand, almsgiving. Let not your vainglory be aware of your almsgiving.

4. That thine alms may be in secret, and thy Father Who seeth in secret Himself shall reward thee openly. When will He reward you? When all things are revealed clearly and openly, and then you will be not merely rewarded, but glorified.

5. And when thou prayest, thou shalt not be as the hypocrites are: for they love to pray standing in the synagogues and in the corners of the streets, that they may be seen of men. Verily I say unto you, They have received their reward. He also calls those men hypocrites who pretend they are looking to God when in fact they are looking to men; and from men they have received the only reward they will receive.

6. But thou, when thou prayest, enter into thine inner chamber and when thou hast shut thy door, pray to thy Father Who is in secret; and thy Father Who seeth in secret shall reward thee openly. Should I not then pray in church? Indeed I should, but with a right mind and not for show. For it is not the place which harms prayer, but the manner and the intent with which we pray. For many who pray in secret do so to impress men.

7. But when ye pray, do not babble as the Gentiles do. "Babbling" means praying foolishly, as when someone asks for such worldly things as fame, wealth, or victory. "Babbling" is also inarticulate, childish speech. Therefore you, O reader, must not pray foolishly. **For they think that they shall be heard for their many words.** It is not necessary to make long prayers, but rather short and frequent prayers, uttering few words, but persevering in prayer.

8. Be not ye therefore like unto them: for your Father knoweth what things ye have need of, before ye ask Him. It is not to inform God of anything that we make our petitions, but instead, that we may detach ourselves from the cares of life and receive benefit by conversing with God.

9. In this manner, therefore, pray ye: Our Father Who art in the heavens. A vow is different from a prayer.[1] A vow is a promise made to God, as, for example, when one vows to abstain from wine, etc. But prayer is a petitioning for good things. By saying "Father", the Lord shows you of what good things you have been deemed worthy, having

---

[1] Bl. Theophylact here draws attention to the similarity, yet difference, between the Greek words for "vow" and "prayer", *euchē* and *pros-euchē*.

become a son of God. By saying "in the heavens" He has revealed to you your fatherland and your paternal home. For if you desire to have God as your Father, then look toward heaven and not toward earth. And you must not say, "My Father", but "Our Father", regarding all men as brothers of one and the same Father. **Hallowed be Thy Name.** This means, Make us holy, so that Thou mightest be glorified through us. For just as God is blasphemed through me, so also is He hallowed through me, that is, He is glorified as the Holy One.

10. Thy kingdom come. This refers to the second coming. He whose clean conscience renders him bold prays that the resurrection and the judgement will come. **Thy will be done on earth as it is in heaven.** Just as the angels do Thy will, the Lord says, so also grant us to do the same.

11. Give us this day our daily bread. By the word "daily" He means what is sufficient for our existence, our essence, and our sustenance.[2] Thus He teaches us not to worry about tomorrow. "Bread for our essence" is also the Body of Christ, of Which we pray that we may partake without condemnation.

12. And forgive us our debts, as we forgive our debtors. Because we sin even after our baptism, we beseech Him to forgive us. But forgive us as we forgive others: if we remember wrongs, God will not forgive us. God takes me as the pattern He will follow: what I do to another, He does to me.

13. And lead us not into temptation. We humans are weak and therefore we should not throw ourselves into temptations. But when we have fallen into temptation, we should pray that we not be swallowed up by it. For he who has been led into the very depth of temptation is the one who has been swallowed up and defeated by temptation. But it is different for him who merely fell into temptation, and then conquered it. **But deliver us from the evil one.** He did not say, from evil men, for it

---

[2] The Greek word here translated as "daily" is *epiousios*, a word virtually unique to the Gospel; the ancient scholarly authority Origen considered that it was coined by the Lord or by the apostles. The word consists of the prefix *epi* and the form *ousia* meaning "existence", "essence", or "substance". Hence, *epi-ousios artos* means literally "bread for [man's] being".

is not they who do us harm, but the devil. **For Thine is the kingdom and the power and the glory unto the ages. Amen.** Here He emboldens us, for if our Father is King, powerful and glorious, then certainly we too will defeat the evil one and we will then be made glorious.

14. For if ye forgive men their trespasses, your heavenly Father will also forgive you. Again He teaches us not to remember wrongs. He reminds us of the Father so that we might revere Him, since we are the children of such a Father, and not act as fierce beasts, refusing to forgive.

15. But if ye forgive not men their trespasses, neither will your Father forgive your trespasses. God, Who is meek, hates nothing more than cruelty.

16. Moreover when ye fast, be not, as the hypocrites, of a sad countenance: for they disfigure their faces, that they may appear unto men to fast. Verily I say unto you, They have received their reward. "Disfigurement of the face" is an artificial discoloration of the face, painting it pale, so that one does not appear as he really is, but feigns mournfulness.

17-18. But thou, when thou fastest, anoint thine head, and wash thy face; that thou appear not unto men to fast, but unto thy Father Who is in secret: and thy Father Who seeth in secret shall reward thee openly. Men of old would anoint themselves with oil after bathing as a mark of their joy and well-being. So you also, O reader, should appear joyful when you fast. The oil used to anoint we also understand to mean almsgiving.[3] Our Head is Christ, Which we should anoint with deeds of mercy; and our face, that is our senses, we should wash with tears of repentance.

19-21. Lay not up for yourselves treasures upon earth, where moth and corruption doth destroy, and where thieves break through and steal: but lay up for yourselves treasures in heaven, where neither

---

[3] On the relationship between olive oil, mercy, and alms, see the footnote at Mt. 3:16 on p. 37, and at Mt. 5:7 on p. 45.

moth nor corruption doth destroy, and where thieves do not break through nor steal. For where your treasure is, there will your heart be also. Having first cast out the sickness of vainglory by what He said before, now He speaks about non-possessiveness. For men possess more than they need because of vainglory. He shows how unprofitable earthly treasure is: moth and corruption consume food and clothing, and thieves steal gold and silver. And then, so that no one should say to Him that not all treasure is stolen, Jesus says, even if nothing is lost in this manner, are you not wretched for being nailed down by your worries over wealth? This is why He says, "Where your treasure is, there will your heart be also."

22-23. The eye is the lamp of the body: if therefore thine eye be sound, thy whole body shall be full of light. But if thine eye be evil, thy whole body shall be full of darkness. If therefore the light that is in thee be darkness, how great is that darkness. This means, if you fill your mind with worries over money, you have extinguished the lamp and darkened your soul. For just as the eye that is "sound" or "healthy" brings light to the body, and the eye that is "evil" or "diseased" brings darkness, so also does the state of the mind affect the soul. If the mind is blinded by these worries, it is cast into darkness; then the soul becomes dark, and how much more so the body as well?

24. No man can serve two lords. What He means is this: no man can serve two lords who command things that are opposed to each other. Such lords are God and mammon. We make the devil our lord when we make the belly our god. But by nature and in truth God is the Lord, and mammon is unrighteousness. **For either he will hate the one, and love the other; or else he will hold to the one, and despise the other. Ye cannot serve God and mammon.** Do you see that it is not possible for a rich and unrighteous man to serve God? His love of money drives him away from God.

25. For this reason I say unto you, Take no thought for your life, what ye shall eat, or what ye shall drink; nor yet for your body, what ye shall put on. "For this reason"—for what reason? Because concern over money drives a man away from God. The soul does not eat, for it is bodiless, but Jesus said this according to the common use of the word.[4] For it is obvious that the soul does not consent to remain in a body if the flesh is not fed. Jesus does not forbid us to work, but rather He forbids us to give ourselves over entirely to our cares and to neglect God. Hence we must work for our livelihood[5] while not neglecting the soul. **Is not life more than food, and the body more than raiment?** This means, will not He Who gave what is greater, life itself, and fashioned the body, will He not also give food and clothing?

26. Behold the birds of the air: for they sow not, neither do they reap, nor gather into barns; yet your heavenly Father feedeth them. Are ye not much more than they? Although He could have given the example of Elijah and John the Baptist, instead He mentions the birds in order to shame us, for we are even more witless than these creatures. God feeds them by having given them the instinctive knowledge for finding food.

27. Which of you by taking thought can add one cubit unto his stature? This means, even if you take the utmost care, you can do nothing if God does not will it. Why then do you drive yourself to exhaustion with futile worries?

28-29. And why take ye thought for raiment? Consider the lilies of the field, how they grow; they toil not, neither do they spin: and yet I say unto you, That even Solomon in all his glory was not arrayed like one of these. He shames us not only by the birds, which lack reason, but also by the lilies, that wither. For if God adorned the lilies in such a manner, without any necessity to do so, how much more will He fulfill our own need for clothing? He shows that though you go to great lengths, you are not able to be adorned as beautifully as the lilies. Even Solomon the most wise and splendid, with all his kingdom at his disposal, could not array himself in such a manner.

---

[4] In the text of St. Matthew, "Take no thought for your life," the Greek word translated as "life" is *psychē*. It also means "soul". Bl. Theophylact has both meanings in mind in his commentary. See also the commentary on Mt. 2:19-20 on p. 30.

[5] Literally, "work the soil", the primary occupation in a non-industrial society.

30. Wherefore, if God so clothe the grass of the field, which today is, and tomorrow is cast into the oven, shall He not much more clothe you, O ye of little faith? We learn from this that we ought not to be concerned with beautifying ourselves, for our adornments wither like the fading flowers. Therefore one who beautifies himself is like grass. But you, He says, are creatures endowed with reason, whom God fashioned with both soul and body. Those "of little faith" are all those who concern themselves with such thoughts. For if they had perfect faith in God, they would not give such anxious thoughts to these things.

31-32. Therefore take no thought, saying, What shall we eat? or, What shall we drink? or, Wherewithal shall we be clothed? For after all these things do the Gentiles seek. He does not forbid us to eat, but to say, "What shall we eat?" The rich say in the evening, "What shall we eat tomorrow?" See that it is luxury and excess that He forbids.

32-33. For your heavenly Father knoweth that ye have need of all these things. But seek ye first the kingdom of God, and His righteousness; and all these things shall be added unto you. The kingdom of God is the enjoyment of all that is good. This comes through righteousness. To him who seeks after spiritual things God in His generosity adds that which is needed for physical life.

34. Take therefore no thought for the morrow: for the morrow shall take thought for the things of itself. Sufficient unto the day is the evil thereof. "The evil of the day" means the crushing burden and pressure. It is sufficient for you that you are afflicted by today's burden. If you also take thought for tomorrow, and continually burden yourself for the sake of bodily things, when will you have time for God?

CHAPTER SEVEN

On not judging anyone. On asking and seeking. Concerning the need to beware of false prophets.

1. Judge not, that ye be not judged. He forbids condemning others, but not reproving others. A reproof is for another's benefit, but condemnation expresses only derision and scorn. You may also understand that the Lord is speaking of one who, despite his own great sins, condemns others who have lesser sins of which God will be the judge.

2-5. For with what judgement ye judge, ye shall be judged: and with what measure ye mete, it shall be measured to you again. And why beholdest thou the speck that is in thy brother's eye, but considerest not the beam that is in thine own eye? Or how wilt thou say to thy brother, Let me pull out the speck out of thine eye; and, behold, a beam is in thine own eye? Thou hypocrite, first cast out the beam out of thine own eye; and then shalt thou see clearly to cast out the speck out of thy brother's eye. He who would rebuke others ought to be blameless himself. If he himself has a plank in his eye, that is, some great sin, and he finds fault with another who has only a speck, he causes that man to be even more shameless in his sin. The Lord shows that he who has sinned greatly is not even able to see clearly the sin of his brother. For how could one who has a plank in his eye even see another man who is only slightly injured.

6. Give not that which is holy unto the dogs, neither cast ye your pearls before swine, lest they trample them under their feet, and turn again and rend you. The dogs are the unbelievers and the swine are believers who lead a filthy and shameful way of life. One ought not therefore to speak of the mysteries to the unbelievers, nor speak brilliant and lustrous words of theology to those who are unclean. For the swine trample them underfoot, that is, despise what is said, while the dogs turn on us and tear us limb from limb. This is what those so-called philosophers do; when they hear that God was crucified, they stab us with their syllogisms, reasoning with their sophistry that this is impossible.

7-8. Ask, and it shall be given you; seek, and ye shall find; knock, and it shall be opened unto you: for every one that asketh receiveth; and he that seeketh findeth; and to him that knocketh it shall be opened. In what has preceded the Lord has commanded us to do great and difficult things. Here He shows us how these things can be accomplished: through unceasing prayer. For He said, "Ask," that is, "keep asking," meaning, "ask continuously."[1] For He did not say, "Ask one time." Then He affirms what He has said by an example from everyday life.

9-10. Or what man is there of you, whom if his son ask bread, will he give him a stone? Or if he ask a fish, will he give him a serpent? Here He teaches us that we must not only ask in a fervent manner, but we must also ask for things that are profitable for us. For, He says, when your children ask for things that are good for them, such as bread and fish, you give them what they are seeking. So too must you seek from God what is profitable for you, that is, spiritual things and not things of the flesh.

11. If ye then, being evil, know how to give good gifts unto your children, how much more shall your Father Who is in heaven give good things to them that ask Him? He calls men evil by comparison with God, for our nature is good, being God's creation. But we become evil by our own choice.

12. Therefore all things whatsoever ye would that men should do to you, do ye even so to them: for this is the law and the prophets. In a few words He shows us the way to virtue. We humans know just by common sense what we ought to do. If you wish others to do good to you, do good to them. If you wish to be loved by your enemies, you must love your enemies. For both the law of God and the prophets speak of those things which even natural law bids us to do.

---

[1] In Greek the present imperative of the verb implies continuous action, while the aorist imperative implies a single, isolated action. The Greek words translated as "ask", "seek", and "knock" in this passage of St. Matthew are all in the present, not the aorist, imperative, so a more accurate translation might be: "keep asking", "keep seeking", "keep knocking".

13. Enter ye in at the narrow gate: for wide is the gate and broad is the way that leadeth to destruction, and many there be which go in thereat. The narrow gate means both trials that are voluntarily undertaken, such as fasting and the like, and trials that are involuntarily experienced, such as imprisonment and persecution. Just as a man who is fat, or who is carrying a great load, cannot go in through a narrow gate, neither can a gourmandizer or a rich man. These go in through the wide gate. To show that narrowness is temporary and that width is likewise transitory, He calls them a ''gate'' and a ''way''. For the gate is hardship, and he who undergoes hardship passes through his hardship as quickly as he would pass through a gate. And the pleasures of the gourmandizer's feast are as transitory as any moment in a journey along a road. Since both are temporary, we ought to choose the better of the two.

14. How narrow is the gate and how hard the way which leadeth unto life, and few there be that find it! The word ''how'' expresses the Lord's wonderment, as if He were saying, ''Alas, how narrow it is!'' But how is it that the Lord says on another occasion, ''My yoke is light''?[2] It is light on account of the future rewards.[3]

15-16. Beware of false prophets, who come to you in sheep's clothing, but inwardly they are ravening wolves. Ye shall know them by their fruits. The heretics are cunning and deceitful, which is why He says, ''Beware.'' They produce sweet words and feign a decent life, but within lies the hook. ''Sheep's clothing'' is meekness, which some pretend to employ, in order to flatter and to deceive. But they are recognized by their ''fruit'', that is, by their deeds and by their life. For though they can dissemble for a time, they are unmasked by those who are heedful.

16-17. Do men gather grapes from thorns, or figs from thistles?

---

[2] Mt. 11:30

[3] A Slavonic scholion adds: ''For the burden and yoke and way and gate signify the commandments. They are light and good for all who sincerely desire to be granted eternal and ineffable blessings, but they are heavy and grievous for the negligent and lazy and all who passionately look for the good things of this age. Thus it is that few are saved. See to it that you are one of the few.''

Even so, every good tree bringeth forth good fruit; but a corrupt tree bringeth forth evil fruit. The hypocrites are called thorns and thistles: they are like thorns in that they prick unexpectedly; they are like thistles in their cunning and deviousness. The corrupt tree is anyone who has been corrupted by a pleasure-loving and dissolute life.

18. A good tree cannot bring forth evil fruit, neither can a corrupt tree bring forth good fruit. A corrupt tree cannot bring forth good fruit as long as it is diseased. But if it has changed its condition, it can bring forth good fruit. See that He did not say, "it will not be able", but only that as long as it is corrupt it does not bear good fruit.

19-20. Every tree that bringeth not forth good fruit is hewn down, and cast into the fire. Wherefore by their fruits ye shall know them. He addresses the Jews, speaking the same words as did John.[4] Jesus likens man to a tree. For by the introduction of a graft, a fruitless tree can bear fruit; so, too, a sinful and fruitless man when engrafted with Christ can bear fruits of virtue.

21. Not every one that saith unto Me, Lord, Lord, shall enter into the kingdom of heaven; but he that doeth the will of My Father Who is in heaven. Here Jesus shows that He is Lord by saying, "Not every one that saith unto Me, Lord, Lord." Jesus in fact is saying that He is God. He teaches us that we derive no benefit from our faith if it is without works. "He that doeth the will of My Father." He did not mean, "that did the will of My Father on one occasion" but "that doeth the will of My Father continually until his death." And He did not say, "that doeth My will," lest He scandalize His listeners, but instead, "that doeth the will of My Father." For the will of a father and his son are one and the same, unless the son rebels.

22-23. Many will say to Me in that day, Lord, Lord, have we not prophesied in Thy name? And in Thy name cast out devils? And in Thy name done many wonderful works? And then will I profess unto them, I never knew you: depart from Me, ye that work iniquity. At

---

[4] Mt. 3:10

the beginning of the preaching many who were unworthy cast out demons that fled at the name of Jesus. For the grace was at work even in the unworthy, just as we may be sanctified by unworthy priests. Judas also worked signs, as did the sons of Sceva.[5] Jesus says, "I never knew you," meaning, "at that time when you were working miracles I did not know you," that is, "I did not love you." Here "know" means "love".

24-25. Therefore whosoever heareth these sayings of Mine, and doeth them, I will liken him unto a wise man, who built his house upon a rock: and the rain descended, and the rivers came, and the winds blew, and beat upon that house; and it fell not: for it was founded upon a rock. No virtue can be accomplished without God, which is why Jesus said, "I will liken him unto a wise man." The rock is Christ and the house is the soul. Therefore nothing will shake the man who builds his soul upon the doing of Christ's commandments. Neither the rain, which is the devil who fell from heaven, nor the rivers, which are mean and harmful men filled to overflowing by such a rain, nor the winds, which are evil spirits, nor, in short, can any temptations cast down such a man.

26-27. And every one that heareth these sayings of Mine, and doeth them not, shall be likened unto a foolish man, who built his house upon the sand: and the rain descended, and the rivers came, and the winds blew, and beat upon that house; and it fell: and great was the fall of it. Speaking of the man who believes but does not act, Jesus did not say, "I will liken him to a foolish man." Instead Jesus says, "He shall be likened" on his own account to a foolish man. Such a man builds the house of his soul upon sand, that is, with no deeds to provide a stable foundation. This is why it collapses under the blows of temptations. For when temptation beats upon it, it falls with a crash. Unbelievers do not fall, for they are always lying on the ground. It is the believer who falls. Therefore "great was the fall", because it was a Christian who fell.

28-29. And it came to pass, when Jesus had ended these sayings, the people were astonished at His teaching: for He taught them as

---

[5] Acts 19:14-17

one having authority, and not as the scribes. It was not the rulers who were astonished: how could that be when they viewed Him with spite? Rather it was the guileless multitude that was astonished. They did not marvel at His turns of phrase, but at His straightforward speech, and that He showed authority beyond that of the prophets. The prophets said, "Thus saith the Lord," but Christ spoke as God, "I say to you."

CHAPTER EIGHT

Concerning the leper. Concerning the centurion.
Concerning Peter's mother-in-law.
Concerning those healed of various diseases.
Concerning the man not permitted to follow Christ.
Concerning the rebuking of the waters.
Concerning those possessed of demons, from whom the demons were cast out and entered the herd of swine.

1-2. When He was come down from the mountain, great multitudes followed Him. And, behold, a leper approached and fell prostrate before Him, saying, Lord, if Thou wilt, Thou canst make me clean. Being a man of good sense, the leper did not go up on to the mountain, so as not to interrupt Jesus' teaching. But when Jesus came down from the mountain, then the leper worshipped Him. And the leper did not say, "If you beseech God, then you will heal me." But he showed great faith, saying, "If Thou wilt." And Christ did.

3-4. And Jesus put forth His hand, and touched him, saying, I will it; be thou clean. And immediately his leprosy was cleansed. And Jesus saith unto him, See thou tell no man; but go thy way, show thyself to the priest, and offer the gift that Moses commanded, for a testimony unto them. He touches the leper to show that He is not subject to the law which forbids one to touch a leper, but rather that He is Master of that law. He also shows that for Him Who is pure, nothing is impure, and that His holy flesh imparts holiness. Fleeing glory, He commands the leper to tell no one, but rather to show himself to the priest. For unless the priest would say that the leper was clean, he would have to remain outside the city.[1] Jesus bids him to offer the gift as a testimony to the Jews, as if to say, "When they accuse Me of abolishing the law, you shall bear witness on My behalf that I commanded you to offer the gifts required by the law."

---

[1] See Levit. 14.

5-6. And when Jesus entered into Capernaum, there came unto Him a centurion, beseeching Him, and saying. This man, too, did not approach Jesus while on the mountain, to avoid interrupting the teaching. This is the same man mentioned by Luke.[2] Although Luke says that the centurion sent to Jesus others who were elders, this does not contradict Matthew who says that the centurion himself came to Jesus. For it is altogether likely that first he sent others, and then, when death was imminent, he himself came and said:

6-7. Lord, my servant lieth at home a paralytic, grievously tormented. And Jesus saith unto him, I will come and heal him. The centurion did not bring his servant lying on his bed to Jesus, as he believed that Jesus could heal him even from a distance. Therefore:

8-10. The centurion answered and said, Lord, I am not worthy that Thou shouldest enter under my roof: but speak the word only, and my servant shall be healed. For I am a man under authority, having soldiers under me: and I say to this man, Go, and he goeth; and to another, Come, and he cometh; and to my servant, Do this, and he doeth it. When Jesus heard it, He marvelled, and said to them that followed, Verily I say unto you, I have not found so great faith, no, not in Israel. The centurion says, "If I who am the servant of the emperor command the soldiers who are under me, how much more so art Thou able to command death and the illnesses, so that they depart from one and beset another?" For illnesses of the body are God's soldiers and officers of punishment. Christ marvels, therefore, saying, "I have not found such great faith among the Israelites as I have in this Gentile."[3]

---

[2] Lk. 7:1-10

[3] A scholion in the Greek text adds:

Others have interpreted these words thus: When Jacob, the renowned patriarch, beheld the ladder reaching up to heaven and the angels of God ascending and descending, he understood that God was present in that place, but not that He is everywhere present. Thus he said, "How fearful is this place! This is none other than the house of God." (Gen. 28:16-17) The Lord now marvels at the great and supernatural faith of this Gentile, saying, "Not even in Israel"—that is, in Jacob—"did I find such faith. For Jacob understood that I could appear in one place, but this man understands that I am everywhere in all places and that by word alone I can do all things." For he said, "Only speak the word, and my servant shall be healed."

11-12. And I say unto you, That many shall come from the east and west, and shall sit at table with Abraham, and Isaac, and Jacob, in the kingdom of heaven. But the sons of the kingdom shall be cast out into outer darkness: there shall be weeping and gnashing of teeth. Jesus did not say outright, "Many Gentiles shall sit at table." But He said it in a roundabout manner, so as not to scandalize the Jews, "Many shall come from the east and west." He mentioned Abraham to show that He does not stand in opposition to the Old Testament. By saying "outer darkness" He shows that there is also an inner darkness which is less severe. For in hell there are varying degrees of punishment. He calls the Jews "the sons of the kingdom", for the promises of the Old Testament were made to them. He is saying, "Israel is my firstborn son."[4]

13. And Jesus said unto the centurion, Go thy way; and as thou hast believed, so be it done unto thee. And his servant was healed in the selfsame hour. And when the centurion returned to his house, at the same hour, he found his servant well. By healing the servant by His word alone, Jesus showed that He also spoke the truth when He said that the Jews would be cast out from the kingdom.

14-15. And when Jesus was come into Peter's house, He saw his mother-in-law lying sick with a fever. And He touched her hand, and the fever left her: and she arose, and ministered unto them. Jesus entered Peter's house so that they could eat. And when He touched the woman's hand, not only did He quench her fever but He restored her to perfect health, so that her strength returned and she was able to serve. Yet we know that it takes a considerable time for the sick to recover their strength. The other evangelists say that first they besought Him and then Jesus healed the woman;[5] but Matthew does not say this, for reasons of brevity. For I told you at the beginning that what one evangelist leaves out, the other mentions. Learn also that marriage does not impede virtue: the chief of the apostles had a mother-in-law.

16-17. When the evening was come, they brought unto Him many

---

[4] Ex. 4:22

[5] See Mk. 1:29-31 and Lk. 4:38-39.

who were possessed with demons, and He cast out the spirits by His word, and healed all that were sick: that it might be fulfilled which was spoken by Isaiah the prophet, saying, He Himself took our weaknesses, and bore our diseases. At the end of the day and on into the evening, they brought the sick to Him and He, in His love for man, healed them all. Then Matthew brings forward the witness of Isaiah,[6] lest you disbelieve that He could heal so many sicknesses in so short a time. Although the prophet spoke concerning sins, Matthew has applied these words to illnesses, for the majority of illnesses occur as a result of sins.

18. Now when Jesus saw great multitudes about Him, He gave commandment to depart unto the other side. Jesus gave this order because He was not a seeker after glory, and also because He wished to avoid the spiteful envy of the Jews.

19-20. And a certain scribe approached, and said unto Him, Master, I will follow Thee wheresoever thou goest. And Jesus saith unto him, The foxes have holes, and the birds of the air have nests; but the Son of Man hath not where to lay His head. A scribe is one who knows the letter of the law.[7] When this scribe saw the many signs which Jesus did, he imagined that Jesus was making money from them; hence his eagerness to follow Him so that he too could collect money. But Christ answers this thought of his as if saying to him, "You expect that by following Me you will make money. Do you not see that I am homeless? So too must My followers be." Jesus said this to persuade him to change his ways and to follow. But the scribe departed. Some say that the foxes and the birds mean the demons. So Jesus is saying, "The demons take their rest in you, and I, therefore, can have no rest in your soul."

21-22. And another of His disciples said unto Him, Lord, suffer me first to go and bury my father. But Jesus said unto him, Follow Me; and let the dead bury their dead. After one has given himself to God, he ought not to turn back to the things of this life. Indeed one must honor

---

[6] See Is. 53:4.

[7] The Greek words for "scribe" and "letter" are *grammateus* and *gramma*, respectively.

one's parents; but God first. That this man's father was an unbeliever is evident from Jesus' words, "Let the dead," that is, the unbelievers, "bury their dead." If this man was not even permitted to bury his father, woe to those who after they have begun the monastic life turn back to worldly things!

23-24. And when He was entered into a boat, His disciples followed Him. And, behold, there arose a great tempest in the sea, insomuch that the boat was covered with waves: but He was asleep. He took only His disciples, so that they could see the miracle. He allows them to be tossed by the waves so as to train them to endure trials and temptations, and also so that their faith would be even greater as a result of the miracle. Jesus slept so that when they had become terrified they would recognize their own weakness and call upon Him. Accordingly the evangelist says:

25-26. And His disciples came to Him, and awoke Him, saying, Lord, save us: we perish. And He saith unto them, Why are ye fearful, O ye of little faith? He did not say, "O ye of no faith," but, "O ye of little faith." The disciples showed their faith when they said, "Lord, save us;" but when they said, "We are perishing," they lacked faith. They ought not to have been afraid, as Jesus was with them in the boat. See how, by chastising them for cowardice, He shows that cowardice itself is a danger. This is why He calms first the turbulence of their souls, and then the storm.

26-27. Then He arose, and rebuked the winds and the sea; and there was a great calm. But the men marvelled, saying, What manner of man is this, that even the winds and the sea obey Him! In appearance He was a man, but His deeds showed that He was God.

28. And when He was come to the other side into the land of the Gergesenes, there met Him two possessed with demons, coming out of the tombs, exceeding fierce, so that no man might pass by that way. While the men in the boat were yet wondering what manner of man this was that even the winds and the sea obeyed Him, the demons come to proclaim the answer. Although Mark and Luke speak of one man who was possessed by a legion of demons,[8] understand that this one man was one of the two mentioned by Matthew, evidently, the more notorious of the two. Jesus came alone towards them, since no one dared to bring them to Him, so fierce were they. They dwelt among the tombs because the demons wish to inspire the belief that the souls of those who have died become demons. Let no one believe this: for when the soul departs from a man, it does not wander about the earth. For the souls of the righteous are in the hand of God,[9] and the souls of sinners are also led away, as was the soul of the rich man.[10]

29. And, behold, they cried out, saying, What have we to do with Thee, Jesus, Thou Son of God? Art Thou come hither to torment us before the time? Behold, they proclaim Him to be the Son of God, but first they declare their enmity. The demons consider it torment to be prevented from harming men. Understand the demons' words, "before the time", to mean that they thought that Christ, not enduring their great wickedness, would not wait for the time of their punishment. But this is not so; for the demons are permitted to contend with us until the end of the world.

30-32. And there was a good way off from them a herd of many swine grazing. So the demons besought Him, saying, If Thou cast us out, suffer us to go away into the herd of swine. And He said unto them, Go. And when they were come out, they went into the herd of swine. The demons asked this so that they could drown the swine, and thus the owners would be grieved and would not welcome Christ. Christ granted the demons their request in order to show how great is their bitterness towards men, and that if they had the power, and were not prevented as they are by God, they would do worse things to us than they did to the swine. For God protects those possessed by demons so that they do not kill themselves.

32-34. And, behold, the whole herd of swine ran violently down a

---

[8] Mk. 5:9, Lk. 8:27.

[9] Wisdom of Solomon 3:1

[10] in the account of the rich man and Lazarus, Lk. 16:19-31.

steep place into the sea, and perished in the waters. And they that kept them fled, and went their ways into the city, and told everything, and what was befallen to those possessed of the demons. And, behold, the whole city came out to meet Jesus: and when they saw Him, they besought Him that He would depart out of their region. The inhabitants of the city begged Jesus to leave because they were grieved and thought that they would suffer something worse thereafter. You, O reader, learn that where there is swinish life, it is not Christ Who dwells there, but demons.

CHAPTER NINE

Concerning the paralytic. Concerning Matthew.
Concerning the Saviour eating with the publicans.
Concerning the daughter of the ruler of the synagogue.
Concerning the woman with a hemorrhage.
Concerning the two blind men.
Concerning the possessed and mute man.

1-2. And He entered into a boat, and passed over, and came into His own city. And, behold, they brought to Him a paralytic, lying on a bed. "His own city" means Capernaum, for it was there that He was living. He was born in Bethlehem, raised in Nazareth, and lived for an extended length of time in Capernaum. This paralytic is not the same as the one mentioned in John,[1] for that one was beside the Sheep's Pool in Jerusalem, while this one was in Capernaum. And that one had no one to help him, while this one was carried by four men, as Mark says,[2] who lowered him through the roof, a fact which Matthew omits.

And Jesus seeing their faith. Either the faith of the men who brought the paralytic, for Jesus often worked a miracle on account of the faith of those who brought the one sick; or, of the paralytic himself. **Said to the paralytic, Take courage, child; thy sins be forgiven thee.** Jesus calls him "child", either as one of God's creatures, or because he believed. To show that the man's paralysis is a result of his sins, Jesus first forgives him his sins.

3-5. And, behold, certain of the scribes said within themselves, This man blasphemeth. And Jesus knowing their thoughts said, Wherefore think ye evil in your hearts? For which is easier to say, Thy sins be forgiven thee; or to say, Arise, and walk? By knowing their thoughts, Jesus shows that He is God. He rebukes them by saying, "You think that I am blaspheming by promising to forgive sins, which is a great thing,

---

[1] Jn. 5:2-9

[2] Mk. 2:3-12

and that I resort to this because it is something which can not be verified. But by healing the body, I shall guarantee that the soul has been healed as well. By doing the lesser deed, though it appears to be more difficult, I shall also confirm the remission of sins, which is indeed something great even though it appears easier to you since it is not visible to the eye."

6-8. But that ye may know that the Son of Man hath power on earth to forgive sins—then saith He to the paralytic—Arise, take up thy bed, and go unto thine house. And he arose, and departed to his house. But when the multitudes saw it, they marvelled, and glorified God Who had given such power unto men. Jesus commanded him to carry his bed so that the event would not appear to have been imaginary, and also, so that the multitudes would see the miracle. For they thought that Jesus, Who is greater than all, was only a man.

9. And as Jesus passed forth from thence, He saw a man, named Matthew, sitting collecting tax: and He saith unto him, Follow Me. And he arose, and followed Him. He did not call Matthew together with Peter and John, but when He knew that he would obey. He likewise called Paul later, when it was time. Marvel at how the evangelist displays his own former way of life, while the other evangelists disguise his name, calling him "Levi".[3] That Matthew is converted by word alone is the work of God.

10-11. And it came to pass, as Jesus sat at table in the house, behold, many publicans and sinners came and sat down with Him and His disciples. And when the Pharisees saw it, they said unto His disciples, Why eateth your Master with publicans and sinners? Joyful because he had received Christ into his house, Matthew invited the publicans. Christ ate with them so that He might benefit them also, even though He was criticized for doing it. For the Pharisees wanted to separate His disciples from Him, and so they slandered Him for eating with publicans.

---

[3] Mk. 2:13-17 and Lk. 5:27-32

12-13. But when Jesus heard that, He said unto them, They that be whole need not a physician, but they that are sick. But go ye and learn what that meaneth, I desire mercy, and not sacrifice: for I am not come to call the righteous, but sinners to repentance. He says, "I have not come now as judge but as physician, and for this reason I endure stench and filth." He also rebukes them for being ignorant when He says, "Go ye and learn." This means, "Since up to the present time you have not managed to learn, so at least from this time on go and learn that God prefers mercy towards sinners above any sacrifice."[4] The words "I am not come to call the righteous" He spoke ironically. That is, "I have not come to call you who consider yourselves to be righteous, but I have come to call sinners. I do this, not so that they remain sinners, but in order for them to repent."

14. Then came to Him the disciples of John, saying, Why do we and the Pharisees fast often, but Thy disciples fast not? John's disciples were envious of Christ's fame and so accused Him of not fasting. And perhaps they were wondering how He conquered the passions without ascetic struggle, something which John could not do. For they did not understand that while John, a mere man, was righteous because of his virtues, Christ is Virtue, as He is God.

15. And Jesus said unto them, Can the sons of the bridechamber mourn, as long as the bridegroom is with them? But the days will come, when the bridegroom shall be taken from them, and then shall they fast. "Now is the time for rejoicing as long as I am with My disciples," Jesus says. He calls Himself the bridegroom, as One Who betroths to Himself the new congregation, the old having died. The "sons of the bridechamber" [i.e. the wedding guests] are the apostles. Jesus says, "After I have suffered and ascended, the time will come for them to fast with great hunger and thirst and to be persecuted." To show that His disciples are not yet perfected, He adds:

16-17. No man putteth a piece of unshrunk cloth unto an old garment, for the patch teareth from the garment, and the rent is

---

[4] Hosea 6:7

made worse. Neither do men put new wine into old wineskins: else the skins burst, and the wine runneth out, and the skins are destroyed: but they put new wine into fresh wineskins, and both are preserved. The disciples, He says, have not yet become strong, and therefore require forbearance. The heavy burden of commandments ought not to be laid upon them. Jesus also said these things to teach the disciples that later, when they would go out into all the world to make disciples, they too should use forbearance.[5] The "piece of unshrunk cloth" means fasting, as does the "new wine". The "old garment" and the "old wineskins" mean the weakness of the disciples.

18-19. While He spake these things unto them, behold, there came a certain ruler, and fell prostrate before Him, saying, My daughter is even now dead: but come and lay Thy hand upon her, and she shall live. And Jesus arose, and followed him, and so did His disciples. It is apparent that this man had faith, although not as great as that of the centurion.[6] For this man beseeches Jesus, not to speak the word only, but to come and lay His hand upon his daughter. Although Luke says that she had not yet died,[7] the ruler says here that his daughter has already died, either because he thought he had left her as she was breathing her last breath, or to exaggerate the calamity so as to move Christ to have mercy.

20-22. And, behold, a woman, who was diseased with an issue of blood twelve years, came behind Him, and touched the hem of His garment. For she said within herself, If I may but touch His garment, I shall be whole. But Jesus turned Him about, and when He saw her, He said, Take courage, daughter; thy faith hath made thee whole. And the woman was made whole from that hour. The woman was unclean due to her illness,[8] and for this reason she did not approach Him

---

[5] The Greek word here rendered as "forbearance" is *synkatabasis*. It means literally "condescension", that is, lowering oneself to another's level of understanding and strength, out of compassion and love for that person. It is what a good teacher must do with a student; but the supreme example is God the Word taking flesh and becoming man for our sake.

[6] Mt. 8:8

[7] Lk. 8:42

[8] Levit. 15:19

openly for fear that she would be prevented. She intended to escape His notice, and yet hoped to obtain healing if only by touching the hem of His garment. But the Saviour revealed her, not because He loved glory, but to show her faith for our benefit, and also to strengthen the faith of the ruler of the synagogue. Jesus tells her, "Take courage," because she was fearful that she had stolen the gift; He calls her "daughter" because she had faith. He shows that if she had not offered faith she would not have received the grace, even though His garments were holy. It is said that this woman made a figure of Christ and at its feet there grew a plant which aided those with hemorrhages. Some impious men destroyed the figure at the time of the Emperor Julian the Apostate.[9]

23-24. And when Jesus came into the ruler's house, and saw the flute players and the people making a noise, He said unto them, Give place: for the maid is not dead, but sleepeth. And they laughed Him to scorn. Since she was unmarried, they were mourning her with flutes used at weddings, which was contrary to the law. Jesus said that she was sleeping, because He was able to resurrect her easily, and so to Him, death was sleep. Do not marvel that they laughed Him to scorn, for by scoffing they bear witness all the more to the miracle that He resurrected one who was truly dead. So that no one could later say that she had only suffered a seizure, it was confessed by all those present that she was dead.

25-26. But when the people were put forth, He went in, and took her by the hand, and the maid arose. And the fame hereof went abroad into all that land. Where there are crowds and distractions, Christ does not perform miracles. He takes her by the hand, thus imparting strength. And you, O reader, who are dead in sins, He will also resurrect when He puts outside the crowd and its tumult and takes you by the hand so that you might act.

27. And when Jesus departed thence, two blind men followed Him, crying, and saying, Thou Son of David, have mercy on us. The blind

---

[9] This is told by the fourth century church historian, Eusebius, in his *Ecclesiastical History*, chapter 8, paragraph 18.

men addressed to God the words "Have mercy," but as to a man, "O Son of David." For it was well known among the Jews that the Messiah would come from the seed of David.

28. And when He was come into the house, the blind men came to Him: and Jesus saith unto them, Believe ye that I am able to do this? They said unto Him, Yea, Lord. He led the blind men along even as far as the house, to show their steadfast faith, and thus to condemn the Jews. He asks them if they believe, showing that faith can accomplish all things.

29-30. Then touched He their eyes, saying, According to your faith be it unto you. And their eyes were opened. He healed within the house and in private, to show us how to avoid vainglory. In everything He did He taught humility.

30-31. And Jesus sternly charged them, saying, See that no man know it. But they, when they were departed, spread abroad His fame in all that country. Do you see Christ's humility? They spread abroad His fame in thanksgiving, not out of disobedience. But if in another place Christ says, "Go and tell of the glory of God,"[10] there is nothing contradictory in this. For He wants them to say nothing about Himself, but to speak of the glory of God.

32-33. As they went out, behold, they brought to Him a mute man possessed with a demon. And when the demon was cast out, the mute spake. The disease was not a natural one, but from the demon. This is why others brought him forward. He himself was not able to call upon Jesus, as the demon had bound his tongue. Therefore Jesus does not require faith of him, but immediately heals him by casting out the demon which had prevented his speech. **And the multitudes marvelled, saying, It was never so seen in Israel.** The multitude marvelled, placing Christ even above the prophets and the patriarchs. For He healed with authority, unlike those who first had to pray. But let us see what the Pharisees said.

---

[10] Lk. 8:39

34. But the Pharisees said, He casteth out demons through the prince of demons. These words are the height of stupidity. For no demon casts out other demons. But let us suppose that He cast out demons as one who served the prince of demons, that is, as a magician. How then did He heal diseases, forgive sins, and preach the kingdom? For the demon does just the opposite: he brings on diseases and separates man from God.

35. And Jesus went about all the cities and villages, teaching in their synagogues, and preaching the Gospel of the kingdom, and healing every disease and every infirmity among the people. As Lover of mankind He did not wait for them to come to Him, but He Himself went all around. Therefore they could not say as an excuse that "no one taught us." He draws them to Himself by word and deed, teaching and working wonders.

36. But when He saw the multitudes, He was moved with compassion on them because they grew faint and were scattered abroad, as sheep having no shepherd. They did not have a shepherd. For their rulers not only failed to correct them, but even harmed them. The mark of the true shepherd is to have compassion for his flock.

37-38. Then saith He unto His disciples, The harvest truly is plenteous, but the labourers are few; pray ye therefore the Lord of the harvest, that He will send forth labourers into His harvest. The multitude in need of healing He calls the "harvest", and those who ought to teach them, "labourers". The "Lord of the harvest" is Christ Himself Who is Lord of prophets and apostles. This is made clear when He ordains the twelve without petitioning God. Listen, then:

CHAPTER TEN

Concerning the instruction of the apostles.

1. And when He had called unto Him His twelve disciples, He gave them authority over unclean spirits, to cast them out, and to heal every disease and every infirmity. He chose twelve disciples according to the number of the twelve tribes. He gave them power, although indeed they were few, and sent them out. For few are they who walk the narrow way. He granted them the power to work miracles so that having first caused astonishment by the miracles, the disciples would then have receptive listeners for their teaching.

2. Now the names of the twelve apostles are these; The first, Simon, who is called Peter, and Andrew his brother. He lists the names of the apostles because of the false apostles. He first gives Peter and Andrew because they were also the First-called, and then the sons of Zebedee. He places James before John, not ranking them by honor, but simply listing them as the names occur. So he says:

2-4. James the son of Zebedee, and John his brother; Philip, and Bartholomew; Thomas, and Matthew the publican; James the son of Alphaeus, and Lebbaeus, whose surname was Thaddaeus; Simon the Canaanite, and Judas Iscariot, who also betrayed Him. See the humility of Matthew, how he ranked himself after Thomas. And when he came to Judas, he did not say, "the defiled, the enemy of God," but he named him Iscariot after his place of birth. For there was another Judas, who was also called Lebbaeus and Thaddaeus. So there are two James's, the son of Zebedee and the son of Alphaeus, and two Judas's, Thaddaeus and the betrayer. And three Simons, Peter, the Canaanite, and the betrayer; for Judas Iscariot was also called Simon.

5-7. These twelve Jesus sent forth, and commanded them, saying, Go not into the way of the Gentiles, and into any city of the Samaritans enter ye not: but go rather to the lost sheep of the house of Israel. And as ye go, preach, saying, The kingdom of heaven is at hand. "These..." Who are they? Fishermen, ordinary people, and publicans. He sends them first to the Jews that they might not be able to say, "The apostles were sent to the Gentiles and because of this we Jews did not believe." Thus He deprives the Jews of any excuse. He links the Samaritans to the Gentiles as they were Babylonians who inhabited Judea, and did not accept the prophets but only the five books of Moses. You must also understand the "kingdom of heaven" to mean the enjoyment of good things to come. He arms them with miracles, saying:

8. Heal the sick, cleanse the lepers, raise the dead, cast out demons: freely ye have received, freely give. Nothing so befits a teacher as humility and non-possessiveness. He indicates these two virtues here by saying, "freely ye have received." Do not think highly of yourselves that you have such good things to give, for you have received them as a gift and by grace. But as you are humble-minded, so also do not be lovers of money. For He says, "freely give." And finally He eradicates the root of all evils, saying:

9-10. Possess neither gold, nor silver, nor copper in your belts, nor satchel for your journey, neither two tunics, neither sandals, nor yet staves: for the workman is worthy of his food. He is training them in all strictness, and for this reason He allows them absolutely nothing in excess, nor to have any cares. He does not even allow them a staff, for this is the strictness of non-possessiveness which makes credible the words of one who would teach this virtue. And then, so that they might not ask, "How shall we eat?" He says, "The workman is worthy of his food"; that is, your disciples shall feed you. For they owe this to you as they would to workmen. But He said, "worthy of his food," not of delicacies, for teachers should not live luxuriously.

11. And into whatsoever city or village ye shall enter, inquire diligently who in it is worthy; and there abide till ye go thence. He bids them not to go to just anyone lest they associate with those who are unworthy and so be slandered. But if they go only to the worthy, their needs will be met in full. He commands them to stay there and not move from one house to the next lest they be accused of being gluttons and appear to insult those who first received them.

12-13. And when ye come into a house, salute it, saying, Peace be

unto this house. And if the house be worthy, let your peace come upon it: but if it be not worthy, let your peace return to you. By "salutation" and "peace" understand "blessing", which remains only upon those who are worthy. Learn, then, from this that it is primarily our own deeds that bring blessing upon us.[1]

14-15. And whosoever shall not receive you, nor hear your words, when ye depart out of that house or city, shake off the dust from your feet. Verily I say unto you, It shall be more tolerable for the land of Sodom and Gomorrah in the day of judgement, than for that city. He wants them to shake the dust from their feet to show that the apostles received nothing from that place because of the inhabitants' unbelief; or, as a testimony to the great distance the apostles had walked, which nonetheless brought no benefit to the inhabitants. It will be more tolerable for the Sodomites than for the unbelievers because the Sodomites, having been chastised here in this life, will be punished less severely there in the next life.

16. Behold, it is I Who send you forth as sheep in the midst of wolves. He armed them with miracles and made them confident of their means of sustenance by opening to them the doors of those who are worthy. Now He also tells them of the terrible things that will occur, thus showing His foreknowledge. He comforts them with the words "It is I".[2] It is I, the Mighty One, He says, so you may take courage; you will not be overcome. He prepares them to undergo suffering. Just as it is impossible for a sheep in the midst of wolves not to suffer harm, so it is with you amidst the Jews. But should you suffer, do not become angry, for I want you to be as meek as sheep and in this very manner so to conquer. **Be ye therefore wise as serpents, and innocent as doves.** He also wants the disciples to be wise. So that you might not imagine,

---

[1] The thought is this: it is good to receive a blessing from one who blesses, but if we are unworthy, that is, living a life of unrepentant sin, then that blessing does not remain upon us, but returns to the giver.

[2] *Egō apostellō ymas* literally means "I send you." But the personal pronoun *egō*, "I", is grammatically unnecessary in Greek as the verb ending already indicates the subject. Its presence here serves to emphasize who it is that is sending, and has been translated by the phrase "It is I", in order to indicate this nuance upon which Theophylact comments.

hearing them referred to as sheep, that a Christian must be foolish, Christ says that he must also be wise, knowing how to act when surrounded by many enemies. For just as the serpent allows all the rest of its body to be struck but guards its head, so let the Christian give all of his belongings and even his body to those who would strike it; but let him guard his Head, which is Christ and faith in Him. And just as the serpent squeezes through a narrow hole and sheds its old skin, so too let us traverse the narrow way and shed the old man. But since a serpent is also poisonous, He commands us to be innocent, that is, sincere, guileless, and harmless as doves. For when the offspring of doves are taken from them and they are driven away, they fly back again to their masters. Be wise, then, as the serpent lest you be tricked in this life, but be blameless in all your ways; and as for harming others, be as the dove that is guileless.

17-18. But beware of men: for they will deliver you up to the councils, and they will scourge you in their synagogues; and ye shall be brought before governors and kings for My sake, for a testimony against them and the Gentiles. You see, this is what it means to be wise: beware not to give cause to those who would afflict you, but to conduct yourselves wisely. If the persecutor wants money or honor, give it to him, that he have no cause against you. But if he would take your faith, then guard your Head. Christ intends to send the disciples not only to the Jews, but to the Gentiles as well, which is why He says, "for a testimony against them and the Gentiles," that is, as a reproof to those who do not believe.

19-20. But when they deliver you up, take no thought how or what ye shall speak: for it shall be given you in that same hour what ye shall speak. For it is not ye that speak, but the Spirit of your Father Which speaketh in you. So that the disciples might not ask, "And how shall we who are ordinary people convince the wise?" He bids them to take courage and not be anxious. For when we intend to converse with believers we must study beforehand and be ready to give an answer, as Peter exhorts us[3]. But when we are caught between the crowds and the raging kings, He promises His own strength, so that we may not be

[3] I Peter 3:15

afraid. It is for us to confess, but it is God Who will enable us to answer wisely. So that you not imagine that skill in such defense is a natural one, He says, "It is not ye that speak, but the Spirit."

21. And the brother shall deliver up the brother to death, and the father the child: and the children shall rise up against their parents, and cause them to be put to death. He foretells to them the things that will happen, so that when they occur the disciples will not be dismayed. He also shows them the power of the Gospel that is preached, how it causes men to hold in contempt nature itself, for such is Christianity. He also reveals the inhuman rage of those who will not spare even their closest kin.

22. And ye shall be hated by all men for My name's sake: but he that patiently endureth to the end shall be saved. "Hated by all men" means "hated by many". For not everyone hated them, as there were those who accepted the faith. It is he who patiently endures until the end, and not only in the beginning, who will partake in eternal life.

23. But when they persecute you in this city, flee ye into another: for verily I say unto you, Ye shall not have gone through the cities of Israel, till the Son of Man be come. The fearful things spoken of above, such as "They will hand you over" and "You will be hated", concerned those things which would take place after the Ascension. What is spoken of now concerns that which would take place before the Cross. "You will not be persecuted through all the cities of Israel before I shall come to you." He commands them to flee from their persecutors. For it is of the devil for a man to throw himself into manifest danger and thus become the cause of condemnation to those who would slay him and the detriment of those whom he was about to benefit by his preaching. "Till the Son of Man be come"—do not understand by this the second coming, but rather, His drawing together with them and the comfort that He would give them yet before the Cross. For when they had been sent out and had preached, they again returned to Christ and were together with Him.

24-25. The disciple is not above his teacher, nor the servant above his lord. It is enough for the disciple that he be as his teacher, and the servant as his lord. Here He teaches them to endure insults. For if

I, your Teacher and Master, have endured them, how much more so should you, My disciples and servants. You may ask, "Why does He say, The disciple is not above his teacher, when we see many disciples who are greater than their teachers?" Learn, then, that while they are disciples they are less than their teachers; if they become greater, they are no longer disciples. In the same way, a servant, while he is a servant, is not above his lord.

25-26. If they have called the master of the house Beelzebub, how much more shall they call them of his household? Fear them not therefore: for there is nothing covered, that shall not be revealed, and hid, that shall not be known. Take comfort, He says, in My example. For if they have called Me the chief of demons, is it such a fearful thing that they should slander you who are members of My household? He calls them "household members" and not "slaves", thus showing His intimacy with them. So take courage; the truth will not be hidden, but time will reveal your virtue as well as the wickedness of those who slander you, for nothing is hidden which shall not be known. They may slander you now, but later they will make you renowned.

27. What I tell you in darkness, that speak ye in light: and what ye hear in the ear, that preach ye upon the housetops. Those things, He says, which I have spoken to you alone and in one place, for that is what is meant by "in the ear" and "in darkness" you must teach with boldness in a strong voice so that all may hear you. But since dangers are also a consequence of boldness, He adds:

28. And fear not them which kill the body, but are not able to kill the soul: but rather fear Him Who is able to destroy both soul and body in gehenna. He teaches them to despise even death, for punishment in gehenna is yet more fearful, He says. Those who slay accomplish the destruction of only the body, while they are perhaps the benefactors of the soul. But God punishes both the soul and the body of those whom He casts into gehenna. He says "in gehenna", indicating the perpetual nature of the punishment, for gehenna is never ending.

29-31. Are not two sparrows sold for a farthing? And not one of them shall fall on the ground without your Father. But the very hairs

of your head are all numbered. Fear ye not therefore, ye are of much more value than sparrows. So that they would not fear that they are abandoned, He says, "If not even a sparrow is caught without My knowledge, how shall I abandon you whom I love?" And to show His precise knowledge and forethought for us He says that even the hairs of our head are numbered by Him. But do not think that the sparrows are snared by God's doing; rather, that even the snaring of sparrows is not unknown to Him.

32-33. Whosoever therefore shall confess in Me before men, him will I confess also before My Father Who is in heaven. But whosoever shall deny Me before men, him will I also deny before My Father Who is in heaven. He exhorts them to bear witness even unto martyrdom. For belief only within one's soul does not suffice; He desires also the belief confessed with the tongue. He did not say, "Whosoever shall confess Me," but "in Me,"[4] that is, in My strength. For he who confesses does so aided by the grace which is from above. But as for him who denies, Christ did not say "in Me," but "whosoever shall deny Me," showing that he denies because he does not have the aid from above. Therefore everyone who confesses that Christ is God will find Christ giving confession of him to the Father, that he is a true servant. But those who deny will hear the words "I do not know you."

34-36. Think not that I am come to send peace on earth: I came not to send peace, but a sword. For I am come to set a man at variance against his father, and the daughter against her mother, and the daughter in law against her mother in law. And a man's foes shall be they of his own household. Harmony is not always a good thing, while separation sometimes is. The sword, then, is the word of faith which severs our bond to our families and relatives when they hinder our piety towards God. For He does not tell us simply to separate ourselves from them, but only when they will not come with us, and especially when they hinder us in our faith.

37. He that loveth father or mother more than Me is not worthy

---

[4] *ostis omologēsei en emoi.*

of Me: and he that loveth son or daughter more than Me is not worthy of Me. Do you see when it is that we must hate our parents and children? When they want us to love them more than Christ. And why should I speak of father, mother, and children? Hear what is even greater than this:

38. And he that taketh not his cross, and followeth after Me, is not worthy of Me. Whoever, He says, does not renounce this present life and give himself over to shameful death, for this is what the cross signified to the ancients, is not worthy of Me. But since there are many who are crucified, such as robbers and thieves, He added, "and followeth after Me," that is, live according to My laws.

39. He that findeth his life shall lose it: and he that loseth his life for My sake shall find it. He who pampers his life in the flesh appears to "find his life", while in fact he is losing it by sending it to eternal punishment. But he who loses his life and dies, not as a thief or one who strangles himself, but for Christ's sake, he it is that saves his life.

40-41. He that receiveth you receiveth Me, and he that receiveth Me receiveth Him that sent Me. He that receiveth a prophet in the name of a prophet shall receive a prophet's reward; and he that receiveth a righteous man in the name of a righteous man shall receive a righteous man's reward. He incites us to welcome those whom Christ sends, for he who honors a disciple of Christ, honors Christ Himself and, through Him, the Father as well. But we must welcome righteous men and prophets in the name of a righteous man and prophet, that is, because they are righteous men and prophets, and not because of any protection or aid of the sort which kings provide. But even if a man should have the appearance of a prophet but in conduct fall short, you should still receive him as a prophet. And God will reward you for having received a true prophet, for this is what it means "shall receive a righteous man's reward". Or you may understand it in another way, that he who receives a righteous man will himself be counted as a righteous man and will receive the reward which the righteous receive.

42. And whosoever shall give to drink unto one of these little ones a cup of cold water only in the name of a disciple, verily I say unto

you, he shall in no wise lose his reward. Lest anyone use poverty as an excuse, He says, ''If you give even a cup of cold water because he is My disciple, you will receive a reward even for this.'' He who gives a cup of cold water is also he who teaches one burning with the fire of anger and desire and causes him to be named a disciple of Christ. The teacher will not lose his reward.

CHAPTER ELEVEN

Concerning those sent by John.

1. And it came to pass, when Jesus had made an end of commanding His twelve disciples, He departed thence to teach and to preach in their cities. When He had sent the disciples, He Himself was quiet, not working miracles but only teaching in the synagogues. For if He Himself were present healing the sick, no one would have approached the disciples. Therefore He departed so that they would have opportunity to heal.

2-3. Now when John had heard in the prison the works of Christ, he sent two of his disciples, and said unto Him, Art Thou He that cometh, or do we look for another? John did not ask as if he himself did not know Christ. How could this be when he had borne witness to Him, saying, ''Behold the Lamb of God''? But because his disciples were jealous of Christ, John sent them to acquire more evidence, so that by seeing the miracles they might believe that Christ is greater than John. This is why he himself pretends to ask, ''Art Thou He that cometh?'' that is, He Whose coming in the flesh is awaited in the Scriptures. Some believe that by saying, ''He that cometh'', he was asking about the descent into hades, as if, not knowing the answer, John were questioning, ''Art Thou He that goeth[1] even into hades, or should we look for another?'' But this is foolishness, for how could John, who was greater than the prophets, not know of the crucifixion of Christ and the descent into hades, when he had called Christ the Lamb Who would be sacrificed for us? John knew, therefore, that the Lord would also go down into hades in the soul so that even there, as St. Gregory the Theologian says, He might save those who would have believed if He had become incarnate in their day. John did not ask this because he did not know the answer, but rather because he wanted to provide his disciples with the

---

[1] The verb *erchomai* which is used in the phrase *o erchomenos*, ''He that cometh'', has the meaning of either ''come'' or ''go''. That is, it indicates movement from one location to another without specifying, as do ''come'' and ''go'' in English, a certain vantage point such as that of the speaker. Therefore *o erchomenos* can be understood equally as well to mean ''He that goeth.''

evidence of Christ's miracles. Look, then, how Christ answers this question:

4-6. Jesus answered and said unto them, Go and declare unto John those things which ye do hear and see: The blind receive their sight, and the lame walk, the lepers are cleansed, and the deaf hear, the dead are raised up, and the poor have the good tidings. And blessed is he, whosoever shall not be offended in Me. He did not say, "Declare unto John that I am He that cometh." But knowing that John had sent his disciples to see the miracles, He said, "Tell John what you see, and certainly he will use that opportunity to bear witness more fully to you concerning Me." By the words "the poor have the good tidings"[2] understand either those preaching the Gospel, that is, the apostles, who were poor fishermen and despised as common lowly people, or those listening to the Gospel and hearing of the eternal good things. And to show John's disciples that the thoughts they were thinking did not escape His notice, He said, "Blessed is he whosoever shall not be offended in Me," for they had many doubts about Him.

7. And as they departed, Jesus began to say unto the multitudes concerning John, What went ye out into the wilderness to see? A reed shaken with the wind? Perhaps the multitudes heard John's question and were scandalized that even John himself might be unsure of Christ and had so quickly changed his opinion, although he had previously borne witness to Him. Christ allays this suspicion, then, by saying, John is not a reed, that is, one who changes easily. For if he were, why would you have gone out to him in the wilderness? You indeed would not have gone out to see a reed, a changeable man, but you went out to see a great and steadfast man. To be sure, he is still now what you thought him to be then.

8. But what went ye out for to see? A man clothed in soft raiment? Behold, they that wear soft clothing are in kings' houses. Denying

---

[2] The verb *euangelizetai* is here rendered as "have the good tidings" in order to capture in English the double meaning present in the Greek to which Bl. Theophylact makes reference. The verb, in the form in which it appears here, can be either active or passive in meaning, hence, either "to evangelize" or "to be evangelized".

them any basis for saying that John later became soft by giving himself over to luxury, He says, This cannot be; that his clothing is made of hair shows that he is an enemy of luxury. For if he were wearing soft clothing and living in kings' houses, if he so desired luxury he would not be in prison. So then, learn that it does not befit a true Christian to wear luxurious clothing.

9. But what went ye out for to see? A prophet? Yea, I say unto you, and more than a prophet. John was more than a prophet because the other prophets only foretold Christ, while he was an eyewitness, indeed a great thing. And the others prophesied after their birth, while he, still in his mother's womb, recognized Christ and leapt.

10. For this is he, of whom it is written, Behold, I send My angel before Thy face, who shall prepare Thy way before Thee. John was called an angel, both because of his angelic and almost immaterial way of life, and because he announced and proclaimed Christ. He prepared Christ's way by witnessing concerning Him and by baptizing unto repentance, for after repentance comes the forgiveness of sins, which Christ gives. Christ said these things after John's disciples had left so that He would not appear to be flattering him. The prophecy mentioned is of the prophet Malachi.[3]

11. Verily I say unto you, Among them that are born of women there hath not risen a greater than John the Baptist. He declares this with certainty, that there is no one greater than John. But by saying "born of women" He excludes Himself, for Christ was born of a virgin, not of a woman, that is, one who is married.[4] **Notwithstanding, He that is younger is greater than he in the kingdom of heaven.** Since He has extolled the praises of John, lest they think that John is greater than He,

[3] Malachi 3:1

[4] The Greek word for "woman", (*gynē*, nominative, *gynaika* accusative) implies married status. Even in modern Greek, it remains today the general word for "wife".

He says here more clearly, I am the younger[5] in age and the lesser in your opinion, yet I am greater than he in the kingdom of heaven, that is, in regards to spiritual and heavenly good things. For here I appear less than he, both because his birth preceded Mine and because he appears great to you, but there in the kingdom of heaven I am greater.

12. And from the days of John the Baptist until now the kingdom of heaven suffereth violence, and the violent take it by force. It would seem that this does not follow the train of thought, but it does. Consider this: Christ, by saying of Himself that He is greater than John, strongly urges them to believe in Him, showing that many are by force acquiring the kingdom of heaven, that is, faith in Him. And there is need of great force, for in order to leave father and mother and to despise one's own life, how much force is needed?

13. For all the prophets and the law prophesied until John. This, too, follows the same train of thought. For He is saying, I am He that cometh, for all the prophets have been fulfilled. They would not have been fulfilled if I had not come. Therefore, await nothing further.

14. And if ye will receive it, this is Elijah, who was to come. If you are willing, He says, to accept it, that is, if you judge the matter with a good disposition of mind, and not spitefully, he is the one whom the prophet Malachi called Elijah who was to come.[6] For both the Forerunner and Elijah have the same ministry. The one was the Forerunner of the first coming, while Elijah will be the forerunner of the second coming. Then, showing that it is an enigma that John is Elijah, and requires wisdom to understand it, He says:

15. He that hath ears to hear, let him hear. Thus urging them to ask

---

[5] *O mikroteros*. This is the comparative, not superlative, form of the adjective *mikros*. Besides the general meaning of "small" or "little", *mikros* also denotes "few in years", i.e. "young". Bl. Theophylact follows St. John Chrysostom in interpreting this passage. Another interpretation given by St. Cyril of Alexandria, Blessed Augustine, Jerome, and others, is: He that is least in the kingdom of heaven (i.e. any baptized believer, or, any of the angels) is greater than John the Baptist. This latter interpretation is the one usually followed in English translations of the New Testament.

[6] Malachi 4:5. "And, behold, I will send to you Elijah the Tishbite before the great and glorious day of the Lord comes."

and to learn.

16-17. But whereunto shall I liken this generation? It is like unto children sitting in the market, and calling unto their fellows, and saying, We have piped unto you, and ye have not danced; we have mourned unto you, and ye have not lamented. It is the malcontent nature of the Jews that He is speaking of here. For as they were cantankerous, neither John's asceticism nor Christ's simplicity pleased them. They were like foolish little children who are never satisfied—whether one cries for them or plays the pipe for them, they are not pleased.

18-19. For John came neither eating nor drinking, and they say, He hath a devil. The Son of Man came eating and drinking, and they say, Behold a man gluttonous, and a drunkard, a friend of publicans and sinners. He compares John's way of life to mourning, for John showed great severity both in words and deeds, and His own life on earth He compares to piping, that is, to the sound of the flute. For the Lord was most gracious and pleasing, condescending to all that He might win all, bringing the good tidings of the kingdom, and He was not severe in appearance as was John. **But Wisdom is justified by her children.** This is what He is saying: so, then, since neither John's life nor My own pleases you, but you scorn all the means of salvation, I Who am Wisdom am justified [that is, shown to be righteous, and vindicated]. Therefore you will have no excuse but will be utterly condemned. For I, on My part, have done everything, yet you, by your refusal to believe, prove that I Who omitted nothing am justified.

20. Then Jesus began to upbraid the cities wherein most of His mighty works were done, because they repented not. After showing that He had done everything that He ought to have done, and they remained unrepentant, then He upbraids them.

21. Woe unto thee, Chorazin! Woe unto thee, Bethsaida! So that you might understand that those who did not believe were evil not by nature, but by choice, He calls to mind Bethsaida, the city of Andrew, Peter, Philip and the sons of Zebedee. Evil does not come from nature, but from our own choice; for if it came from nature, these apostles too would have been evil.

21-22. For if the mighty works, which were done in you, had been done in Tyre and Sidon, they would have repented long ago in sackcloth and ashes. But I say unto you, It shall be more tolerable for Tyre and Sidon at the day of judgement, than for you. He says that the Jews are worse than the inhabitants of Tyre and Sidon, for the Gentile inhabitants of Tyre transgressed only the natural law while the Jews transgressed the Mosaic law as well. For the former did not see miracles, but the latter have both seen and slandered. Sackcloth is a symbol of repentance, and ashes and dust are what mourners put on their heads.

23-24. And thou, Capernaum, which art exalted unto the heavens, shalt be brought down to hades: for if the mighty works which have been done in thee, had been done in Sodom, it would have remained until this day. But I say unto you, That it shall be more tolerable for the land of Sodom in the day of judgement, than for thee. Capernaum was exalted as the city of Jesus, for it was made as glorious as if it were His birthplace, yet it derived no benefit from this because it did not believe. On the contrary, it is rather because of this that it has been condemned to hades, that, while having such a citizen, it derived no benefit from Him. From the fact that the name "Capernaum" means "place of comfort and consolation", see that even though one has once been deemed worthy to become a place of the Comforter, that is, of the Holy Spirit, but then becomes haughty in mind, though he had been lifted up to heaven, he falls on account of his haughtiness. Tremble, then, O man!

25. At that time Jesus answered and said, I thank Thee, O Father, Lord of heaven and earth, because Thou hast hid these things from the wise and prudent, and hast revealed them unto babes. This is what He is saying: I thank Thee, Father, that the Jews who seem to be wise and knowledgeable of the Scriptures did not believe, while the unlearned and the babes believed and recognized the mysteries. God hid the mysteries from those who seemed wise, not out of malice, or so as to cause ignorance, but because of their unworthiness, stemming from the very fact that they thought that they were wise. For he who thinks himself to be wise and is bold in his own knowledge does not call upon

God. So then God, not having been called upon, gives him neither help nor revelation. Furthermore, God, out of His very love for man, does not reveal the mysteries to the multitude lest they be punished the more for first knowing the mysteries and then scorning them.

26. Even so, Father: for such was Thy good will. Here He shows the Father's love for man, in that the Father revealed the mysteries to the babes, without having been called upon by anyone to do so, but because it so pleased Him to do from the beginning. For [the Greek word for "good will"] *eudokia* means both "will" and "pleasure".

27. All things are given unto Me by My Father. In His preceding words, He said to the Father, "Father, Thou hast revealed." Lest you think that He Himself does nothing and that everything is of the Father, He says, "All things have been given to Me and both the Father and I have the same authority." And when you hear "given" do not think that means given as to a servant or a subordinate, but rather as bestowed upon a son. It is because He was begotten of the Father that those things were given to Him. For if He were not begotten and yet were of the same essence as the Father, those things need not have been given to Him because He would have already possessed them. See what He says: all things have been given, not by a master, but by My Father. As, for example, when a handsome child is born of a handsome father, the child says, "I have been given, that is, I have inherited, my father's beauty."

27. And no man knoweth the Son, but the Father; neither knoweth any man the Father, save the Son, and he to whomsoever the Son willeth to reveal Him. He says something great, "There is nothing marvelous in My being the Master of all things since I possess something even greater, that is, to know the Father, and knowing Him, to reveal Him to others." Consider, then: He said, above, that the Father has revealed the mysteries to babes, and here, that the Son reveals the Father. You see, then, the single power of the Father and the Son, since both the Father and the Son reveal.

28. Come unto Me, all ye that labour and are heavy laden, and I will give you rest. He calls all mankind, not only the Jews, but also the Gentiles. By those "that labour" understand the Jews, who follow the strict observances of the law and labor in the occupation of fulfilling the commandments of the law. Those who are "heavy laden" are the Gentiles, who are oppressed by the burden of sins. To all these does Christ give rest. For to believe, to confess, and to be baptized, what labor is it? Is it not, rather, rest? For here in this life you are unburdened of the things which you did before your baptism, and there in the next life rest awaits you.

29-30. Take My yoke upon you, and learn from Me that I am meek and lowly in heart: and ye shall find rest unto your souls. For My yoke is easy, and My burden is light. The yoke of Christ is humility and meekness. For he who humbles himself before all men has rest and remains untroubled; but he who is vainglorious and arrogant is ever encompassed by troubles as he does not wish to be less than anyone but is always thinking how to be esteemed more highly and how to defeat his enemies. Therefore the yoke of Christ, which is humility, is light, for it is easier for our lowly nature to be humbled than to be exalted. But all the commandments of Christ are also called a yoke, and they are light because of the reward to come, even though for a time they appear heavy.

CHAPTER TWELVE

Concerning the disciples
when they plucked grain on the sabbath.
Concerning the man with the withered hand.
Concerning the blind and dumb demoniac.
Concerning those who asked for a sign.
Concerning the mother and brothers of Christ.

1-4. At that time Jesus went on the sabbath day through the grainfields; and His disciples were hungry, and began to pluck the heads of grain, and to eat. Setting aside for the while observances of the law, He leads His disciples through the grainfields, so that by eating they might set aside the law of the sabbath. **But when the Pharisees saw it, they said unto Him, Behold, Thy disciples do that which is not lawful to do upon the sabbath day. But He said unto them, Have ye not read what David did, when he hungered, and they that were with him; how he entered into the house of God, and did eat the loaves of oblation which were not lawful for him to eat, neither for them which were with him, but only for the priests?** Again the Pharisees find fault with the physical passion, hunger, while they themselves committed worse sins, but the Lord reproves them with a story of David. For David dared, He says, because of hunger to do something even greater. The loaves of oblation, the showbread, are the twelve loaves which were set out each day on the altar, six on the right side and six on the left. Although David was a prophet, he ought not to have eaten them for it was only permitted for priests to eat them. And how much more so was it unlawful for those with him to eat? Nevertheless, because of hunger he could be forgiven. So, too, with the disciples.

5-6. Or have ye not read in the law, how that on the sabbath days the priests in the temple profane the sabbath, and are blameless? But I say unto you, That here is One greater than the temple. The law prohibited work on the sabbath; so, then, the priests as they split wood and lit fires on the sabbath were profaning, that is, defiling, the sabbath, by your reckoning. But you will say to Me, "They were priests, the disciples are not." I say, then, that something greater than the temple is here. I am the Master Who is greater than the temple, and since I am with My disciples, they have greater authority to set aside the law of the sabbath than do the priests.

7-8. But if ye had known what this meaneth, that I desire mercy, and not sacrifice, ye would not have condemned the guiltless. For the Son of Man is Lord even of the sabbath day. He also shows them up as unlearned, not knowing the words of the prophets.[1] For was it not right, He says, to show mercy to men who were hungry? Furthermore, I, the Son of Man, am Lord of the sabbath for I am the Creator of all things, including the days. Hence it is I as Master Who sets aside the sabbath. Understand this also in a spiritual sense. As the apostles were laborers, and the believers were the harvest and the heads of grain, so the apostles were plucking and eating them, that is, they took the salvation of men to be their food. This they were doing on the sabbath, made for rest and cessation from evils. The Pharisees were vexed; and so it is even in the Church, that those who are pharisaical and envious are displeased with teachers who constantly teach and bring benefit.

9-10. And when He was departed thence, He went into their synagogue: and behold, there was a man whose hand was withered. And they asked Him, saying, Is it lawful to heal on the sabbath days? that they might accuse Him. The other evangelists say that Jesus put the question to the Pharisees. It can be said that the Pharisees out of spite first asked Him, as Matthew says. Then Christ in turn asks them the same, mocking them and ridiculing their callousness, as the other evangelists say. The Pharisees asked Him this question so that they might have a pretext to slander Him.

11-12. And He said unto them, What man shall there be among you, that shall have one sheep, and if it fall into a pit on the sabbath day, will he not lay hold of it, and lift it out? How much then is a man better than a sheep? Wherefore it is lawful to do good on the sabbath days. He shows that for love of money and so as not to lose a sheep they would set aside the sabbath, but they could not tolerate that

[1] Hosea 6:7

the sabbath be set aside so that a man might be healed. By this He shows that they were not only lovers of money and cruel men, but even despisers of God. For they hold the sabbath in contempt so as not to suffer the loss of a sheep, and yet without mercy they condemn the healing of a man.

13. Then saith He to the man, Stretch forth thine hand. And he stretched it forth; and it was restored whole, like as the other. Many, even now, have withered hands, that is, they are merciless and tightfisted. But when the word of the Gospel resounds within them, they stretch out their hands in giving. They do this even though the Pharisees, that is, the proud demons who are cut off from us,[2] on account of their enmity for us do not want our hands to be stretched out to others in mercy and almsgiving.

14-15. Then the Pharisees departed, and held a council against Him, how they might destroy Him. But Jesus, aware of this, withdrew Himself from thence. What spite! When good is done to them they become enraged. Jesus withdrew, as it was not yet the time for His Passion, and also to spare them from falling to the crime of murder. He did this to show that it is not God-pleasing to throw oneself into danger. Notice the word "departed"; it is when they departed from God that they plotted to destroy Jesus. For no one who abides in God would plot such things.

15-16. And great multitudes followed Him, and He healed them all; and charged them that they should not make Him known. He does not want to be made known so that He might soften the spite of the Pharisees, for He was eager to heal them in any way possible.

17-19. That it might be fulfilled which was spoken by Isaiah the prophet, saying, Behold My Servant, Whom I have chosen; My Beloved, in Whom My soul is well pleased: I will put My Spirit upon Him, and He shall proclaim judgement to the Gentiles. He shall not strive, nor cry; neither shall any man hear His voice in the streets.

---

[2] The word "Pharisee" in Hebrew means "cut off" or "set apart".

Matthew brings in the prophet as a witness to Jesus' meekness.[3] For whatever the Jews want, he says, Christ will do. If they do not want Him to be made known, then He will not make Himself known. He will not stand up against them like one seeking renown, nor will He dispute contentiously. He will bid the multitudes not to make Him known, but He will also proclaim judgement to the Gentiles, that is, He will teach the Gentiles. For "judgement" (*krisis*) is teaching, knowledge, and discernment (*diakrisis*) of the good. Or, in another sense, He will also proclaim the coming judgement to the Gentiles who have never heard of this judgement. "Neither shall any man hear His voice in the streets." For He did not teach in the middle of the market place, as did the vainglorious, but in the temple and in the synagogues and on the mountain and along the shores.

20. A bruised reed shall He not break, and a smoldering wick shall He not quench. He could have crushed the Jews, he says, like a broken reed, and could have quenched their anger like a smoldering wick, but Jesus did not wish to do so until He had fulfilled His dispensation and defeated them in every way. For this is the meaning of what follows.

20-21. Till He send forth judgement unto victory, and in His name shall the Gentiles hope. So that the Jews would have no excuse, Christ endured all things, so that later He might condemn and overcome those who could say nothing in their own defense. What did He not do to win them over? But the Jews were not willing; therefore the Gentiles shall hope in Him.

22-23. Then was brought unto Him one possessed with a demon, blind, and dumb: and He healed him, insomuch that the blind and dumb both spake and saw. And all the people were amazed, and said, Is not this the Son of David? The demon had stopped up the avenues towards faith, that is, the eyes, the hearing, and the tongue. But Jesus healed, and was called the Son of David by the multitude. For the Christ was expected to come from the seed of David. And so now, if you see a man who neither understands the good, nor accepts the words of

---

[3] Is. 42:1-4

another, consider him blind and dumb, and may God touch his heart and heal him.

24. But when the Pharisees heard it, they said, This fellow doth not cast out demons, but by Beelzebub the prince of the demons. Although the Lord had departed for their sake, nevertheless they heard of it even from afar and slandered Him as He was doing good to men, and thus they were enemies of nature, as is the devil.

25-26. And Jesus, knowing their thoughts, said unto them, Every kingdom divided against itself is brought to desolation; and every city or house divided against itself shall not stand: and if Satan cast out Satan, he is divided against himself; how then shall his kingdom stand? By divulging their thoughts He shows that He is God. He defends Himself from their accusation by means of everyday examples, and reveals their foolishness. For how is it that demons cast out one another when in fact they strive to assist one another? ''Satan'' means ''the adversary''

27. And if I by Beelzebub cast out demons, by whom do your sons cast them out? Therefore they shall be your judges. Let us suppose, He says, that I am such as you say. But by whom do your sons, that is, My disciples, cast them out? Surely they do not also cast them out by Beelzebub? But if they cast them out by divine power, how much more so do I? For they work miracles in My name. Therefore they will be to your condemnation, since you saw them, too, working miracles in My name, and still you slander Me.

28. But if I cast out demons by the Spirit of God, then the kingdom of God is come unto you. This means, if it is by divine power that I cast out demons, then I am the Son of God, and I have come for your sake, to do good to you. So, then, I have come unto you, and this is the kingdom of God. Why do you slander My coming which is for your sake?

29. Or else how can one enter into a strong man's house, and plunder his goods, except he first bind the strong man? And then he will plunder his house. I do not, He says, keep demons as friends; just the opposite, I war against them and bind them who were strong men before My coming. For when Christ entered the house, that is, the world, He seized from the demons their goods, which are men.

30. He that is not with Me is against Me; and he that gathereth not with Me scattereth abroad. How, He says, could Beelzebub work with Me, when, on the contrary, he acts against Me? For I teach virtue, but he, evil. How then is he with Me? And I gather men unto salvation, but he scatters them. Christ also hints at the Pharisees, who, while He was teaching and bringing benefit to many, were dispersing the people so that they could not approach Him. He shows that in reality it is they who are demonic.

31-32. Wherefore I say unto you, Every sin and blasphemy shall be forgiven unto men: but the blasphemy against the Spirit shall not be forgiven unto men. And whosoever speaketh a word against the Son of Man, it shall be forgiven him: but whosoever speaketh against the Holy Spirit, it shall not be forgiven him, neither in this age, nor in the age to come. He is saying here that every other sin, such as fornication or theft, has some defense, however slight. For we take refuge in human weakness and we may be forgiven. But when one sees miracles performed by the Spirit and slanders them as being the work of a demon, what defense will he have? For it is clear that such a slanderer knows that these things are of the Holy Spirit, yet he speaks evil of his own will. How then can such a man be forgiven? When the Jews saw the Lord eating and drinking, associating with publicans and harlots, and doing all the other things He did as the Son of Man, then they slandered Him as a glutton and drunkard; yet for this they deserve forgiveness, and not even repentance will be required. For they were understandably scandalized. But when they saw Him working miracles and were slandering and blaspheming the Holy Spirit, saying that it was something demonic, how will this sin be forgiven them, unless they repent? So, then, know that he who blasphemes the Son of Man, seeing Him living as a man, and says that He is a friend of harlots, a glutton, and a drunkard because of those things which Christ does, such a man will not have to give an answer for this, even if he does not repent. For he is forgiven, as he did not realize that this was God concealed. But he who blasphemes the Holy Spirit, that is, the spiritual deeds of Christ, and calls them demonic, unless he repents, he will not be forgiven. For he does not have a reasonable excuse to slander, as does the man who sees Christ with harlots and publicans and then slanders. He will not be forgiven either here or there, but both here and there he will be punished. For many are punished here, but there, not at all, such as the poor man, Lazarus; while others are punished both here and there, as the Sodomites and those who blaspheme the Holy Spirit. But some, like the apostles and the Forerunner, are punished neither here nor there. For though they who are persecuted appear to suffer punishment, these are not punishments for sins, but rather trials and crowns.

33. Either call the tree good, and its fruit good; or else call the tree corrupt, and its fruit corrupt: for the tree is known by its fruit. Since the Jews were not able to slander the miracles as bad, they blasphemed as demonic the One Who did them, Christ. So He says: either say that I am a good tree, and then all My miracles, which are the fruit, are good as well; or if you say that I am a corrupt tree, then it is clear that the fruit, that is, the miracles, are corrupt as well. But you say that the miracles, the fruit, are good; therefore, I, the tree, am also good. For indeed, just as the tree is known by its fruit, so I am known by the miracles which I do.

34. O brood of vipers, how can ye, being evil, speak good things? Look, He says, you who are evil trees bear evil fruit when you speak ill of Me. And I also, if I were evil, would bring forth evil fruit and not these miracles. He calls them ''brood of vipers'' because they boasted of Abraham. He shows that they are not of Abraham, but of ancestors worthy of their own wickedness.

34-35. For out of the abundance of the heart the mouth speaketh. A good man out of the good treasure of the heart bringeth forth good things: and an evil man out of the evil treasure bringeth forth evil things. When you see a speaker of obscenities, know that he does not have in his heart the same quantity of evil that he speaks, but many times more. For it is the excess that spills over, and he who has a hidden treasure displays only a small part. Likewise he who speaks good has even more in his heart.

36-37. But I say unto you, That every idle word that men shall speak, they shall give account thereof in the day of judgement. For by thy words thou shalt be deemed righteous, and by thy words thou shalt be condemned. Here He strikes fear into our hearts, that we will give an account for even a careless word, that is, any lying, slanderous, indecent, or mocking word. Then He brings forward testimony from Scripture, lest He appear to be speaking His own words. "By thy words thou shalt be deemed righteous, and by thy words thou shalt be condemned."[4]

38. Then certain of the scribes and of the Pharisees answered, saying, Master, we would see a sign from Thee. The evangelist is amazed and so writes the word "then". For when they should have submitted to Him because of His preceding miracles, it was then that they asked for a sign. They wanted to see a sign from heaven, as the other evangelist says.[5] For they thought that He performed the miracles which He did on earth by the power of the devil, as the devil is the ruler of this world. How, then, does the Saviour answer?

39-40. But He answered and said unto them, An evil and adulterous generation seeketh after a sign; and there shall no sign be given to it, but the sign of the prophet Jonah: for as Jonah was three days and three nights in the whale's belly, so shall the Son of Man be three days and three nights in the heart of the earth. He calls them an evil generation as they were deceiving tempters, and adulterous, because they had abandoned God and followed after demons. He calls His Resurrection a sign as it is marvelous beyond belief. For having descended into the heart of the earth, the nethermost part, which is hades, He arose on the third day. The three days and three nights you must understand as spoken of in part and not in their entirety. For He died on Friday, which is one day. He was dead on Saturday—behold, the second day. And the night of Sunday[6] held Him still dead. The three days and

---

[4] Job 15:6; cf. Ecclesiastes 10:12.

[5] Lk. 11:16

[6] The Jewish, the Byzantine, and the Church's "day" (that is, the twenty four hour cycle) is calculated as beginning at sunset. So the "night of Sunday" is what we would call Saturday night.

nights, then, are counted by parts, in just the same way as we often count them ourselves.

41. The men of Nineveh shall rise in judgement with this generation, and shall condemn it: because they repented at the preaching of Jonah; and, behold, a greater than Jonah is here. Jonah, He says, after he left the belly of the whale, preached and was believed. But you will not believe Me even after My Resurrection. Wherefore you will be condemned by the Ninevites, who believed in My servant Jonah without any signs, and, what is more, were barbarians. But you who were nourished on the prophets and have seen signs, have not believed in Me, the Master. For this is what is meant by "Behold, a greater than Jonah is here."

42. The queen of the south shall rise up in the judgement with this generation, and shall condemn it: for she came from the ends of the earth to hear the wisdom of Solomon: and, behold, a greater than Solomon is here. The queen, He says, came from a great distance, despite her tender womanhood, to hear about trees and woods and certain things of nature. But though I came to you, speaking of ineffable things, you have not accepted Me.

43-45. When the unclean spirit is gone out of a man, he walketh through dry places, seeking rest, and findeth none. Then he saith, I will return into my house from whence I came out; and when he is come, he findeth it empty, swept, and garnished. Then goeth he, and taketh with himself seven other spirits more wicked than himself, and they enter in and dwell there: and the last state of that man is worse than the first. Even so shall it be also unto this wicked generation. He shows that they have been brought to utter perdition by not accepting Him. For just as those who have been delivered from demons suffer worse things if they become lazy and careless, so it is that your generation was possessed of a demon when it worshipped the idols. But this demon was cast out by means of the prophets. Then I Myself came, wishing to cleanse you further. But since you rejected Me, and, indeed, are eager to slay Me, as your sin is worse, so will your punishment be worse, and your last captivity will be more grievous than the former. You, O reader, must also understand this, that the unclean spirit is cast out by baptism and goes forth among waterless and unbaptized souls; but it does not find rest in them. Rest for demons is to harass with evil deeds those who are baptized, for they already possess those who are unbaptized. Therefore the demon returns with seven other spirits to the one who is baptized. For just as there are seven gifts of the Holy Spirit, so, on the contrary, there are seven spirits of evil. When the demon re-enters the one who is baptized, the disaster is worse. For, previously, there was hope of being cleansed through baptism. But now there is no hope of a second baptism, unless it be by the baptism of repentance, which is exceedingly toilsome.

46. While He yet talked to the people, behold, His mother and His brethren stood without, desiring to speak with Him. Subject to a certain human foible, His mother wanted to show that she had authority over her child, for she did not yet comprehend His greatness. This is why, while He was still speaking, she wished to summon Him to herself, seeking to draw attention to her son's obedience to her. What does Christ do? He knew her intentions; hear what He says:

47-50. Then one said unto Him, Behold, Thy mother and Thy brethren stand without, desiring to speak with Thee. But He answered and said unto him that told him, Who is My mother? and who are My brethren? And He stretched forth His hand toward His disciples, and said, Behold My mother and My brethren! For whosoever shall do the will of My Father Who is in heaven, the same is My brother, and sister, and mother. He did not say this to offend His mother, but to correct this vainglorious and human thought of hers. For He did not say, "She is not My mother," but "Unless she does the will of God, that she bore Me is of no benefit to her." He does not deny the relationship by birth, but He adds to it the relationship by virtue. For no unworthy person derives benefit from a relationship by birth. When He had corrected the sickness of vainglory, He once again obeyed His mother who was calling Him. For the evangelist says:[7]

[7] The evangelist shows that Jesus did obey His mother, saying in the following verse that Jesus went outside, where His mother and brothers were.

CHAPTER THIRTEEN

Concerning the parables of the sower and of the kingdom of heaven.

1-2. The same day went Jesus out of the house, and sat by the sea side. And great multitudes were gathered together unto Him so that He went into a boat, and sat; and the whole multitude stood on the shore. He sat in the boat so that He could face all His listeners, and so that all could hear. Then as a fisherman He casts His net from the sea toward those on land.

3. And He spake many things unto them in parables, saying. To the simple and sincere multitudes on the mountain He spoke without parables. But as the deceitful Pharisees are here, He speaks in parables so that those who do not understand can ask and learn. Moreover it is not right to lay bare the teachings before those who are unworthy. For it is not right to cast pearls before swine. First He tells a parable which makes the listener more attentive. Listen: **Behold, a sower went forth to sow his seed.** He calls Himself the sower, and His word, the seed. He went forth, but not from a place, for He was in all places. But He drew near to us, taking on human flesh, and thus it is said, "He went forth", that is, from the bosom of the Father. He went forth to us because we were not able to come to Him. And what did He go forth to do? To scorch the earth because of the tangle of thorns? To punish? No, but rather to sow. He said "his seed" because the prophets also sowed; but He sowed, not their seed, but God's. He being God, sowed His own seed. He was not made wise by divine grace—far from it! He Himself was the Wisdom of God.

4-7. And as he sowed, some seeds fell by the way side, and the winged creatures of the sky came and devoured them up: some fell upon rocky ground, where they had not much earth: and forthwith they sprang up, because they had no deepness of earth: and when the sun rose, they were scorched: and because they had no root, they withered away. Those by the way side are they who are lazy and indolent, who do not accept the word. For their minds are a pathway that is trodden and hard, and not in the least bit tilled. The word is snatched from them by the birds of the sky, that is, the spirits of the air, who are the demons. Those on rocky ground are they who hear but out of weakness do not resist trials and afflictions, but abandon their own salvation. By the rising sun understand temptations, which, like the sun, show men as they really are and reveal things which are hidden. **And some fell among thorns; and the thorns sprang up and choked them.** These are they who choke the word with worldly thoughts. For though a rich man thinks he is doing a good deed, yet the deed does not grow and flourish, hindered as it is by worldly cares.

8. But other seed fell upon good ground, and brought forth fruit, one a hundredfold, another sixtyfold, and another thirtyfold. Three quarters of the seed perished and only a quarter was saved. For few are they who are saved. At the end He speaks of the good ground, thus giving us hope of repentance. For although a man be rocky ground, or by the way side, or among the thorns, yet it is possible for him to become good ground. Nor do all who accept the word bear fruit equally: but "one a hundredfold", perhaps he who has attained perfect non-possessiveness and extreme asceticism; "another sixtyfold", perhaps the monk dwelling in a monastic community, and he, too, yields fruitfully; "and another thirtyfold", he who has chosen honorable marriage and diligently practices the virtues as much as he is able. See the goodness of God, how He accepts everyone: those who achieve great things, those who achieve moderate things, and those who achieve small things.

9. He who hath ears to hear, let him hear. He shows that those who have spiritual ears must understand these things in a spiritual sense. For many have ears but do not use them for hearing. This is why He added, "He who hath ears to hear, let him hear."

10-12. And the disciples came, and said unto Him, Why speakest Thou unto them in parables? He answered and said unto them, It is given unto you to know the mysteries of the kingdom of heaven, but to them it is not given. For whosoever hath, to him shall be given, and he shall have in abundance: but whosoever hath not, from him shall be taken away even what he hath. The disciples found great obscurity in the words spoken by Christ, and being solicitous of the common people came to Him and asked the question. And He said, "It is given unto you to know the mysteries," that is, since you have willingness and zeal to learn, it is given to you. But to those who do not have zeal, it is not given. For it is he that asks who receives. Ask, therefore, He says, and it will be given to you. See here how the Lord told the parable and only the disciples, who asked, received. So we can truly say that to him who has zeal, knowledge is given and in abundance. But from him who does not have zeal and a worthy mind, even that which he imagines he has will be taken away. That is to say, if he has even the slightest spark of good, he extinguishes it if he does not blow on it with the Spirit and spiritual deeds, and kindle it.

13. Therefore speak I to them in parables: because they seeing see not; and hearing they hear not, neither do they understand. Take heed. Here the problem is solved of those who say that some are evil by nature, or by God's intent. For they argue that Christ Himself said, "It is given unto you to know the mysteries, but to the Jews it is not given." But we say, with God, to those who speak such things, that God makes everyone by nature to understand what is necessary. For God "enlighteneth every man that cometh into the world."[1] But it is our own will and inclination that casts us into darkness. This is made clear even here. For Christ says that although they see by nature, that is, they were created by God to understand, they by their own choice do not see. And hearing, that is, by nature created by God to hear and to understand, they by their own choice do not hear, nor do they understand. Tell me, did they not see the miracles of Christ? Yes, they did, but they made themselves blind and condemned Him. So this is the meaning of "seeing they see not." Then He brings forward the prophet as further witness to His argument.

14-15. And in them is fulfilled the prophecy of Isaiah, which saith, By hearing ye shall hear, and shall not understand: and seeing ye shall see, and shall not perceive: for this people's heart has grown fat, and their ears are dull of hearing, and their eyes they have closed; lest at any time they should see with their eyes, and hear with their ears, and should understand with their heart, and should turn back,

---

[1] Jn. 1:9

and I should heal them. Do you see what the prophecy[2] is saying? You do not understand, not because I created your heart fat and dull, but because it has grown fat, although it is obvious that before it was fine and subtle. For something which grows fat was first thin. And when their heart had grown fat, then they closed their eyes. He did not say that God closed their eyes, but they did, of their own choice. They did this, He says, so that they would not turn back and be healed by Me. For they chose evil and went to great lengths to remain unhealed and unrepentant.

16-17. But blessed are your eyes, for they see: and your ears, for they hear. For verily I say unto you, That many prophets and righteous men have desired to see those things which ye see, and have not seen them; and to hear those things which ye hear, and have not heard them. Even the physical eyes and ears of the apostles are blessed. But even more so are their spiritual eyes and ears worthy of blessedness, because they recognized the Christ. He esteems them more highly than the prophets because the prophets saw the Christ only spiritually, while the apostles saw Him both spiritually and physically. But also because the prophets were not deemed worthy of such great mysteries and knowledge as were the apostles. In two ways, then, the apostles surpass the prophets: that they saw Christ bodily and that they were initiated into a deeper, more spiritual, understanding of the divine mysteries. Then He explains the parable to the disciples, saying:

18-19. Hear ye therefore the parable of the sower. When any one heareth the word of the kingdom, and understandeth it not, then cometh the evil one, and catcheth away that which was sown in his heart. This is he who received seed by the way side. He urges us to understand what is spoken by those who teach, lest we too be like those who are "by the way side". For it may be said, since Christ is the way, those who are outside of Christ are by the way side. For they are not in the way, but outside of the way.

20-21. As for that which was sown on rocky ground, this is he that heareth the word, and straightway with joy receiveth it; yet hath he

---

[2] Is. 6:9-10

not root in himself, and dureth but for a while: for when tribulation or persecution ariseth because of the word, straightway he stumbleth and falleth. He speaks of tribulation because there are many who, when they are hard-pressed by their parents, or by some misfortunes, immediately blaspheme. And of persecution, on account of those who fall into the hands of tyrants.

22. As for that which was sown among the thorns, this is he that heareth the word; and the care of this world, and the deceitfulness of riches, choke the word, and he becometh unfruitful. He did not say this world chokes, but the care of this world. Nor did He say wealth chokes, but the deceit of wealth. For wealth, when it is distributed, does not choke the word, but instead makes it grow. The thorns are cares and pleasures, for they kindle the flame both of desire and of gehenna. And just as the thorn is sharp and pierces the body and is removed with difficulty, so also with pleasure, once it takes hold of the soul, it enters it and is eradicated only with difficulty.

23. As for that which was sown upon the good ground, this is he that heareth the word, and understandeth it; who also beareth fruit, and bringeth forth, one a hundredfold, another sixty, and another thirty. The forms of virtue vary, and those who progress in virtue vary. Do you see the order in the parable? We must first hear and understand it so that we may not be like those who are by the way side. Then we must hold steadfastly to what we have heard, and, finally, we must not be lovers of money. For what benefit is it to me to hear and retain the word, only to be choked by the love of money?

24-30. Another parable put He forth unto them, saying, The kingdom of heaven is likened unto a man which sowed good seed in his field: but while men slept, his enemy came and sowed tares among the wheat, and went his way. But when the blade was sprung up, and brought forth fruit, then appeared the tares also. So the servants of the householder came and said unto him, Sir, didst not thou sow good seed in thy field? From whence then hath it tares? He said unto them, An enemy hath done this. The servants said unto him, Wilt thou then that we go and gather them up? But he said, Nay; lest while ye gather up the tares, ye root up also the wheat with them. Let

both grow together until the harvest: and at the time of harvest I will say to the reapers, Gather ye together first the tares, and bind them in bundles to burn them: but gather the wheat into my barn. In the previous parable He spoke of the fourth part of the seed which fell on the good soil, while in this parable He shows that the enemy does not allow even that part which fell on good soil to remain incorrupted, because we sleep and grow indolent. The field, then, is the world, or, each one's soul. The sower is Christ. The good seed is good people, or, good thoughts. The tares are heresies, or, evil thoughts. The one who sows them is the devil. The men who were sleeping are those who by their indolence give entry to heretics and evil thoughts. The servants are the angels, who are indignant that there are heresies or any wickedness in the soul, and wish to seize and cut off from this life the heretics and those who think evil thoughts. But God does not allow the heretics to be destroyed by wars, lest the righteous suffer and be destroyed along with them. Likewise, neither does God wish to cut down a man on account of his evil thoughts, lest the wheat be destroyed along with them. If, for example, Matthew had been cut down while he was a tare, the wheat of the word which was later to spring up from him would have been cut down with him. Similarly with Paul and the thief. While they were tares they were not cut down, but were permitted to live so that later their virtue might grow. Therefore He says to the angels, At the end of the world you will gather the tares, namely, the heretics. But how? Into bundles, that is, binding them hand and foot. For at that time a man will no longer be able to do anything, but all his power to act will be bound. The wheat, namely, the saints, will be gathered by the angelic reapers into heavenly granaries. So it is with the evil thoughts which Paul had when he persecuted: they were burnt in the fire which Christ came to light upon the earth, while the wheat, that is the good thoughts, was gathered into the granaries of the Church.

31-32. Another parable put He forth unto them, saying, The kingdom of heaven is like to a grain of mustard seed, which a man took, and sowed in his field. It is the least of all seeds: but when it is grown it is the greatest among plants, and becometh a tree, so that the winged creatures of the sky come and lodge in the branches thereof. The grain of mustard seed is both the preaching and the apostles. For though they appeared to be few, they encompassed the whole earth, with the result that the birds of the air, that is, those with frivolous and feathery knowledge of the things above, could find rest in them. You, too, O reader, must be as a grain of mustard seed, small in appearance (for it is not right to make a show of virtue) but hot, zealous, pungent, and reproving. Thus you will become greater than the shrubs, that is, greater than those who are weak and imperfect, by yourself being perfect, so that even the winged creatures of heaven,[3] that is, the angels, will take their rest in you who are living the angelic life. For they, too, rejoice in the righteous.

33. Another parable spake He unto them; The kingdom of heaven is like unto leaven, which a woman took, and hid in three measures of flour, till the whole was leavened. He calls the apostles leaven as well as a grain of mustard seed. For just as the leaven, although it is small, transforms to itself all the flour, so you will transform the whole world, though you are few. Some understand the leaven to be the preaching; the three measures are the three faculties of the soul—the abilities to reason, to be stirred into action, and to desire—and the woman is the soul which hides the preaching within all three of its faculties, so that it is all mixed together, leavened, and sanctified. So every part of us must be leavened and transformed into that which is more Godlike. For He says, "till it was all leavened."

34-35. All these things spake Jesus unto the multitude in parables; and without a parable spake He not unto them: that it might be fulfilled which was spoken by the prophet, saying, I will open My mouth in parables; I will utter things which have been kept secret from the foundation of the world. He brings forward as witness the prophet who had proclaimed beforehand that Jesus would teach in parables,[4] lest you think that Christ had invented some new form of teaching. But do not understand the prophecy in terms of cause and effect, but rather from the outcome of the event. For Christ did not teach in this manner in order to fulfill the prophecy, but rather, because He

---

[3] The same word in Greek, *ouranos*, means either "sky" or "heaven". Bl. Theophylact here and in the lines above is simply drawing upon both meanings.

[4] Ps. 77:2

taught in parables, the word of the prophet is found in the outcome to have been fulfilled in Him. "Without a parable spake He not unto them" on this occasion only, for indeed He did not always speak to them in parables. The Lord uttered those things which were hidden since the foundation of the world. For He Himself revealed to us the mysteries of the heavens.

36. Then Jesus left the multitude, and went into the house. He left the multitude at that time because they were not benefiting from His teaching. For He was speaking in parables so that they would question Him. But they were not concerned with this, neither did they ask to learn anything, so it was reasonable that He should leave them. **And His disciples came unto Him, saying, Declare unto us the parable of the tares of the field.** They only asked about this parable as the others seemed clearer to them. Tares are anything that grow among wheat and are harmful to it, such as weeds and the like.

37-42. He answered and said unto them, He that soweth the good seed is the Son of Man; the field is the world; the good seed are the children of the kingdom; but the tares are the children of the evil one; the enemy that sowed them is the devil; the harvest is the end of the world; and the reapers are the angels. As therefore the tares are gathered and burned in the fire; so shall it be at the end of this world. The Son of Man shall send forth His angels, and they shall gather out of His kingdom all things that cause temptation, and them which do iniquity; and shall cast them into the furnace of fire: there shall be wailing and gnashing of teeth. What needed to be said has been said above. We said that He is speaking here of the heresies which are permitted to exist until the end of the world. For if we were to slay the heretics and cut them down, there would be uprisings and pitched battles, and perhaps many of the faithful would be destroyed in the uprisings. But even Paul and the thief had tares before they believed, but they were not cut down at that time, for the sake of the wheat that would spring up in them, for they later bore fruit for God. But the tares were consumed by the fire and heat of the Spirit.

43. Then shall the righteous shine forth as the sun in the kingdom of their Father. He who hath ears to hear, let him hear. Since the sun appears brighter to us than all the stars, He compares the radiance of the righteous to the sun. For they will shine more resplendently than the sun. Since, perhaps, Christ is the Sun of Righteousness, so the righteous will shine as Christ Himself, for they, too, will be gods.[5]

44. Again, the kingdom of heaven is like unto treasure hid in a field; the which when a man hath found, he hideth, and for joy thereof goeth and selleth all that he hath, and buyeth that field. The field is the world, the treasure is the preaching and knowledge of Christ. It is hidden in the world. For as St. Paul says, We preach a wisdom that is hidden.[6] He who seeks knowledge of God, finds it. And all that he has, be it pagan doctrines, wicked practices, or money, he immediately throws away and buys the field, that is, the world. For he who has knowledge of Christ has the world as his own possession. For having nothing he possesses everything, and has the elements as his servants and commands them, as did Joshua and Moses.

45-46. Again, the kingdom of heaven is like unto a merchant man, seeking goodly pearls: who, when he had found one pearl of great price, went and sold all that he had, and bought it. The sea is the present life. The merchants are those who traverse it in search of some knowledge. Many think that the pearls are the opinions of the multitude of philosophers. But one is of great price. For there is One Truth, which is Christ. It is like the story that is told of how the pearl comes into being within the oyster: the oyster opens its folds and a bolt of lightning strikes within; the folds are again shut and the pearl is conceived from the lightning and a droplet of moisture, giving it its pure whiteness. So Christ also was conceived from the lightning from above, the Holy Spirit. And as a man who has a pearl turns it over and over in his hands, and he knows what great wealth he possesses, while others are ignorant, so too the preaching is hidden among the unnoticed and the simple. To obtain this pearl one must give all.

---

[5] There are two aspects to the mystery of the Incarnation. The first is that the Son of God, in assuming our flesh, united the divine nature to human nature. The second is that those who are perfected in Christ will find their human nature transformed to the divine, and in this sense they will become "gods".

[6] See I Cor. 2:7.

47-50. Again, the kingdom of heaven is like unto a net, that was cast into the sea, and it brought together of every kind: which, when it was full, they drew to shore, and sat down, and gathered together the good into vessels, but cast the bad away. So shall it be at the end of the world: the angels shall come forth, and sever the wicked from among the righteous, and shall cast them into the furnace of fire: there shall be wailing and gnashing of teeth. Fearful is this parable, for it shows that though we believe, if we do not lead a good life we shall be cast into the fire. The net is the teaching of the fishermen apostles, woven from miracles and the prophets' testimonies. For what the apostles taught, they confirmed with miracles and the voices of the prophets. This net, then, caught all kinds—barbarians, Greeks, Jews, harlots, publicans, and thieves. When it has been filled, that is, when the world has ended, then those in the net are separated. And though we may have believed, if we are found to have become corrupt, we are thrown out. But those who are not, are placed into vessels which are, in fact, the places of eternal dwelling. Every deed, be it good or evil, is called the food of the soul. And the soul, too, has teeth, but they are spiritual in nature. Then the corrupted soul will gnash its teeth, that is, grind together its now impotent faculties of action, because it practiced such things.

51-52. Jesus saith unto them, Have ye understood all these things? They say unto Him, Yea, Lord. Then said He unto them, Therefore every scribe who is instructed in the kingdom of heaven is like unto a man that is a householder, who bringeth forth out of his treasure things new and old. Do you see how the parables have made them more attentive? For behold, they who before were unthinking and unlearned have understood these difficult things that were spoken. Therefore the Saviour praises them and says "every scribe". He calls them scribes, students of the law, but though they were students of the law, they did not remain within the law, but were instructed in the kingdom, that is, in the knowledge of Christ, and they are able to speak of both the old and the new. The householder, then, is Christ, the rich man. For in Him are the treasures of wisdom. He taught new things and then brought forward testimony from the old. For example, He said, "You will be called to account for every idle word''[7]—this is new. Then He brought forward testimony, ''By your words you will be judged and condemned''[8]—this is the old. In this the apostles were similar, for Paul says, ''Be ye imitators of me, as I am of Christ.''[9]

53-54. And it came to pass, that when Jesus had finished these parables, He departed thence. And when He was come into His own country, He taught them in their synagogue. Matthew says ''these parables'' because in a short time He would tell them other ones. He departed so that He could benefit others by His presence. ''His own country'' means Nazareth, for He was raised there. He was teaching in the synagogue, speaking openly in public, that they might not later have grounds to claim that He was teaching things contrary to the law.

54-57. Insomuch that they were astonished, and said, Whence hath this man this wisdom, and these mighty works? Is not this the carpenter's son? Is not his mother called Mary? and his brethren, James, and Joses, and Simon, and Jude? And his sisters, are they not all with us? Whence then hath this man all these things? And they were offended in Him. The Nazarenes were foolish to think that low birth and plain ancestry hinder anyone from pleasing God. Let us suppose that Jesus was simply man and not God. What would have prevented Him from being a great wonderworker? So they are proven to be foolish and spiteful. They ought rather to have taken pride that their native city had produced such a good man. The Lord had brothers and sisters, the children of Joseph which he begat by the wife of his brother Cleopas. For when Cleopas died childless, Joseph took his wife in accordance with the law and had six children by her, four boys and two girls, Mary, who was called the daughter of Cleopas, in accordance with the law, and Salome. The Nazarenes also took offense at Jesus, perhaps themselves saying that He was casting out demons by Beelzebub.

57-58. But Jesus said unto them, A prophet is not without honour,

---

[7] See Mt. 12:36.

[8] Mt. 12:37; cf. Lk. 19:22, Job 15:6.

[9] See I Cor. 4:16.

save in his own country, and in his own house. And He did not many mighty works there because of their unbelief. See how Christ did not insult them, but said meekly, ''A prophet is not without honour.'' For it is our human habit to despise those who are familiar, and to give a friendly welcome strangers. He added ''and in his own house'' because even His brothers who were of the same house bore Him ill-will. ''He did not many mighty works there'' because of their unbelief, sparing them further punishment lest they remain unbelieving even after the miracles which He might have done there. ''He did not many mighty works,'' but He did perform a few, that they might not have excuse to say later, ''If He had done something, we would have believed.'' You, O reader, understand this: to this day Jesus is without honor in His own country, that is, among the Jews. But we who are foreigners give Him honor.

CHAPTER FOURTEEN

Concerning John and Herod.
Concerning the five loaves and the two fish.
Concerning Jesus' walking on the water.

1-2. At that time Herod the tetrarch heard of the fame of Jesus, and said unto his servants, This is John the Baptist; he is risen from the dead; and therefore mighty works do show forth themselves in him. This Herod was the son of him who slew the infants in Bethlehem.[1] From this passage consider the dimness in which a ruler lives his life. See how long it takes for Herod to hear of Jesus. Those in power learn slowly about such things because they are not concerned about those who shine forth in virtue. He appears to fear the Baptist. This is why he does not dare to speak out to anyone except his servants. Since John did not work any signs when he was alive, Herod thought that by his resurrection he had also received from God the gift of working miracles.

3-5. For Herod had laid hold on John, and bound him, and put him in prison for Herodias' sake, his brother Philip's wife. For John said unto him, It is not lawful for thee to have her. And when he would have put him to death, he feared the multitude, because they counted him as a prophet. In what has gone before, Matthew has not given an account of John, as it was his intent to write only about Christ. Nor would he have mentioned it now if it did not relate to Christ. John had rebuked Herod for unlawfully taking the wife of his brother. For the law decreed that a man should take the wife of his brother only when that brother had died childless. But in this case Philip had not died childless, for the dancing girl was his child. Some say that Herod had seized both wife and tetrarchy from Philip while he was still living. Whether the former or the latter is correct, what was done was a transgression of the law. He postponed the murder because he feared the multitude, not because he feared God; yet the devil found the opportune moment for him.

---

[1] See footnote on p. 23.

6-8. But when Herod's birthday was kept, the daughter of Herodias danced before them, and pleased Herod. Whereupon he promised with an oath to give her whatsoever she would ask. And she, being prompted by her mother, said, Give me here John Baptist's head on a platter. Behold, the wantonness! The princess dances, and the better she dances, the more evil it is. For it is shameful for a princess to be skilled at doing something unbefitting. And consider this additional foolishness of Herod's, that he promised to give whatever she asked. If she had asked for your own head, would you have given it to her? She says, "Give me here John Baptist's head." Why did she add the word "here"? She feared that Herod might later come to his senses and change his mind, so she urges him on by saying, "Give me it here and now."

9-12. And the king was sorry: nevertheless for the oath's sake, and them which sat with him at table, he commanded it to be given her. And he sent, and beheaded John in the prison. And his head was brought on a platter, and given to the damsel: and she brought it to her mother. And his disciples came, and took up the body, and buried it. And they went and told Jesus. He was sorry because of John's virtue, for even the enemy in war marvels at valor displayed by his adversary.[2] But because of his oaths, he gives the inhuman gift. Let us learn from this that it is sometimes better to perjure oneself than to do something ungodly because of an oath. The body of the Baptist was buried in Sebaste Caesarea. But his precious head was buried the first time in Emesa. "And they went and told Jesus." What did they tell Jesus? Not that John had died, for the account of John's death was given parenthetically. But rather, they told Jesus what Herod was saying about Him, that Jesus was John.

13. When Jesus heard of it, He departed thence by boat into a desert place apart. Jesus departed on account of Herod's bloodthirstiness, teaching us also not to cast ourselves openly into danger. He also departed so that He would not seem to have been incarnate only in appearance. For if Herod had seized Jesus, he would have attempted to

---

[2] The original meaning of the Greek word for "virtue", *aretē*, is "valor displayed in battle".

kill Him, and if Jesus had snatched Himself from such danger because it was not yet time for His death, then He would have seemed to be only an apparition. He departed "to a desert place apart" so that He might perform the miracle with the loaves.

13-14. And when the people had heard thereof, they followed Him on foot out of the cities. And Jesus went forth, and saw a great multitude, and was moved with compassion toward them, and He healed their sick. The multitude show their faith by running to Jesus even as He is departing, for which they receive healing as the reward of faith. Their following on foot and without any provisions are also signs of faith.

15-16. And when it was evening, His disciples came to Him, saying, This is a desert place, and the hour is now late; send the multitude away, that they may go into the villages, and buy food for themselves. But Jesus said unto them, They need not depart; give ye them to eat. The disciples are compassionate and concerned about the multitude, not wanting them to go without food. What, then, does the Saviour do? "Give ye them to eat," He says, not in ignorance of the extreme poverty of the apostles—far from it. But so that when they had said, "We do not have," He might appear to proceed to work a miracle out of necessity and not from vainglory.

17-19. And they say unto Him, We have here but five loaves, and two fishes. He said, Bring them hither to Me. And He commanded the multitude to recline on the grass, and took the five loaves, and the two fishes, and looking up to heaven, He blessed. "Bring the loaves here to Me. Though it be evening, I Who created the hours am here. Though it be a deserted place, it is I Who giveth food to all flesh." We learn from this that we must spend in hospitality even the little that we have, just as the apostles gave to the crowds the little that they had. As that little was multiplied, so too will your little be multiplied. He bids the multitude to recline on the grass, teaching frugality, so that you also, O reader, may not take your ease on expensive beds and couches. He looks up to heaven and blesses the loaves, as if both to confirm that He is not opposed to God but that He came from the Father and from heaven, and also to teach us to give thanks when we begin a meal and only then to eat.

19-21. And He brake, and gave the loaves to His disciples, and the disciples gave them to the multitude. And they did all eat, and were filled: and they took up of the fragments that remained twelve baskets full. And they that had eaten were about five thousand men, beside women and children. He gives the loaves to the disciples so that they might always retain the miracle in their memory and not have it fade from their minds, although they did in fact immediately forget. There was food left over lest you think that He performed the miracle only in appearance. There were twelve baskets so that Judas too might carry one and thus remembering the miracle not rush headlong into betrayal. And He multiplies both the loaves and the fish to show that He is the Creator of earth and sea, and the Giver of what we eat everyday, and it is multiplied by Him. He performed the miracle in a deserted place lest anyone think that He bought the loaves from a neighboring town and distributed them to the multitude, for it was deserted. This is the explanation of the literal account. But in its spiritual sense, learn that when Herod, who represents the fleshly and superficial mind of the Jews (for "Herod" means "fleshly" and "skinlike"), cut off the head of John who was the head and chief of the prophets, it showed that Herod rejected those who prophesied of Christ. Whereupon Jesus withdrew to a desert place, to the nations who were desolate without God, and He healed the sick in soul and then He fed them. For if He had not forgiven our sins and healed our sicknesses by baptism He could not have nourished us by giving us the immaculate Mysteries, for no one partakes of Holy Communion who has not first been baptized. The five thousand are those who are sick in their five senses and who are healed by the five loaves. Since the five senses were diseased, there are as many poultices as there are wounds. The two fish are the words of the fishermen. The one fish is the Gospel and the other the Epistles. Some have understood the five loaves to signify the Pentateuch of Moses: Genesis, Exodus, Leviticus, Numbers, and Deuteronomy. Twelve baskets were lifted up and carried by the apostles; for whatever we, the multitude, are unable to eat, that is, to understand, the apostles carried and held, that is, they accepted and understood. "Besides women and children." This means, allegorically, that a Christian man, woman, or child, must not in any way be childish, womanly, or unmanly.

22. And straightway Jesus constrained His disciples to get into a

boat, and to go before Him unto the other side, while He sent the multitudes away. By saying "constrained", Matthew suggests how inseparable the disciples were from Jesus, for they wanted to be with Him at all times. He sends the multitudes away, not wishing to draw them after Him lest He appear to vaunt in His powers.

23-24. And when He had sent the multitudes away, He went up onto a mountain apart to pray: and when the evening was come, He was there alone. But the boat was now in the midst of the sea, tossed with waves: for the wind was contrary. He went up on the mountain to show that we should pray in an undistracted manner; everything He did was for our sake as He Himself had no need of prayer. He prayed on into the evening, teaching us not to cease praying after a short time, and also to pray especially at night, for it is very quiet then. He permits the disciples to be caught in a storm, so that they might learn to endure trials bravely and that they might know His power. The boat was out in the very middle of the sea so that their fear would be greater.

25-27. And in the fourth watch of the night Jesus went unto them, walking on the sea. And when the disciples saw Him walking on the sea, they were troubled, saying, It is a spirit; and they cried out for fear. But straightway Jesus spake unto them, saying, Take courage; it is I; be not afraid. He did not appear immediately to them to calm the storm, but at the fourth watch, [that is, as the night was coming to its end], teaching us not to ask for a swift solution to our misfortunes but to endure them bravely. The night was divided into four parts by soldiers who stood guard in shifts, each "watch" lasting three hours. So then, sometime after the ninth hour of the night, the Lord appeared to them as God, walking on the water. But they thought it was a phantom, so extraordinary and strange was the sight. For they did not recognize Him by figure, because it was night and because of fear. He first strengthens their resolve by saying: It is I Who can do all things; take courage.

28. And Peter answered Him and said, Lord, if it be Thou, bid me come unto Thee on the water. As Peter had the most fervent love for Christ, he desires immediately, before the others, to be near Him. For he believes not only that Jesus Himself walks on the water, but that He will grant this to him as well. Peter did not say, "Bid me to walk," but rather "to come unto Thee." The former would have been ostentation; the latter is love for Christ.

29-30. And He said, Come. And when Peter was come down out of the boat, he walked on the water, to go to Jesus. But when he saw the mighty wind, he was afraid; and beginning to sink, he cried out, saying, Lord, save me. The Lord laid the sea down beneath Peter's feet, revealing His power. See how Peter prevailed over that which was greater, the sea, but was afraid of the lesser peril, the wind; such is the weakness of human nature. And it was as soon as he became afraid that he began to sink. For when his faith weakened, then Peter went down. The Lord did this so that Peter would not become puffed up, and to console the other disciples who perhaps envied him. Whereupon Christ also showed how much greater He was than Peter.

31-33. And immediately Jesus stretched forth His hand, and caught him, and said unto him, O thou of little faith, of what didst thou doubt? And when they were come into the boat, the wind ceased. Then they that were in the boat came and worshipped Him, saying, Of a truth Thou art the Son of God. Showing that the cause of his sinking was not the wind but faintheartedness, Christ does not rebuke the wind, but the fainthearted Peter. This is why He raised him up and set him on the water, but allowed the wind to blow. Peter did not doubt in everything, but in part. Inasmuch as he was afraid, he showed lack of faith; but by crying out, "Lord, save me," he was healed of his unbelief. This is why he hears the words "O thou of little faith" and not "O thou of no faith." Those in the boat were also delivered from fear, for "the wind ceased." And then, indeed, recognizing Jesus by these things, they confessed His divinity. For it is not an attribute of man to walk on the sea, but of God, as David says, "In the sea are Thy byways, and Thy paths in many waters."[3] The spiritual meaning of the miracle is this: the boat is the earth; the waves, man's life that is troubled by evil spirits; the night is ignorance. In the fourth watch, that is, at the end of the ages, Christ appeared. The first watch was the covenant with Abraham; the second, the law of Moses; the third, the prophets; and the fourth, the

---

[3] Ps. 76:19

coming of Christ. For He saved those who were drowning when He came and was with us so that we might know and worship Him as God. See also how Peter's later denial, return, and repentance were prefigured by what happened to him here on the sea. Just as there he says boldly, "I will not deny Thee", so here he says, "Bid me to come on the water." And just as then he was permitted to deny, so now he was permitted to sink. Here the Lord gives His hand to him and does not let him drown, but there, by Peter's repentance, Christ drew him out of the abyss of denial.

34-36. And when they had crossed over, they came to the land of Gennesaret. And when the men of that place had knowledge of Him, they sent out into all that country round about, and brought unto Him all that were diseased; and besought Him that they might only touch the hem of His garment: and as many as touched were made perfectly whole. Jesus stayed for some time in Gennesaret, and the people recognized Him not only by sight but by the signs which He worked, and they showed fervent faith. So much so that they even desired to touch the hem of His garment, and indeed, when they did so, they were healed. You also, O reader, touch the edge of Christ's garment, which is the end of His sojourning in the flesh. For if you believe that He ascended, you will be saved. The garment means His flesh, and its hem, the end of His life on earth.

CHAPTER FIFTEEN

Concerning the transgression of the commandment of God on account of the tradition of men.
Concerning the Canaanite woman.
Concerning the multitudes who were healed.
Concerning the seven loaves.

1-2. Then came to Jesus scribes and Pharisees, which were of Jerusalem, saying, Why do thy disciples transgress the tradition of the elders? For they wash not their hands when they eat bread. Although there were scribes and Pharisees in every place, those in Jerusalem were the most honored. Hence they envied Christ all the more as they were the most vainglorious. As a custom from ancient tradition, the Jews did not eat with unwashed hands. Seeing the disciples disdain this tradition, they thought that the disciples held the elders in contempt. What then does the Saviour do? He says nothing in defense of this, but accuses them in return.

3-6. But He answered and said unto them, Why do ye also transgress the commandment of God by your tradition? For God commanded, saying, Honour thy father and mother: and, He that curseth father or mother, let him surely die. But ye say, Whosoever shall say to his father or his mother, That which thou mightest have gained from me, is a gift; and honour not his father or his mother, [he shall be absolved.] Thus have ye made the commandment of God of none effect by your tradition. The Pharisees were accusing the disciples of transgressing the commandment of the elders, but Christ shows that the Pharisees were transgressing the law of God.[1] For they were teaching sons to give nothing to their parents but to offer whatever they had to the treasury of the temple. There was a coffer in the temple in which he who so wished could put money, and the contents were distributed to the poor. So the Pharisees first persuaded sons not to give anything to their parents but to offer it instead to the treasury of the

[1] See Ex. 20:12; 21:16.

temple, and then taught them to say, "O my father, the help that you seek from me is a gift, that is, it is offered to God." And then the Pharisees and the sons would divide the money among themselves, and the parents were being left uncared for in their old age. The money lenders had the same practice. For if one of them would lend money to someone who proved to be a bad debtor who did not pay back what was owed, then the money lender would say to the ungrateful debtor, "What you owe me is Corban," that is, a gift offered to God. Then the debtor, as one who was now in debt to God, would pay up although unwillingly. This is what the Pharisees were teaching sons to do.

7-9. Ye hypocrites, well did Isaiah prophesy of you, saying, This people draweth nigh unto Me with their mouth, and honoureth Me with their lips; but their heart is far from Me. But in vain they do worship Me, teaching for doctrines the commandments of men. Through the voice of the prophet Isaiah[2] Christ shows that the Pharisees and scribes are disposed to Him in the same way that they are to His Father. For they were evil, and by their evil deeds they had distanced themselves from God, and so were speaking the words of God only with their mouth. For it is utterly in vain for those who dishonor God by their deeds to worship Him and to believe that by so doing they honor Him.

10-11. And He called the multitude to Himself, and said unto them, Hear, and understand: not that which goeth into the mouth defileth a man; but that which cometh out of the mouth, this defileth a man. He no longer converses with the Pharisees, as they were incurable, but with the multitude. Christ sees fit to honor the multitude by calling them to Himself so that they might accept His word, and He says, "Hear and understand," urging them to be attentive. As the Pharisees had blamed the disciples for eating with unwashed hands, the Lord speaks of food, saying that no food defiles a man. And if food does not defile, how much less does eating with unwashed hands? What defiles the inner man is to say those things which he should not. Here He is alluding to the Pharisees who defile themselves by speaking spiteful words. Behold His wisdom, how He neither openly enjoins the eating with unwashed hands,

---

[2] Is. 29:13

nor forbids it. But He teaches something different, not to spew evil words from the heart.

12. Then came His disciples, and said unto Him, Knowest Thou that the Pharisees were offended, after they heard this saying? The disciples spoke on behalf of the Pharisees, saying that the Pharisees had taken offense. But that the disciples also were troubled is made clear when Peter approached and asked about this. When Jesus heard, then, that the Pharisees had taken offense, He said:

13-14. But He answered and said, Every plant, which My heavenly Father hath not planted, shall be rooted up. Let them alone: they are blind leaders of the blind. And if the blind lead the blind, both shall fall into the ditch. It is the Judaic ordinances and the traditions of the elders that He says will be rooted up, not the commandments of the law, as the Manichean heretics believe. The law is a plant of God, so it has not been rooted up. Its root, that is, the hidden Spirit, remains, but its leaves, namely, the visible letter, have fallen. For we no longer understand the law according to the letter, but according to the Spirit. As the Pharisees were hopeless and incurable, He said, "Let them be." Here we learn that it is not to our detriment to give offense to those who willingly take offense and are incorrigible. He calls them blind teachers of the blind; He says this to draw the multitudes away from them.

15. Then answered Peter and said unto Him, Explain to us this parable. Peter knew that the law did not allow the eating of all foods, and he was afraid to say to Jesus, "I too am scandalized by this saying of Thine, which appears to transgress the law." Therefore he questions Jesus, feigning ignorance.

16-20. And Jesus said, Are ye also yet without understanding? Do not ye yet understand, that whatsoever entereth in at the mouth goeth into the belly and is cast out into the drain? But those things which proceed out of the mouth come forth from the heart; and they defile the man. For out of the heart proceed evil thoughts, murders, adulteries, fornications, thefts, false witness, blasphemies: these are the things which defile a man: but to eat with unwashed hands defileth not a man. The Saviour rebukes the disciples and censures their lack of sense, either because they took offense or because they did not understand the obvious. For He says, "That which is understood and is apparent to all, you do not understand; that food does not remain within but passes out below, not at all polluting a man's soul, for it does not remain inside. But thoughts are engendered within and remain there, and when they come out, that is, proceed to deed and act, they pollute the man." For the thought of fornication stains while it remains within, but when it issues forth into deed and act, it utterly defiles.

21-23. Then Jesus went thence, and departed into the region of Tyre and Sidon. And behold, a woman of Canaan came from that region, and cried unto Him, saying, Have mercy on me, O Lord, Thou Son of David; my daughter is grievously vexed with a demon. But He answered her not a word. Why did He not allow the disciples to go by way of the Gentiles,[3] while He Himself went to Tyre and Sidon, which were Gentile cities? Learn then, that He did not go there to preach, since, as Mark says, "He hid Himself."[4] But rather, when He saw that the Pharisees had not accepted His words about food, He went to the Gentiles. The woman said, "Have mercy, not on my daughter, who is unconscious, but on me who am suffering and experiencing these terrible things." And she did not say, "Come and heal," but "Have mercy." He did not answer her a word, not out of contempt, but to show that He had come, in the first place, for the Jews, and to shut the mouths of those Jews who might later slanderously accuse Him of doing good to Gentiles. He also did not answer her so that He might reveal the persevering faith of the woman.

23-24. And His disciples came and besought Him, saying, Send her away; for she crieth after us. But He answered and said, I am sent only unto the lost sheep of the house of Israel. The disciples were oppressed by the cry of the woman and so begged Christ to send her away. They did this, not out of a lack of compassion, but rather with the desire to persuade the Lord to have mercy on her. But He said, "I was sent only to the Jews, who are lost sheep because of the wickedness of

---

[3] Mt. 10:5

[4] Mk. 7:24

those shepherds to whom they had been entrusted.'' In this manner He discloses more fully the faith of the woman.

25-27. Then came she and fell prostrate before Him, saying, Lord, help me. But He answered and said, It is not meet to take the children's bread, and to cast it to dogs. And she said, Yea, Lord: yet even the dogs eat of the crumbs which fall from their masters' table. When the woman saw that her advocates, the apostles, had not succeeded, again she approaches fervently and calls upon the Lord. Christ speaks of her as a dog, because the Gentiles led an unclean life and were involved with the blood of meat sacrificed to idols, while the Jews He speaks of as children. But she answers wisely and indeed profoundly, ''Even though I am a dog and not worthy to receive a loaf of bread, that is, a mighty act and a great sign, nevertheless grant this to me which is a small thing by comparison with Thy power, though to me it is great. For crumbs are not large in the eyes of those who eat loaves, but to dogs they are large, and they feed on them.''

28. Then Jesus answered and said unto her, O woman, great is thy faith: be it unto thee even as thou wilt. And her daughter was made whole from that very hour. Now Jesus shows the reason why He put off healing her at the beginning. So that the faith and understanding of the woman might be made manifest, Christ did not immediately give His assent at the beginning and even drove her away. But now when her faith has been revealed she hears the words of praise, ''Great is thy faith.'' By saying, ''Be it unto thee even as thou wilt,'' Christ showed that if she had not had faith she would not have obtained her request. So, too, if we desire to obtain something, nothing prevents us from obtaining what we desire. Notice that even if saints should ask on our behalf, as the apostles did for the woman, still, we accomplish even more when we ask for ourselves. The Canaanite woman is also a symbol of the Church gathered from among the Gentiles. For Gentiles who first were even driven away, later were advanced to the rank of sons and were deemed worthy of the Bread, I mean, the Body of the Lord; while the Jews became dogs, thinking that they were being fed by the crumbs, that is, the minute and insignificant details of the letter of the law. ''Tyre'' means ''besieged'', ''Sidon'' ''they who hunt'', and ''Canaan'' ''made ready by humility''. Therefore the Gentiles, who were besieged by evil in that the demons were among them hunting for souls, were also made ready by humility. For the righteous were made ready for the heights of the kingdom of God.

29-31. And Jesus departed from thence, and came nigh unto the sea of Galilee; and went up on to a mountain, and sat down there. And great multitudes came unto Him, having with them those that were lame, blind, dumb, maimed, and many others, and they cast them down at Jesus' feet, and He healed them: so that the multitude marveled, when they saw the dumb to speak, the maimed whole, the lame to walk, and the blind to see: and they glorified the God of Israel. He does not visit Judea frequently, as He does Galilee, because the unbelief of the Judeans was so great. For the Galileans had more faith than they. Behold their faith, how they even ascend a mountain although they are lame and blind. And they do not move sluggishly but throw themselves at the feet of Jesus as if believing that He is more than a man and then, indeed, they obtain healing. So you also, O reader, must ascend the mountain of the commandments where the Lord is seated. And though you are blind and unable to see the good for yourself; and though lame, seeing the good but unable to go towards it; and though deaf and dumb, unable to hear another exhorting you and unable to exhort another; and though maimed, that is, unable to stretch out your hand to give alms; and though diseased in any other way, if you fall at Jesus' feet and touch the foot prints of His life, you will be healed.

32. Then Jesus called His disciples unto Him, and said, I have compassion on the multitude, because they continue with Me now three days, and have nothing to eat: and I will not send them away fasting, lest they faint on the way. The multitude did not dare to ask for bread, as they had come for healing. But He Who loves mankind takes thought for them. So that no one could say, "They have other provisions," He says, "Even if they had, they would have been used up, for it has already been three days." He shows that they came from a distance when He says, "lest they faint on the way." He says these things to the disciples, wishing to encourage them to say to Him, "You are able to feed them as you did the five thousand." But the disciples still lack understanding.

33. And His disciples say unto Him, From where should we have so much bread in the wilderness, as to fill so great a multitude? They should have understood that on the previous occasion even a greater number had been fed in the desert. But they are senseless here, so that later when you see them filled with such great wisdom, you may marvel at the grace of Christ.

34-38. And Jesus saith unto them, How many loaves have ye? And they said, Seven, and a few little fishes. And He commanded the multitude to sit down on the ground. And He took the seven loaves and the fishes, and gave thanks, and brake them, and gave to His disciples, and the disciples gave to the multitude. And they did all eat, and were filled: and they took up of the broken pieces that were left seven baskets full. And they that did eat were four thousand men, beside women and children. He teaches frugality by having them sit on the ground; and He teaches us to give thanks before eating by Himself giving thanks. Do you ask why it is that when there were five loaves and five thousand being fed, twelve baskets [*kophinoi*] remained, but here where there are more loaves and fewer people only seven baskets [*spyrides*] were left over? It could be said either that *spyrides* were a larger type of basket than *kophinoi*, or that He did not wish the numerical equality of this miracle with the previous one to cause it to be forgotten. For if on this occasion, too, twelve baskets [*kophinoi*] had been left over, because of the numerical equality they would have forgotten that He performed the miracle with the loaves a second time. But you, O reader, must also know this, that the four thousand, that is, they who are perfect in the four virtues,[5] are fed with seven loaves, that is, with more spiritual and perfected words, for the number seven is a symbol of the seven spiritual gifts. They fall down to the earth putting beneath them all earthly things and treading them down, just as the five thousand fell down onto the grass, that is, putting beneath them the flesh and its glory. "For all flesh is grass and all the glory of man as the flower of grass."[6] Here there are seven baskets of remnants, because it was the spiritual and more perfect things that they were unable to eat. For the amount left over

---

[5] Bl. Theophylact explains the "four universal virtues" in his preface above on p. 7.

[6] Is. 40:6; cf. Ps. 102:15.

was what seven baskets could contain, that is, what only the Holy Spirit knew. "For the Spirit searches all things, even the depths of God."[7]

39. And He sent the multitude away, and got into a boat, and came to the region of Magdala. Jesus went away because the miracle of the loaves drew more people to follow Him than any other that He performed; so much so that they were even about to make Him king, as John says.[8] Therefore Jesus went away to avoid the suspicion of Herod the tyrant.

---

[7] I Cor. 2:10

[8] Jn. 6:15

CHAPTER SIXTEEN

Concerning the leaven of the Pharisees.
Concerning the questioning in Caesarea.
Concerning the rebuking of Peter
who objected that Christ would suffer.

1. The Pharisees also with the Sadducees came, and tempting Him, asked that He show them a sign from heaven. Although the Pharisees and Sadducees were at odds over their teachings, they conspired together against Christ. They ask for a sign from heaven, such as making the sun or the moon stand still, as they believed that signs on earth were by demonic power and by Beelzebub. But they were mindless not to remember that even Moses in Egypt did many signs on the earth and that the fire from heaven which descended on Job's flocks was from the devil. So, then, not all things from heaven are of God and neither are all things on the earth of the demons.

2-4. He answered and said unto them, When it is evening, ye say, It will be fair weather: for the sky is red. And in the morning, It will be foul weather today: for the sky is red and threatening. O ye hypocrites, ye can discern the face of the sky; but can ye not discern the signs of the times? He reproves them for their request, the purpose of which was only to test, and He calls them hypocrites, saying, "As it is with the phenomena of the sky where the sign of a storm differs from the sign of calm weather, and one who sees the sign of a storm would not expect calm weather, nor would one seeing the sign of calm weather expect a storm, so too must you think about Me. For this time of My appearing differs from that which is to come. Now there is need for signs on earth, but signs in heaven are reserved for that time when the sun will be extinguished, the moon will be hidden, and the heavens will be changed." **A wicked and adulterous generation seeketh after a sign: and there shall no sign be given unto it, but the sign of the prophet Jonah. And He left them and departed.** He calls them "a wicked generation" for tempting Him, and "adulterous" for deserting God and going over to the devil's side. Although they asked for a sign from heaven, He gives only the sign of Jonah, which is, that for three days He will be in the belly of the great whale of death, and then He will rise. Yet you might say that this sign too is from heaven, for at His death the sun was darkened and all creation was changed. Mark the words "there shall no sign be given unto it, but the sign of the prophet Jonah." It was for them that the signs were given, that is, the signs took place for their sakes, yet they did not believe. This is why He left them as incurable and departed.

5-6. And when His disciples were come to the other side, they had forgotten to take bread. Then Jesus said unto them, Take heed and beware of the leaven of the Pharisees and of the Sadducees. Just as leaven is both sour and old, so too the sour teaching of the Pharisees and Sadducees, with its moldering traditions of the elders, ate away at souls. And just as leaven is a mixture of water and flour, so the teaching of the Pharisees is a mixture of their speech and their corrupted life. He did not say openly to them, "Beware of the teaching of the Pharisees," so that He might remind them of the signs done with the loaves.

7-12. And they reasoned among themselves, saying, It is because we have taken no bread. But Jesus, aware of this, said unto them, O ye of little faith, why reason ye among yourselves, because ye have brought no bread? Do ye not yet understand, neither remember the five loaves of the five thousand, and how many baskets (*kophinoi*) ye took up? Neither the seven loaves of the four thousand, and how many baskets (*spyridas*) ye took up? How is it that ye do not understand that I spake it not to you concerning bread, that ye should beware of the leaven of the Pharisees and of the Sadducees? Then understood they how that He bade them not beware of the leaven of bread, but of the doctrine of the Pharisees and of the Sadducees. They thought that He was telling them to guard themselves against the stain of Jewish food, which is why they discussed among themselves that they had not brought any bread. He upbraids them for being mindless and of little faith. They were mindless by not remembering how many He had fed with how many loaves; they showed little faith by not believing that Christ Himself could provide bread even if they had not bought any bread from the Jews. As He rebuked them rather sharply—for meekness is not good on every occasion—they immediately understood that by "leaven" He meant "teaching"; such is the effect of a judicious rebuke on any occasion.

13. When Jesus came to the region of Caesarea Philippi, He asked His disciples, saying, Whom do men say that I the Son of Man am? The evangelist mentions the founder of the city, Philip, because there is another Caesarea, of Strato,[1] and it was not in the latter, but in the former, that Christ asked them the question. He leads the disciples far away from the Jews so that they could speak boldly without fear of anyone. First He asks for the opinion of the multitude so that the disciples would be directed upwards to a greater understanding and not fall into the same lowliness of understanding as that of the people. He does not ask them, "Who do the Pharisees say that I am?" but "Who do men say?" referring to the guileless multitude.

14. And they said, Some say that Thou art John the Baptist: some, Elijah; and others, Jeremiah, or one of the prophets. Among those who called Him John was Herod, who thought that John after rising from the dead had also received the gift of working miracles. Those who thought He was Elijah did so because of the way in which Christ rebuked and because Elijah was expected to return. Those who thought He was Jeremiah, did so because of His natural wisdom acquired without any instruction. For while Jeremiah was yet a child, he was commanded to prophesy.

15-16. He saith unto them, But whom say ye that I am? And Simon Peter answered and said, Thou art the Christ, the Son of the living God. Once again Peter leaps forward with fervor and confesses that He is truly the Son of God. He did not say, "Thou art the anointed one, a son of God", without the article "the", but with the article, "the Son", that is, He Who is the One and the Only, not a son by grace, but He Who is begotten of the same essence as the Father. For there were also many other christs, anointed ones, such as all the priests and kings; but the Christ, with the article, there is but One.

---

[1] Caesarea Philippi is north of the Sea of Galilee at the foot of Mt. Hermon; only in this episode of Christ's life is it mentioned in the New Testament (see Mk. 8:27). The other Caesarea is on the coast of the Mediterranean and is mentioned several times in the Acts of the Apostles.

17. And Jesus answered and said unto him, Blessed art thou, Simon Bar Jona: for flesh and blood hath not revealed it unto thee, but My Father Who is in heaven. He calls Peter blessed for having received knowledge by divine grace. And by commending Peter, He thereby shows the opinions of other men to be false. For He calls him "Bar Jona", that is, "son of Jona", as if saying, "Just as you are the son of Jona, so am I the Son of My Father in heaven, and of one essence with Him." He calls this knowledge "revelation", speaking of hidden and unknown things that were disclosed by the Father.

18. And I say also unto thee, That thou art Peter, and upon this rock I will build My Church; and the gates of hades shall not prevail against it. The Lord gives Peter a great reward, that the Church will be built on him. Since Peter confessed Him as Son of God, the Lord says, "This confession which you have made shall be the foundation of those who believe, so that every man who intends to build the house of faith shall lay down this confession as the foundation." For even if we should construct a myriad of virtues, but we do not have as a foundation the orthodox confession, our construction is rotten. By saying "My Church" He shows that He is the Master of all, for the whole universe is the servant of God. The gates of hades are those persecutors who from time to time would send the Christians to hades. But the heretics, too, are gates leading to hades. The Church, then, has prevailed over many persecutors and many heretics. The Church is also each one of us who has become a house of God. For if we have been established on the confession of Christ, the gates of hades, which are our sins, will not prevail against us. It was from these gates that David, too, had been lifted up when he said, "O Thou that dost raise me up from the gates of death."[2] From what gates, O David? From those twin gates of murder and adultery.

19. And I will give unto thee the keys of the kingdom of the heavens: and whatsoever thou shalt bind on earth shall be bound in the heavens; and whatsoever thou shalt loose on earth shall be loosed in the heavens. He spoke as God, with authority, "I will give unto

---

[2] Ps. 9:13

thee.'' For as the Father gave you the revelation, so I give you the keys. By ''keys'' understand that which binds or looses transgressions, namely, penance or absolution; for those who, like Peter, have been deemed worthy of the grace of the episcopate, have the authority to absolve or to bind. Even though the words ''I will give unto thee'' were spoken to Peter alone, yet they were given to all the apostles. Why? Because He said, ''Whose soever sins ye remit, they are remitted.''[3] Also, the words ''I will give'' indicate a future time, namely, after the Resurrection.[4] ''The heavens'' also mean the virtues, and the keys to the heavens are labors. For by laboring we enter into each of the virtues as if by means of keys that are used to open. If I do not labor but only know the good, I possess only the key of knowledge but remain outside. That man is bound in the heavens, that is, in the virtues, who does not walk in them, but he who is diligent in acquiring virtues is loosed in them. Therefore let us not have sins, so that we may not be bound by the chains of our own sins.

20. Then charged He His disciples that they should tell no man that He was the Christ. Before the Cross, Christ wanted to obscure His own glory. For if, before the Passion, men heard that He was God and then saw Him suffering, how could they not be scandalized? This is why He hid Himself from the multitude, so that after the Resurrection He might be known without causing any scandal, the Holy Spirit removing all doubt by means of the miracles performed.

21. From that time forth began Jesus to show unto His disciples how that He must go unto Jerusalem and suffer many things of the elders and chief priests and scribes, and be killed, and be raised again the third day. To them He foretells the Passion, lest it come upon them unexpectedly and they be scandalized, thinking that He suffered unwillingly and without foreknowing it. When they had heard, in Peter's

---

[3] Jn. 20:23. The verb in Greek for ''ye remit'', *aphēte*, is second person plural, obviously not referring to one person only. Had the authority been granted to Peter alone, the text in John's Gospel would read, ''Whose soever sins thou remittest'', but since ''ye'' is plural, we understand that the gift was given to all the apostles.

[4] The actual granting of the authority to remit sins takes place on the occasion described in Jn. 20:23, when, after the Resurrection, the Lord breathes on all the assembled disciples.

confession, that He was the Son of God, then He also revealed the Passion to them. But to the sorrow He adds the joy, that He would rise on the third day.

22. Then Peter took Him and began to rebuke Him, saying, Be it far from Thee, Lord, this shall not be unto Thee. Peter rightly confessed what had been revealed; in what had not been revealed, he erred: that we may learn that Peter did not utter that great truth without God's help. Not wanting Christ to suffer, and being ignorant of the mystery of the Resurrection, Peter said, "Be it far from Thee, Lord, this shall not be unto Thee."

23. But He turned and said unto Peter, Get thee behind Me, Satan: thou art an offense unto Me: for thou savourest not the things that be of God, but those that be of man. When Peter spoke rightly, Christ called him blessed, but when he was irrationally dismayed, and did not want Him to suffer, then Christ rebuked him and said, "Get thee behind Me, Satan." "Satan" means "the adversary". "Get thee behind Me," that is, do not oppose Me, but follow My will. He calls Peter this because Satan, too, did not wish Christ to suffer. What He is saying, then, is this: with human reasoning you think that suffering does not befit Me, but you fail to understand that by this means God is accomplishing salvation and that this, on the contrary, greatly befits Me.

24. Then said Jesus unto His disciples, If any man desireth to come after Me, let him deny himself and take up his cross and follow Me. "Then"—when? When He had rebuked Peter. Wishing to show that Peter erred in hindering Him from suffering, He said, "You are hindering Me, but I say to you that not only is My not suffering harmful to you [since without it you cannot be saved], but neither can you be saved unless you yourself also die, nor can anyone else, whether man or woman, rich or poor. He says "desireth" to show that virtue hinges on free will and not coercion. He who follows behind Jesus is not he who only confesses Him to be the Son of God, but rather it is he who also undergoes all tribulations and endures them. Christ's words, "Let him deny himself," indicate utter denial.[5] That is to say, let him not be kindly disposed towards his own body, let him look down on it, just as we have the expression "So and so denied so and so,"[6] meaning, he has neither friend nor acquaintance. Therefore no one should have any friendship towards the body, so that he can take up his cross, that is, choose death and even eagerly desire the most ignominious death, for this is what the cross meant to the ancients. But He also said, "Let him follow Me, for many robbers and thieves are crucified but they are not My disciples." So "let him follow", that is, let him also show forth every other virtue. The one who yesterday was dissolute denies himself and today he is temperate. Such was Paul who had denied himself when he said, "I live yet it is no longer I, but Christ that liveth in me."[7] He that has mortified and crucified himself to the world is he that takes up his cross.

25. For whosoever would save his life shall lose it, and whosoever would lose his life for My sake shall find it. He exhorts us to confess Christ even at the cost of a martyr's death. For he who denies Christ, finds his life in the present, that is, he saves his own life, but he also loses it later. But he who confesses Christ as a martyr, loses his life, but for Christ's sake, and so he "shall find it" incorrupt and eternal.

26-27. For what is a man profited, if he shall gain the whole world, and lose his own soul? Or what shall a man give in exchange for his soul? For the Son of Man shall come in the glory of His Father with His angels; and then He shall reward every man according to His works. Let us suppose, He says, that you have gained the whole world: what profit is it if your body prospers while your soul suffers ill? That would be as if the lady of the house dressed in tattered rags, while her maidservants were gorgeously arrayed. For in the age to come a man can give nothing in exchange for his soul. Here one can give tears, sighs, and

---

[5] Bl. Theophylact comments upon the form of the word used by St. Matthew, *ap-arnēsasthō*, "let him utterly deny himself." The prefix *ap-*, which is the preposition *apo*, serves to intensify the meaning of the verb *arnoumai*, to deny oneself.

[6] This is an expression of the Greek language of Bl. Theophylact's own time (12th century), which does not have an idiomatic English equivalent.

[7] Gal. 2:20

alms, but there, nothing. For it is a Judge who takes no bribes that will receive us, and He judges each one according to his deeds. But He is also awesome and dreadful, and comes in His glory with His angels, not in lowly form.

28. Verily I say unto you, there be some standing here, who shall not taste of death, till they see the Son of Man coming in His kingdom. He had said that the Son of Man would come in His glory. So that they would not disbelieve Him, He says "there be some here" who would see, as far as they were able, the glory of the second coming in the Transfiguration. At the same time He shows what great glory will belong to those who suffer for His sake. For as His flesh shone like lightning on that occasion, so in due proportion will the saints shine forth then at His second coming. Here He is hinting at Peter, James and John, whom He took with Him on the mountain and showed them His kingdom, that is, the future condition in which He would come and both He and the righteous would be radiant. He is saying, therefore, "Some of you here shall not die until you have seen Me transfigured." See, then, that it is those who stand firm in goodness who see Jesus radiantly transfigured, and they are ever advancing in faith and in the commandments.

CHAPTER SEVENTEEN

Concerning Christ's Transfiguration.
Concerning the lunatic.
Concerning the two-drachma piece.

1. And after six days Jesus taketh Peter, James, and John his brother. This does not contradict what Luke says, "And it came to pass about eight days after these sayings."[1] For Luke counts both the first day and the last day on which they ascended the mountain. But Matthew counts only the days in between. Christ took Peter because of Peter's strong love for Him; He took John, because Christ loved him; and He took James, because James, too, was zealous. That James had zeal is evident from his promise to drink the cup that Christ would drink[2] and from the fact that Herod slew him with the sword to please the Jews.

1-2. And bringeth them up onto a high mountain apart, and was transfigured before them: and His face did shine as the sun, and His raiment was white as the light. He brings them up onto a high mountain, showing that unless a man is raised up high, he does not become worthy of such divine visions. A mountain set "apart", because Christ would often perform the most wondrous of His miracles in secret, lest the multitude see Him as God and think that He was human in appearance only. When you hear "He was transfigured," do not think that He had cast off His body at that moment, for His body remained in its own form, as you hear mention of His face and His clothing. But it appeared more resplendent, the divine exhibiting in small part its effulgence as much as they were able to see. This is why He had also previously spoken of the Transfiguration as "the kingdom" of God,[3] for it exhibited the indescribable majesty of His power, it showed that He is the true Son of the Father, and it had the aspect of the second coming on account of the ineffable radiance of Jesus' face.

---

[1] Lk 9:28

[2] Mt. 20:22

[3] Mt 16:28

3. And, behold, there appeared unto them Moses and Elijah talking with Him. What were they talking about? "The ending," says Luke, "which He should accomplish in Jerusalem,"[4] namely, the Cross. Why did Moses and Elijah appear? To show that He is Lord of the law and of the prophets, and of the living and of the dead. For Elijah was a prophet and still lived, while Moses was a lawgiver and had died. They also appeared so that it might be seen that He was opposed neither to the law nor to God, for Moses would not have spoken with one opposed to his own laws, nor would Elijah the zealot have endured one who was opposed to God. And they appeared for yet another reason, to prove false the opinion of those who said that He was Elijah or one of the prophets. How did the disciples know that these two were Moses and Elijah? Not of course from icons, for at that time it was considered impious to draw pictures of men. It would seem, then, that they recognized them by the words which they were speaking. For Moses perhaps was saying, "Thou art He whose Passion I prefigured when I slaughtered the lamb and performed the Pascha;"[5] and Elijah, "Thou art He Whose Resurrection I prefigured when I raised the widow's son;" and such words as these. By showing Moses and Elijah to the disciples, Christ teaches the disciples to imitate them, to be both meek and leaders of men, as was Moses, to be zealous and, when necessary, unyielding, as was Elijah, and to be fearless, as they both were, for the truth.

4. Then answered Peter, and said unto Jesus, Lord, it is good for us to be here: if Thou wilt, let us make here three tabernacles; one for Thee, and one for Moses, and one for Elijah. Peter, out of great love, did not want Christ to suffer, and so he said, "It is good to stay here and for Thee not to go down and be slain. And if anyone should come here we have both Moses and Elijah to help us. For Moses contended with the Egyptians, and Elijah called down fire out of heaven: such opponents do we have for any enemies who might come here." He spoke these things out of great fear, not knowing, as Luke says, what he was saying.[6] For either the extraordinary nature of the event had dumb-

---

[4] Lk. 9:31

[5] i.e., the Passover. See note on Mt. 26:1, p. 222, 223.

[6] Lk. 9:33

founded him, or he truly did not know what he was saying, when he spoke of wanting Jesus to remain on the mountain and not come down and suffer for our sake. But fearing to appear presumptuous, Peter said, "If Thou wilt."

5. While he yet spake, behold, a bright cloud overshadowed them: and behold a voice out of the cloud, which said, This is My beloved Son, in Whom I am well pleased; hear ye Him. You, Peter, desire tabernacles made with hands, but the Father has formed around them another tabernacle not made with hands, the cloud, showing that just as He Himself appeared as God in a cloud to the men of old, so also does His Son now appear in a cloud. Here the cloud is bright, not dark as in the time of old, for He desires not to bring fear but to teach. Out of the cloud came the voice, to show that it was of God. "In Whom I am well pleased," that is, in Whom I rest and take pleasure. And He teaches: "Hear ye Him and if He willeth to be crucified, oppose Him not."

6-8. And when the disciples heard it, they fell on their faces, and were sore afraid. And Jesus came and touched them, and said, Arise, and be not afraid. And when they had lifted up their eyes, they saw no man, save Jesus only. Not able to endure the brightness of the cloud, nor the voice, the disciples fell to the ground. Their eyes were also heavy with sleep, as Luke says,[7] ("sleep" indicating the daze caused by the vision). Lest the fear grip them for a long time and obliterate the memory of what they had seen, the Lord rouses them and reassures them. He is seen to be alone, so that you will not imagine that the voice was for Moses or Elijah; indeed, the voice was for Christ, as He is the Son.

9. And as they came down from the mountain, Jesus charged them, saying, Tell the vision to no man, until the Son of Man be risen again from the dead. Out of humility He orders them to tell no one, and also, so that those who might hear such things would not later be scandalized when they saw Him crucified. For they would think that He was a deceiver who had conjured up God-like visions. But you, O reader, learn that after six days, that is, after the six days in which the world was

---

[7] See Lk. 9:32.

created, comes the vision of God. For if you do not transcend the world and are not raised up on the mountain top, you will not see glorious things: neither Jesus' face, which is His divinity, nor His clothing, which is His flesh. May you then also see Moses and Elijah conversing with Jesus. For the law, the prophets, and Jesus speak harmoniously as one. But also, when you find someone brilliantly interpreting the meaning of Scripture, know that this man is beholding the brilliant face of Jesus; and if that man is rendering the words of Scripture clear and bright, know that he is beholding the white clothing of Jesus. For the words are the clothing of the thoughts. But do not say, as did Peter, "It is good for us to be here." For one must always be advancing and not standing still on the same level of virtue and vision, but moving on to another place.

10. And His disciples asked Him, saying, Why then say the scribes that Elijah must first come? The scribes were deceiving the people, saying that Jesus was not the Christ, for if He were, Elijah would first have come. But they did not know that there are two comings of Christ, the Forerunner of the first being John, and of the second, Elijah. Christ then explains this to the disciples. Listen:

11-13. And Jesus answered and said unto them, Elijah truly shall first come, and restore all things. But I say unto you, That Elijah is come already, and they knew him not, but have done unto him whatsoever they desired. Likewise shall also the Son of Man suffer at their hands. Then the disciples understood that He spake unto them of John the Baptist. By saying, "Elijah truly shall come," Christ shows that he has not yet come, but that he will appear as the forerunner of the second coming; and when he appears, he will restore all teachable Jews to faith in Christ, as if restoring them to their paternal inheritance which they had lost. But when Christ says, "Elijah is come already," He is speaking of John the Forerunner; for the Jews "did unto him whatsoever they desired" when they slew him; they slew him when they permitted Herod to slay John, though they could have prevented it. Then the disciples became keener in perception and understood that He was calling John Elijah, as John was the Forerunner of the first coming, just as Elijah would be the forerunner of the second coming.

14-15. And when they were come to the multitude, there came to

Him a certain man, kneeling down to Him, and saying, Lord, have mercy on my son: for he is lunatic, and sore vexed: for ofttimes he falleth into the fire, and oft into the water. That this man is exceedingly faithless is clear from the words which Christ spoke in reply to him, "O faithless generation," and from the fact that the man himself blamed the disciples. The moon was not the cause, but rather, the demon would take note when the moon was full, and then would set upon his victim, so that men would blaspheme the created works of God as maleficent. You, then, O reader, understand that it is a foolish man that changes as the moon, as it is written,[8] at times waxing great in virtue, at other times waning and vanishing altogether. Then the foolish man becomes deranged and falls down into the fire of anger and lust, and into water, that is, the waves of the many cares of life, in which Leviathan the devil dwells, he who reigns over the waters. For are not the cares of the rich like waves that follow each other in quick succession?

16-18. And I brought him to Thy disciples, and they could not cure him. Then Jesus answered and said, O faithless and perverse generation, how long shall I be with you? How long shall I endure you? Bring him hither to Me. And Jesus rebuked him; and the demon departed out of him; and the child was cured from that very hour. Do you see how the man has shifted the blame for his own lack of faith upon the disciples, saying that they were too weak to heal? The Lord, therefore, is shaming him for accusing the disciples, saying, "O faithless generation," that is, "It is not so much the fault of the weakness of the disciples as it is of your lack of faith, which, being great, has prevailed over the equal measure of their strength." He rebukes not only this man, but everyone who lacks faith, even the bystanders. By saying, "How long shall I be with you?" Christ shows that He longs for the Passion upon the Cross and His departure from them. For He is saying, "How long shall I live among scoffers and unbelievers?" "And Jesus rebuked him"—whom? He who was lunatic. From this it appears that he, too, lacked faith and his lack of faith had given occasion for the demon to enter him.

---

[8] Sirach 27:11

19-21. Then came the disciples to Jesus apart, and said, Why could not we cast him out? And Jesus said unto them, Because of your unbelief: for verily I say unto you, If ye have faith as a grain of mustard seed, ye shall say unto this mountain, Remove hence to yonder place; and it shall remove; and nothing shall be impossible unto you. But this kind goeth not out but by prayer and fasting. The apostles were afraid that they had lost the grace against demons that had been given to them; this is why they asked Jesus in private and with great anxiety. But the Lord reproves them for being imperfect in faith, saying, "Because of your unbelief." For if you had fervent, ardent faith, you would accomplish great things even though they appeared to be small. The location of the mountains which the apostles moved is nowhere recorded, yet it is likely that they did move them, but the event was not written down; for not everything was written down. Or, by another interpretation, they did not move a mountain because the occasion did not present itself, but they did even greater things than that. Note how the Lord said, "Ye shall say unto this mountain, Remove hence," in other words, the mountain shall move when you say the word. But the apostles did not say the word as there was neither occasion nor necessity, and so they did not move mountains. But if indeed they had spoken, they would have moved. "This kind" of demon is cast out by prayer and fasting. For they themselves who are demonized must fast, as well as those who would heal them; then comes the prayer, preceded by fasting, not drunkenness. Understand, then, that even perfect faith is as the grain of mustard seed, considered worthless on account of the foolishness of the preaching. Yet if it should find good soil, it grows into a tree in which the winged creatures of heaven, that is, soaring thoughts, may alight. Whoever, then, has perfect faith can say to this mountain, that is, to the demon, "Remove hence." For Christ was also referring to the demon that had gone out.

22-23. And while they abode in Galilee, Jesus said unto them, The Son of Man shall be betrayed into the hands of men: and they shall kill Him, and the third day He shall be raised again. And they were exceeding sorry. He continually foretells the Passion, so that no one would think that He suffered unwillingly, and also, to train them so that they would not be shaken by the unexpected when it occurred. To the sorrow He weds the joy, that He will rise.

24. And when they were come to Capernaum, they that received the two-drachma tax came to Peter and said, Doth not your master pay the tax? He saith, Yes. God wished to consecrate to Himself the tribe of Levi in the place of the first-born sons of the Hebrews. The tribe of Levi was found to number only 22,000; yet the first-born sons of all twelve tribes numbered 22,273.[9] In place of those first-born sons that exceeded the number of the tribe of Levi, God decreed that for each such first-born son two drachmas be given to the priests. From then on it became the custom simply for every first-born son to pay the two-drachma tax, which is the equivalent of five shekels, or two hundred obols. As the Lord, too, was a first-born son, He also paid the tax. Perhaps in awe of Christ because of His wonderworking, they did not ask Christ, but Peter; but, more likely, they asked craftily, as if they were saying, "Surely your teacher, who is opposed to the law, has not agreed to pay the two-drachma tax?"

25-26. And when he was come into the house, Jesus spake first to him, saying, What thinkest thou, Simon? Of whom do the kings of the earth take custom or tribute? Of their own sons, or of strangers? Peter saith unto him, Of strangers. Jesus saith unto him, Then indeed are the sons free. Being God, Christ knew what they had said to Peter although He had not heard the question. So He spoke first to Peter and said, "If earthly kings do not collect tax from their own sons, but from strangers, how would the heavenly King collect the two-drachma tax from Me, His own Son?" For this was paid, as I said above, to the priests and to the temple. "If earthly sons are free," that is, they pay nothing, "how much more so am I?"

27. Notwithstanding, lest we should offend them, go thou to the sea, and cast a hook, and take up the fish that first cometh up; and when thou hast opened his mouth, thou shalt find a piece of money: that take, and give unto them for Me and thee. Pay the tax, Christ says, lest they think that we despise and disdain the law, and we give offence. I am not paying because I owe the tax, but I make allowance for their weakness. We learn from this that we should not cause offense to

---

[9] Num. 3:43-50

anyone over things that do not harm us, but when we would be harmed by some action, then neither should we concerned about those who unreasonably take offense. To show, therefore, that He is God and Ruler of the sea, He sent Peter to take the coin from the fish. At the same time we learn a mystery: the fish is our nature immersed in the depths of unbelief, but the apostolic word drew us up and found in our mouth the coin, the words of the Lord and the confession of Christ. For he who confesses Christ has in his mouth the coin which equals two of the two-drachma pieces. For Christ also has two natures, being both God and man. Thus the coin is Christ, which was given for two, the Jews and the Gentiles, the righteous and the sinners. And if you should see a miser who has nothing in his mouth except gold and silver, know that this man is like a fish swimming in the sea of life, and if a teacher like Peter can be found, he will hook this fish and extract from his mouth the gold and silver.

CHAPTER EIGHTEEN

Concerning those who said, Who is the greatest? On not causing temptation. Concerning the parable of the hundred sheep. On admonishing one's neighbor. Concerning the power to bind and to loose. Concerning the man who owed ten thousand talents.

1. In that same hour came the disciples unto Jesus, saying, Who is the greatest in the kingdom of heaven? When they saw that Peter had been honored by Christ (for he had been honored by being instructed to give the coin for Christ and for himself), they fell prey to a human weakness and were stung by jealousy. So they approached and asked the Lord craftily, "Who is the greatest?"

2-4. And Jesus called a little child unto Him, and set him in the midst of them, and said, Verily I say unto you, Except ye be turned back, and become as little children, ye shall not enter into the kingdom of heaven. Whosoever therefore shall humble himself as this little child, the same is greatest in the kingdom of heaven. When the Lord sees the disciples under the sway of the passion of vainglory, He restrains them, showing them the way of humility by means of an unassuming child. For we must be as children in the humility of our mind, but not be infantile in our thoughts; and we must be as children in guilelessness, but not in foolishness. By saying, "Except ye be turned back," He showed that they had gone from humility to vainglory. You must turn back again to that place, which is humility, from which you departed.

5-6. And whoso shall receive one such little child in My name receiveth Me. But whoso shall offend one of these little ones which believe in Me, it were better for him that a millstone were hanged about his neck, and that he were drowned in the depth of the sea. Not only, He says, must you be humble, but if for My sake you honor others who are humble, you shall receive your reward. For when you receive the children, that is, the humble, you are receiving Me. Then He says by contrast, "But whoso shall offend one of these little ones," that is, give insult to those who make themselves small and who humble themselves although they are great, "it would be better for him that a millstone were hanged about his neck." He brings to the fore the sensory punishment, wishing to show that those who insult and give offense to the humble in Christ will endure great punishment. And you, O reader, understand that even if a man gives offense to one who is truly small, that is, weak, and does not instead use every means to bear him up, he will be punished. For it is not a great man who easily takes offense, but a small man.

7. Woe unto the world because of temptations! For it must needs be that temptations come; but woe to that man by whom the temptation cometh! As One Who loves mankind He laments for the world which is going to be harmed by temptations.[1] But one might ask, "Why lament when there is need to assist and extend a helping hand?" To which we would reply that to lament for someone is of itself assistance. For often we benefit those whom our admonition has not benefitted, when we weep for them and thus bring them to an awareness of themselves. And if "it must needs be that temptations come," how can we avoid them? They must needs come but we need not perish, rather we must resist the temptations. Understand "temptations" to mean those who are an obstacle and a stumbling-block to our doing good. The "world" means those people who are low and crawl along the ground, who are easily hindered by every obstacle.

8-9. Wherefore if thy hand or thy foot cause thee temptation, cut it off, and cast it from thee: it is better for thee to enter into life halt or maimed, rather than having two hands or two feet to be cast into everlasting fire. And if thine eye cause thee temptation, pluck it out, and cast it from thee: it is better for thee to enter into life with one eye, rather than having two eyes to be cast into the gehenna of fire. Hand, foot, and eye understand to mean friends whom we rank as dear as our own members. And even though it may be these, our close friends, who harm us, we must disregard them as gangrenous members and cut them off, lest they harm others as well as themselves. From this it is clear

---

[1] On the Greek word *skandalon* here rendered as "temptation" see the footnote on Mt. 5:29 above, on p. 52.

that even if it is necessary that temptations come, that is, those who would harm us, it is not necessary that we be harmed. But if we shall do as the Lord has said, and cut off from ourselves those that would harm us even though they are our friends, we shall not be harmed.

10-11. Take heed that ye despise not one of these little ones; for I say unto you, that in heaven their angels do always behold the face of My Father Who is in heaven. For the Son of Man is come to save that which was lost. He commands them not to disdain those thought to be of little importance, that is, those poor in spirit who are great in God's eyes. They are so greatly loved by God, He says, that they have angels watching over them so that they may not be harmed by the demons. Every believer, and indeed, every one of us human beings, has a guardian angel. The angels of those who are little and humble in Christ are so intimate with God that they always stand before Him and behold His face. From this it is apparent that although we all have angels, the angels of us sinners are ashamed on account of our lack of boldness,[2] and neither do they have boldness to behold the face of God and perhaps even to pray for us. But the angels of those who are humble minded behold the face of God because of the boldness with which they can approach Him. And, the Lord goes on to say, "Why should I say merely that such ones as these have angels? I Myself have come for this very reason, to save that which was lost, and to make those who are thought by many to be of no account My intimate friends."

12-14. How think ye? If a man have a hundred sheep, and one of them be gone astray, doth he not leave the ninety and nine on the mountains, and goeth to seek that which is gone astray? And if so be that he find it, verily I say unto you, he rejoiceth more of that sheep, than of the ninety and nine which went not astray. Even so it is not the will of your Father Who is in the heavens, that one of these little ones should perish. What man had a hundred sheep? Christ. For all of the reason-endowed creation, both angels and men, are the hundred sheep, of which Christ is the shepherd, not another sheep. For He is not a

---

[2] i.e. our lack of boldness to freely and sincerely approach God, due to the fact that we have distanced ourselves from God by our unrepentant sinfulness.

creature but the Son of God. So He left the ninety and nine in the heavens, and taking on the form of a servant He came to seek the one sheep, which is the fallen human nature. And He rejoices more over it than over the steadfastness of the angels. This shows in a few words how diligently God pursues the conversion of sinners, and rejoices more over them than over those who are constant in virtue.

15-17. Moreover if thy brother shall trespass against thee, go and admonish him between thee and him alone: if he shall hear thee, thou hast gained thy brother. But if he will not hear thee, then take with thee one or two more, that in the mouth of two or three witnesses every word may be established. And if he shall neglect to hear them, tell it unto the Church: but if he neglect to hear the Church, let him be unto thee as a Gentile and a publican. Having spoken strong words against those who are a cause of temptation, now He corrects those who have been offended. Lest you, O reader, who have been offended, should utterly fall into error, imagining that the "woe!" was spoken only to him who gave offence, He says, "I want you who have been offended, that is, harmed, to admonish those who have dealt unjustly with you and harmed you, if they are Christians." See what He is saying: "if thy brother," that is, a Christian, "shall trespass against thee." But if an unbeliever wrongs you, then concede to him even what is yours. If it is a brother, admonish him; He did not say "revile" but "admonish". "If he shall hear thee" means "if he shall acknowledge his fault." He desires that sinners first be admonished in private, lest they become even more shameless when admonished before many. But if when admonished before two or more witnesses the sinner still is not ashamed, then divulge his sin to those who preside in the Church. Since he would not listen to two or three, even though the law says that every charge is confirmed by the evidence of two or three witnesses, then let him be chastised by the Church. And if he will not hear the Church, then let him be put out of the Church lest he transmit his wickedness to others as well. Such brethren as these He likens to the publicans, for the publican was notorious for evil doing and was an outcast. It is a consolation to the one who has been wronged, that the wrongdoer is considered as a publican or a Gentile, that is, a sinner or an unbeliever. Is this the only punishment of the wrongdoer? Indeed not, but hear what follows:

18. Verily I say unto you, Whatsoever ye shall bind on earth shall be bound in heaven: and whatsoever ye shall loose on earth shall be loosed in heaven. If you, He says, who have been wronged deem the wrongdoer a publican and a Gentile, he shall be so in heaven as well. And if you loose, that is, forgive him, he shall be forgiven in heaven as well. For it is not only what the priests loose that is loosed, but also whatever we who have been wronged bind or loose, those things too shall be either bound or loosed.

19-20. Again verily I say unto you, That if two of you shall agree on earth as touching any thing that they shall ask, it shall be done for them of My Father Who is in heaven. For where two or three are gathered together in My name, there am I in the midst of them. By these words He draws us together in love. After forbidding us to give offence to each other, either to harm and to be harmed,[3] now He speaks of mutual agreement and harmony. Those who agree are those who collaborate, not in evil, but in good. Mark what He said: "if two of you," that is, of believers who are virtuous. For Annas and Caiaphas also agreed, but in a manner deserving blame. This is why we often pray but do not receive, because we do not agree among each other. He did not say, "I will be there," for He does not merely intend to be there at some future time, nor does He delay, but rather He said, "there am I," that is, I am present at once. You may also understand that when the flesh and the spirit agree, and the flesh does not desire something in opposition to the spirit, then is the Lord there in the midst. And so also do the three faculties of the soul—the abilities to reason, to be stirred to action, and to desire—all agree. But the Old and the New agree as well and Christ is in their midst, proclaimed by both.

21-22. Then came Peter to Him, and said, Lord, how oft shall my brother sin against me, and I forgive him? till seven times? Jesus saith unto him, I say not unto thee, Until seven times: but, Until seventy times seven. This is what Peter is asking: how many times, if one sins and then comes and begs forgiveness repentantly, should I forgive him? He added "sin against me," for if he sins against God, I,

---

[3] "To be harmed" means to take offence and to revile the one who harms us.

a layman, cannot forgive him, but only the priest who has this authority from God. But if he sins against me, then I will forgive him and he will be forgiven, though I am a layman and not a priest. He said, "until seventy times seven," not to limit forgiveness within a number, for it would be absurd for someone to sit and count the occasions until they numbered 490 (that is, seventy times seven). But what He means here is an infinite number, as if He were saying, "However many times he sins and repents, forgive him." He also tells us that we should be compassionate by means of the following parable.

23. Therefore is the kingdom of the heavens likened unto a man who was a king, who wanted to settle accounts with his servants. The gist of the parable teaches us to forgive our fellow servants who have sinned against us, especially if they fall down before us begging forgiveness. To interpret the parable in its particulars should be done only by one who has the mind of Christ. Nevertheless, we shall attempt it. The kingdom is the Word of God, but it is not a kingdom of small extent, but of the heavens. The Word is likened to a man who was a king, that is, He Who became incarnate for our sake and appeared in the likeness of men, and He settles accounts with His servants as a Good Judge. He does not punish without first judging: that would be cruel.

24-25. And when he had begun to reckon, one was brought unto him, who owed him ten thousand talents. But forasmuch as he had not to pay, his lord commanded him to be sold, and his wife, and children, and all that he had, and payment to made. It is we ourselves who owe ten thousand talents, receiving benefaction every day yet giving back nothing good to God in return. He who owes ten thousand talents is also that ruler who has received from God the protection and allegiance of many men, each man being like a talent, and then does not employ his sovereignty well. Selling the debtor along with his wife and children indicates alienation from God, for the one who is sold goes to another master. And is the wife not the flesh, being the mate of the soul, and the children, the evil deeds done by the soul and the body? He commands the flesh to be given to Satan for ravaging, that is, to be given over to illnesses or to the torment of the demons, but the children, that is to say, the doing of evil deeds, are given over to torture on the rack, as, for example, when God withers the hand that has stolen, or constricts it by means of a demon. See how the woman, which is the flesh, and the children, which is the doing of evil, have been given over to affliction so that the spirit might be saved, as in the case of that man who can no longer steal because his hand is crippled.

26-27. The servant therefore fell down prostrate before him, saying, Lord, have patience with me, and I will pay thee all. Then the lord of that servant was moved with compassion, and loosed him, and forgave him the debt. Behold the power of repentance and the Lord's love for mankind. For repentance caused the servant to fall down prostrate before the king and cease from wickedness, since he who stands firmly in wickedness cannot be forgiven. In His love for man God forgave the debt entirely although the servant was not asking for complete forgiveness of the debt, but for an extension of time in which to repay it. Learn, therefore, that God gives more than we ask for. His love for man is such that even what seems to be severe, the command that the servant be sold, God did not speak out of severity, but to terrify the servant in order to induce him to fix all his hope on entreaty and supplication.

28-30. But the same servant went out, and found one of his fellowservants, who owed him an hundred pence: and he laid hands on him, and took him by the throat, saying, Pay me that thou owest. And his fellowservant fell down at his feet, and besought him, saying, Have patience with me, and I will pay thee all. And he would not: but went and cast him into prison, till he should pay the debt. He who had been forgiven "went out", departed, and as a consequence, took his fellow servant by the throat: the one who lacks compassion is not he who remains in God, but rather he who departs from God and is a stranger to Him. So great was the servant's inhumanity that, although he had been forgiven the greater amount (ten thousand talents), he could not at all forgive the smallest amount (a hundred pence), nor even grant a postponement. And this despite the fact that the fellow servant spoke the very same words to him, reminding him of the words by which he himself had been saved: "Have patience with me and I will pay thee all."

31. So when his fellowservants saw what was done, they were very

sorrowful, and came and told unto their lord all that was done. The fellowservants are the angels, who are shown here to be haters of evil and lovers of good. They do not tell these things to the Lord as if He were unaware of them, but in order for you, O reader, to learn that the angels watch over us and are angered by man's inhumanity.

32-34. Then his lord, after he had called him, said unto him, O thou wicked servant, I forgave thee all that debt, because thou desiredst me: shouldest not thou also have had compassion on thy fellowservant, even as I had pity on thee? And his lord was wroth, and delivered him to the tormentors, till he should pay all his debt. The master in his love for mankind takes issue with the servant, to show that it is not the master, but the savagery and the ingratitude of the servant that has revoked the gift. To what tormentors does he deliver him? To the punitive powers for eternal punishment. For the meaning of "till he should pay all his debt" is this: "let him be punished till that he should pay all that was due." But he will never be able to pay his debt, and therefore his punishment will never end.

35. So likewise shall My heavenly Father do also unto you, if ye from your hearts forgive not every one his brother their trespasses. He did not say "your Father", but "My Father". For such as these are unworthy to have God as their Father. He wants us to forgive from our hearts and not only from our lips. Understand, then, what a great evil is remembrance of wrongs, since it revokes the gift of God; though God does not repent of His gifts, nevertheless they are revoked.

CHAPTER NINETEEN

Concerning those who asked whether it is lawful to divorce one's wife. Concerning the rich man who questioned Jesus.

1-2. And it came to pass, that when Jesus had finished these sayings, He departed from Galilee, and came into the region of Judea beyond Jordan. And great multitudes followed Him; and He healed them there. Again He sojourns in Judea so as not to give the unbelievers in Judea any excuse to say, "He did not visit us frequently, as He did the Galileans." Once again, when the teaching and the speaking are finished, the miracles follow, for we must both teach and act. When the mindless Pharisees saw the miracles, they ought to have believed, but instead they put Him to the test. Hear, then:

3-6. The Pharisees also came unto Him, testing Him, and saying unto Him, Is it lawful for a man to put away his wife for every cause? And He answered and said unto them, Have ye not read, that He Who made them at the beginning made them male and female, and said, For this cause shall a man leave father and mother, and shall cleave to his wife: and they twain shall be one flesh? Wherefore they are no more twain, but one flesh. What therefore God hath joined together, let not man put asunder. O what mindlessness! They thought they would confound Christ by their questions, for if He said it was lawful to divorce one's wife for any reason, they would say to Him, "Why then did you say, Let not a man divorce his wife unless only she be an adulteress?"[1] But if He said it was not lawful for a man to divorce his wife they would slander Him as a lawgiver at variance with Moses. For Moses had decreed that if a man hated his wife he should divorce her even without reasonable cause.[2] What then does Christ say? He shows that monogamy is the work and law of Him Who created us at the beginning. For at the beginning, He says, God joined together one man

---

[1] Mt. 5:32

[2] Deut. 24:3

and one woman. So it is not right that one man should be joined to many women, or one woman to many men. But as they were joined together at the beginning, so they should remain, not sundering the marital union without good cause. Jesus did not say, "It is I Who made them male and female," not wanting to vex the Pharisees; but He phrased it more indefinitely, "He Who made them". The goodness of wedded union is of such importance to God that He even permitted women to leave their parents and to cleave to their husbands. But why is it written in Genesis[3] that Adam said, "Therefore shall a man leave his father and his mother," while here Christ says that it was God Who said, "For this cause shall a man leave father and mother." We say, therefore, that what Adam spoke, he spoke from God, so that the speech of Adam is of God. Therefore, since they have become one flesh, joined together by means of marital relations and physical affection, just as it is accursed to cut one's own flesh, so is it accursed to separate husband and wife. He did not say, "Let not Moses put asunder," so as not to scandalize them, but simply "Let not man," showing the gap between God Who joins together and man who dissolves.

7-9. They say unto Him, Why did Moses then command to give a writing of divorcement, and to put her away? He saith unto them, Moses because of the hardness of your hearts permitted you to put away your wives: but from the beginning it was not so. And I say unto you, Whosoever shall put away his wife, except it be for fornication, and shall marry another, committeth adultery: and whoso marrieth her who is put away doth commit adultery. When the Pharisees saw that the Lord had confuted them, they were compelled to bring forward Moses as a lawgiver who contradicted Christ, and they asked, "Why did Moses then command to give a writing of divorcement, and to put her away?" Then the Lord, turning every accusation upon their own head, defends Moses by saying, "Moses did not set this law in contradiction to God, but rather he addressed this law to your depravity, so that when you in your licentiousness desired to come together with other women, you would not put to death your first wife." For the Israelites, being cruel, would have murdered their wives if they were

[3] Gen. 2:24

constrained to keep them. So Moses provided in the law for a writ of divorce to be given to those wives who were hated by their husbands. But I say to you, Christ says, that it is good to divorce as an adulteress a wife who has committed fornication, but if one divorces a wife who has not committed fornication, he becomes in part the cause of adultery for her if she should marry again. Understand this also, that "he that is joined unto the Lord is of one spirit with Him"[4] and a union takes place between the believer and Christ. For we have all become one body with Him and we are, each one of us, members of Christ. So indeed no one can separate such a union, as Paul said, Who can separate us from the love of Christ? For what God has joined together, nothing can separate, as Paul says, neither man nor any other created thing, not angels, principalities, or powers.[5]

10. His disciples say unto Him, If the case of the man be so with his wife, it is not good to marry. The disciples are troubled and say, "If they are joined together so that they are one and remain inseparable their whole life, so that even if the wife should be a schemer, or worse, he dare not divorce her, it is not expedient to marry. For it would be easier not to marry, and to war and struggle against physical desires, than to endure a wicked woman." "The case of the man with his wife" means the unbreakable union. But some interpret it this way: if the case of man be so, that is, if the man who unlawfully divorces his wife draws such a charge, or blame and accusation, against himself, it is not expedient to marry.

11. But He said unto them, Not all can receive this saying, save they to whom it is given. Since the disciples had said that it would be better not to enter into marriage, the Lord says that virginity is a great thing but not everyone can achieve it, but only those with whom God acts in synergy.[6] "They to whom it is given" refers to those with whom God acts in synergy. It is given to those who ask. For He says, "Ask, and it

---

[4] I Cor. 6:17

[5] See Rom. 8:38-39.

[6] The verb in Greek, *synergein*, from which we get the word "synergy", means literally, "to work together". God's grace and power act together with man's own will and effort in order to accomplish any virtue in a person.

shall be given you. For everyone that asketh receiveth.''[7]

12. For there are some eunuchs, which were so born from their mother's womb: and there are some eunuchs, which were made eunuchs by men: and there be eunuchs, which have made themselves eunuchs for the kingdom of heaven's sake. He that is able to receive it, let him receive it. There are few, He says, who can achieve this virginity. For there are some who are eunuchs from their mother's womb, that is, by their physical temperament are never aroused towards sexual intercourse, so they are chaste without thereby deriving any profit. And there are those who have been made eunuchs by men. Those who have made themselves eunuchs for the kingdom of heaven's sake are not those who have castrated themselves (for that is an accursed deed), but those who exercise self-control. You may also understand it this way. He is a eunuch by nature who, on account of his physical temperament, is not easily aroused to carnal pleasures. He who is made a eunuch by men is he who is guided by human teaching to cut off the burning of carnal desires. He who makes himself a eunuch is he who is instructed by no one else but by himself, and who, self-taught, inclines towards chastity. So this one is best who is guided not by another but by himself to the kingdom of heaven. Christ wants us of our own free will to practice virtue, saying, ''He that is able to receive it, let him receive it.'' For Christ neither demands virginity, nor dissolves marriage, but He puts virginity first.

13-14. Then there were brought unto Him little children, that He should put His hands on them, and pray: and the disciples rebuked them. But Jesus said, Let the little children come unto Me and forbid them not: for of such is the kingdom of heaven. Mothers were bringing their children to be blessed by the touch of His hands. But they were crowding in towards Him in an unruly manner, which is why the disciples forbade them. The disciples also thought that bringing children to Him diminished His dignity as Teacher and Master. Christ therefore shows that He especially accepts the guilelessness of a little child, saying, ''Let the little children come unto Me, for of such is the kingdom of

[7] Lk. 11:9

heaven.'' He does not say, ''of these,'' but ''of such,'' that is, the kingdom of heaven belongs to those who have simplicity, guilelessness and innocence. And if one is teaching and some draw near asking childish questions, let the teacher accept them and not forbid them.

15-17. And He laid His hands on them, and departed thence. And, behold, one came and said unto Him, Good Teacher, what good thing shall I do, that I may have eternal life? And He said unto him, Why callest thou Me good? There is none good but One, that is, God. The man did not come testing Christ, but desiring to learn and thirsting for eternal life. He approached Christ as if Christ were a mere man. That is why the Lord says, ''Why callest thou Me good? There is none good but One, that is, God.'' This means, if you call Me good thinking I am one of the teachers, you speak wrongly, for no man is essentially good; both because we are changeable and easily turned away from good, and because, by comparison with God's goodness, human goodness is counted as wickedness.

17-19. But if thou wilt enter into life, keep the commandments. He saith unto Him, Which? Jesus said, Thou shalt do no murder, Thou shalt not commit adultery, Thou shalt not steal, Thou shalt not bear false witness, Honour thy father and thy mother, and, Thou shalt love thy neighbour as thyself. The Lord directs the enquirer to the commandments of the law, so that the Jews could not say that He despised the law. What happened then?

20. The young man saith unto Him, All these things have I kept from my youth up: what lack I yet? Some accuse him of boasting and arrogance. For how could he have achieved love for neighbor if he were rich? For no one who loves his neighbor as himself is wealthier than his neighbor. Others understand it thus: suppose, he says, that I have kept all these things—what do I still lack?

21-22. Jesus said unto him, If thou wilt be perfect go and sell what thou hast, and give to the poor, and thou shalt have treasure in heaven: and come and follow Me. But when the man heard that saying, he went away sorrowful: for he had great possessions. Everything, He says, which you say you have accomplished, you have done by fulfilling only the letter of the law, as do the Jews. But if you would be perfect, that is, be My disciple and a Christian, go and sell all that you have, and give everything all at once, keeping nothing back with which to give alms continuously. For He did not say, "give repeatedly to the poor," but "give" once and for all and be stripped of your wealth. But since there are some who give alms but who lead a life full of every kind of filth, He adds, "and come and follow Me," that is, possess every other virtue as well. The young man, however, was sorrowful, for though he desired eternal life, and the soil of his heart was deep and fertile, yet the thorns of wealth were choking him. For it says, "he had great possessions." He who has few possessions is not similarly restrained by them, for the bond of many possessions is more tyrannical. Because the Lord was conversing with a rich man, He said, "Do you love wealth? Know that you will have treasure in heaven."

23-24. Then said Jesus unto His disciples, Verily I say unto you, That it is hard for a rich man to enter into the kingdom of heaven. And again I say unto you, It is easier for a camel to go through the eye of a needle, than for a rich man to enter into the kingdom of God. As long as a man is rich and he has in excess while others do not have even the necessities, he can in no way enter the kingdom of heaven. But when all riches have been shed, then he is not rich and so he can enter. For it is just as impossible for a man with wealth to enter the kingdom of heaven as it is for a camel to go through the eye of a needle. See how Christ first said it was difficult to enter, but here that it is completely impossible. Some say that "camel" is not the animal, but the thick cable used by sailors to cast their anchors.

25-26. When His disciples heard it, they were exceedingly amazed, saying, Who then can be saved? But Jesus beheld them, and said unto them, With men this is impossible: but with God all things are possible. The disciples, being compassionate, did not ask this question for their own sake, for they were poor, but for all men. The Lord therefore teaches us not to gauge salvation by human weakness, but by God's power. For if one only begins to cease from greed, he will advance to reducing his excess, and from there he will proceed to eliminating even his necessities, and thus he will be prospered along the way by God acting in collaboration with him.

27. Then answered Peter and said unto Him, Behold, we have forsaken all and followed thee; what shall we have therefore? Even though it seems that Peter had not forsaken very much, as he was poor, understand that in actuality he, too, forsook much. For the fewer possessions we humans have, the greater the attachment. But Peter also rejected every worldly pleasure, even natural affection for his parents. For these passions[8] war against the poor as well as the rich. What then does the Lord answer?

28. And Jesus said unto them, Verily I say unto you, That ye which have followed Me, in the regeneration when the Son of Man shall sit on the throne of His glory, ye also shall sit upon twelve thrones, judging the twelve tribes of Israel. Surely they will not be seated?[9] Of course not, but He indicated by means of a throne the great honor they will enjoy. Will Judas also be seated? No; for Christ said, "which have followed Me," that is, "followed Me to the end," but Judas did not follow to the end. By a different interpretation, God often promises good things to those who are worthy. But if they should change and become unworthy, as Judas did, those good things are denied. Similarly with more menacing things, He often threatens but does not carry out the threat, because we have repented. By "regeneration" understand the resurrection of the dead at the Last Judgement.

29. And every one that hath forsaken houses, or brethren or sisters, or father, or mother, or wife, or children, or lands, for My name's sake, shall receive a hundredfold, and shall inherit everlasting life. So that no one would think that what was said applied only to the disciples, Christ broadened the promise to include everyone who does likewise. For they will have, instead of family of the flesh, intimacy and brotherhood with God; instead of lands, Paradise; instead of houses of stone, the heavenly Jerusalem; instead of a mother, the venerable mothers in the Church; instead of a father, the priests; instead of a wife, all the faithful women, not in marriage—far from it!—but in affection and spiri-

---

[8] Natural affection for one's family becomes a passion when it is placed before love of God.

[9] In the ancient world, the privilege to sit in the presence of others indicates a high office or rank such as that of a king or one representing him, or of the father in the presence of his children.

tual relation and compassionate care for them. The Lord does not bid us simply to separate from our families, but only when they impede our piety. In the same manner, He bids us to despise even our own life and body, but not with the result that we slay ourselves. See how good God is: He not only gives us these good things, but adds to them eternal life. You, then, O reader, hasten to sell your possessions and give to the poor. Possessions are, to the wrathful person, his anger; to the fornicator, his disposition for debauchery; to the resentful person, his remembrance of wrongs. Sell these things and give them to the poor demons who are in want of every good thing. Return the passions to the creators of the passions, and then you will have treasure, which is Christ, in your heaven, that is, in your mind which has been exalted above this world. For he who becomes like the heavenly One has heaven within himself.

30. But many that are first shall be last; and the last shall be first. Christ is suggesting here the Jews and the Gentiles. For the Jews, who were first, became last, while the Gentiles, who were last, were put first. But so that you might clearly understand and learn what this means, He adds the following parable.

CHAPTER TWENTY

Concerning the hired laborers.
Concerning the sons of Zebedee.
Concerning the two blind men.

1-7. For the kingdom of heaven is like unto a man that is an householder, which went out early in the morning to hire labourers into his vineyard. And when he had agreed with the labourers for a penny a day, he sent them into his vineyard. And he went out about the third hour, and saw others standing idle in the marketplace, and said unto them: Go ye also into the vineyard, and whatsoever is right I will give you. And they went their way. Again he went out about the sixth and ninth hour, and did likewise. And about the eleventh hour he went out, and found others standing idle, and saith unto them, Why stand ye here all the day idle? They say unto him, Because no man hath hired us. He saith unto them, Go ye also into the vineyard; and whatsoever is right, that shall ye receive. The kingdom of heaven is Christ, Who is likened to a man inasmuch as Christ took on our form. He is the householder, as He is Master of the house, that is, of the Church. This Christ, then, went out from the bosom of the Father and hired laborers into the vineyard, namely, into the study of the Scriptures and into the doing of the commandments. Or, He hired each one to labor in the vineyard which is his own soul. He hires one in the morning, that is, in his childhood; another, at the third hour, in his youth; others at the sixth and ninth hours, when they are twenty five or thirty years of age, or simply, in their manhood; and others at the eleventh hour, in their old age. For there are many who came to believe even as old men. Or, in another manner as well, the day is this present age, for in it we labor as if for one day. The Lord, then, called at the first hour those living at the time of Enoch and Noah; at the third hour, those living at the time of Abraham; at the sixth hour, those living at the time of Moses; at the ninth hour, those living at the time of the prophets; at the eleventh hour, namely, at the close of the age, the Gentiles, who had been idle from every good work. No one had hired them because no prophet had been sent to the Gentiles.

8-16. So when even was come, the lord of the vineyard saith unto his steward, Call the labourers, and give them their hire, beginning from the last unto the first. And when they came that were hired about the eleventh hour, they received every man a penny. But when the first came, they supposed that they should have received more; and they likewise received every man a penny. And when they had received it, they murmured against the master of the house, saying, These last have laboured but one hour, and thou hast made them equal unto us, which have borne the burden and heat of the day. But he answered one of them, and said, Friend, I do thee no wrong: didst not thou agree with me for a penny? Take what is thine, and go thy way: I desire to give unto this last, even as unto thee; or am I not allowed to do what I will with mine own? Is thine eye evil, because I am good? So the last shall be first, and the first last: for many be called, but few chosen. Evening means the end of the world. Therefore at the end each one receives his penny, which is the gift of the Holy Spirit re-fashioning man into the image of God and making him a sharer in the divine nature. Those who lived before Christ's incarnation labored more, because death was not yet then destroyed, nor the devil crushed, but sin still had its full vitality. But we who by the grace of Christ have been made righteous through baptism receive power to conquer our opponent who has already been cast down and slain by Christ. Also, according to the first interpretation, those who believed in their youth have a greater labor than those who approached in old age, for the youth, warring with passions, must bear the burden of anger and the heat of desires, while the old man is in tranquility. Nevertheless, all are deemed worthy of the one gift of the Holy Spirit. The parable, then, teaches us that it is possible even in old age to repent and obtain the kingdom, for this is the eleventh hour. Surely the saints are not envious of those who receive the same reward? Far from it. But this shows here that the good things given to the righteous are so great as to even incite one to envy.

17-21. And Jesus going up to Jerusalem took the twelve disciples apart in the way, and said unto them, Behold, we go up to Jerusalem; and the Son of Man shall be betrayed unto the chief priests and unto the scribes, and they shall condemn Him to death, and shall deliver Him to the Gentiles to mock, and to scourge, and to crucify Him: and the third day He shall rise again. Then came to Him the mother of

Zebedee's children with her sons, falling prostrate before Him and desiring a certain thing of Him. And He said unto her, What wilt thou? She saith unto Him, Grant that these my two sons may sit, the one on Thy right hand, and the other on the left, in Thy kingdom. The sons of Zebedee, James and John, were thinking that if the Lord went to Jerusalem, He would rule over a temporal kingdom. For they heard Him say continually, "We go up to Jerusalem." They fell, then, to human weakness and persuaded their mother to approach Him, as they themselves were afraid to approach openly. For they too approached secretly, as Mark says,[1] writing that James and John came to Him, meaning that they approached Him secretly and by themselves.

22. But Jesus answered and said, Ye know not what ye ask. Are ye able to drink of the cup that I shall drink of, and to be baptized with the baptism that I am baptized with? They say unto Him, We are able. He turns away from the mother and converses with the sons[2] in order to show that He was not unaware that they had pushed her forward. Jesus says to them, "Ye know not what ye ask," that is, you ask for something so great as to amaze even the angelic powers. Then directing them away from such thoughts, He instead exhorts them to face dangers. He asks the question, knowing full well the answer, in order to compel them to reveal their wound of pride by their answer, and so that they might undertake in earnest to fulfill their promise. For this is what He is saying: since no one can share in My kingdom if he does not also share in My sufferings, tell Me if you are able to suffer such things as these. For the cup means martyrdom and one's own death, at the same time showing that it is an easy thing, like drinking a cup of wine, and that we too ought to embrace martyrdom as easily. He also makes clear that He Himself approaches death gladly. For just as one who drinks a cup of wine is overwhelmed by sleep, so he who drinks the cup of martyrdom is weighed down by the sleep of death. He also calls His death a baptism, as it is the cleansing of us all. They readily promised everything, not knowing what they were saying, but only to obtain what they wanted.

---

[1] Mk. 10:35

[2] That this is so is at once apparent from the fact that the Lord responds in the second person plural, *ouk oidate*, "ye do not know," instead of "thou dost not know."

23. And He saith unto them, Ye shall drink indeed of My cup, and be baptized with the baptism that I am baptized with: but to sit at My right hand, and at My left, is not Mine to give, but it shall be given to them for whom it is prepared by My Father. "You will bear witness even unto martyrdom, this I know"—and so it happened. For James was killed by Herod, and John was condemned by Trajan for bearing witness to the Word of Truth. "But to sit is not Mine to give, but it shall be given to those for whom it is prepared." That is, if one can be found who, along with bearing witness, also possesses every other virtue, that man will receive the gift. It is prepared for him who has labored, just as wreathes are prepared for those who contest in the games. When a foot race is held, sponsored by the king, and a man who did not even compete in the race approaches the king and says, "O holder of the games, give the wreath to me, though I did not compete," the king would answer him, "It is not for me to give out the wreath freely. For it goes to him for whom it has been prepared, that is, to him who ran and won the victory." So Christ here says, "I am not able to freely grant you to sit at My right hand. For it belongs to others who have labored for it and for them it has been prepared." You might ask, then, "Are there some who will sit?"[3] Learn, that no one will sit there in the kingdom, for that is the prerogative of the divine nature alone. For to which of the angels said He at any time, "Sit thou at My right hand?"[4] But John and James supposed that the Lord had said this, and they asked for such a seat, not understanding that to sit on the twelve thrones means they would be glorified on account of their virtue.

24-28. And when the ten heard it, they were moved with indignation against the two brethren. But Jesus called them unto Him, and said, Ye know that the princes of the Gentiles lord it over them, and they that are great exercise authority upon them. But it shall not be so among you: but whosoever will be great among you, let him be your minister; and whosoever will be chief among you, let him be your servant: even as the Son of Man came not to be ministered

---

[3] For the significance of the word "sit" in the ancient world see the footnote to Mt. 19:28 on p. 167.

[4] Heb. 1:13. See Ps. 109:1.

unto, but to minister, and to give His life a ransom for many. When the ten saw the two being rebuked by the Lord, then they, too, became indignant, revealing that even prior to this they had been annoyed at the honor which these two were given. For they were yet imperfect, the two rising up against the ten, and the ten envious of the two. As the ten were stirred up when they heard this, He called them to Himself, and by His calling, before any words were spoken, He calmed them. For the sons of Zebedee spoke to Him after they had separated themselves from the others. Therefore He speaks to them all together. Knowing how tyrannical is the pride of status, requiring a severe rebuke, He touches them to the quick by consigning them to the lot of Gentiles and infidels if they would be vainglorious. So He shames them by saying, "Other men are renowned as princes and rulers, and the lust for high position is a passion of the Gentiles; but My disciples are made honorable by their humility. So that he who would be great ought to serve the most inferior in rank; this is the mark of extreme humility. I Myself show this. I am the Prince and King of those who dwell in the heavens, Who humbled Myself to minister to you for your salvation, and I am your servant to the extent that I even give My life as a ransom for many, that is, for all." For "all" are "many".

29-34. And as they departed from Jericho, a great multitude followed Him. And, behold, two blind men sitting by the way side, when they heard that Jesus passed by, cried out, saying, Have mercy on us, O Lord, Thou Son of David. And the multitude rebuked them, because they should hold their peace; but they cried the more, saying, Have mercy on us, O Lord, Thou Son of David. And Jesus stood still, and called them, and said, What will ye that I shall do unto you? They say unto Him, Lord, that our eyes may be opened. So Jesus had compassion on them, and touched their eyes: and immediately their eyes received sight, and they followed Him. The blind men knew of the Lord by His fame, and so they seized the opportunity when they heard that He was passing by on the way. They believed that Jesus, of the seed of David according to the flesh, was able to heal them, and as their faith was exceedingly fervent, they did not fall silent when they were rebuked but cried out all the more. Therefore Jesus does not ask them if they have faith, but rather, what it is they want, so that no one would think that He gave them something other than what they desired. He shows that they were not shouting out to ask for money, but for healing. By His touch He heals them, that we may learn that every member of His holy flesh was also a life-creating member of God. And if Luke and Mark say that there was one blind man, this does not conflict, for they mentioned what was most noteworthy. Another explanation is that Luke says that He healed a blind man before He entered Jericho, but Mark, after He left Jericho. But Matthew in his succinctness included both in one account. Understand the blind men as the Gentiles who were healed in passing. For Christ did not come, in the first place, for the Gentiles but for the Israelites. Just as the blind men by hearing learned of Jesus, so too the Gentiles by hearing believed. Those who rebuked the blind men, telling them not to shout the name of Jesus, are the persecuting tyrants who attempted to shut the mouth of the Church, but She all the more confessed the name of Christ. Therefore She was healed and sees ever more clearly the light of the Truth, and follows Christ, imitating His life.

CHAPTER TWENTY-ONE

Concerning the ass and the colt.
Concerning the halt and the blind.
Concerning the withered fig tree.
Concerning the chief priests and elders who questioned the Lord. Concerning the parable of the two sons. Concerning the vineyard.

1-5. And when they drew nigh unto Jerusalem, and were come to Bethphage, unto the Mount of Olives, then sent Jesus two disciples, saying unto them, Go into the village over against you, and straightway ye shall find an ass tied, and a colt with her: loose them, and bring them unto Me. And if any man say aught unto you, ye shall say, The Lord hath need of them; and straightway he will send them. All this was done, that it might be fulfilled which was spoken by the prophet, saying, Tell ye the daughter of Sion, Behold, thy King cometh unto thee, meek, and sitting upon an ass, and a colt the foal of an ass. He sat upon an ass for no other reason than to fulfill the prophecy and to show us that our means of conveyance should be humble, for He was mounted not on a horse but on a lowly ass. He fulfills the prophecy[1] both literally, and in a spiritual sense. He fulfills it literally by sitting as He did in view of all. He fulfills it in a spiritual sense by sitting upon the ass, the burdened Jews, and also upon the foal, the Gentiles who were coltish, untamed and unruly.[2] For the ass and the colt had been tethered by the reins of their own sins. Two were sent to loose them, Paul to the Gentiles, and Peter to the circumcised, that is, to the Jews. And even now, there are two that loose us from our sins, the Epistles and the Gospel. Christ comes meekly, for He did not come to judge the world at the first coming, but to save. The other kings of the Hebrews were pillagers and wrongdoers, but Christ is a meek king.

6-7. And the disciples went, and did as Jesus commanded them,

---

[1] Zech. 9:9

[2] See Gen. 49:10-11.

and brought the ass, and the colt, and put on them their clothes, and He sat thereon. Luke and Mark mention only one beast of burden, but Matthew mentions both ass and foal; yet they do not contradict. The mother followed the foal which was led. "He sat thereon," not on the two beasts, but on the clothes. Or, first He sat on the ass and later on the foal, since He first took His rest in the synagogue of the Jews and later among the people of the Gentiles.

8-9. And a very great multitude spread their garments in the way; others cut down branches from the trees, and strewed them in the way. And the multitudes that went before, and that followed, cried out, saying, Hosanna to the Son of David: Blessed is He that cometh in the name of the Lord; Hosanna in the highest. In the literal account, laying down of clothing is a sign of great reverence, and the cutting of branches is a sign of festivity. But in the spiritual sense, learn that the apostles first laid down their garments, which are their virtues, and then the Lord sat upon them. For God is not conveyed by a soul that has not been adorned with apostolic virtues. Those that went before are the prophets who lived before Christ's incarnation, while those who followed are the martyrs and teachers who lived after these events. They laid down their garments for Christ, that is, they subjected the flesh to the spirit, for the body is a garment and covering for the soul. They laid them down in the way, that is, in Christ Who said, "I am the Way." For unless a man lays down his garment in the way, that is, unless he humbles his flesh, abiding in the Way which is Christ, and not turning to heresy, the Lord will not be carried by him. Some say that "Hosanna" means "hymn" or "psalm"; others say, more accurately, that it means "Save now". "He that cometh" means the Lord Whose coming was long awaited by the Hebrews. Thus John the Forerunner and Baptist also says, "Thou art He that cometh," meaning "He Whose coming has been long awaited". In another sense, "He that cometh" means "He Whose second coming is awaited day by day". For each of us should always be in hopeful expectation of the end of the world and the coming of the Lord, and should be ready.

10-11. And when He was come into Jerusalem, all the city was moved, saying, Who is this? And the multitude said, This is Jesus the prophet of Nazareth of Galilee. The multitude, being simple and guileless, were not spiteful towards Christ, but neither did they have the proper understanding of Who He was. Therefore they call Him "prophet". Yet since they said it with the article, "the prophet", it could be understood as "the long awaited Prophet", of whom Moses said, "God will raise them up a Prophet."[3] For they did not say, "This is a prophet," but "the Prophet", that is, He Who is awaited with hope.

12-13. And Jesus went into the temple of God, and cast out all them that sold and bought in the temple, and overthrew the tables of the moneychangers, and the seats of them that sold doves, and said unto them, It is written, My house shall be called the house of prayer; but ye have made it a den of thieves. As Master of the house, which is the temple, He cast out the sellers, showing that the things of the Father are also His own. He did this out of concern for the good order of the temple, but also to show the transformation that would take place in the sacrifices. He cast out the cattle and the doves and thus foretold that there would no longer be any need of animal sacrifice and slaughter, but rather, of prayer. For My house, He says, is a house of prayer, but you have made it a den of thieves, in which there is slaughter and bloodletting. But He also called the temple a den of thieves because of the hawkers and the buyers and sellers, for the love of profit is a thieving passion. The "money changers" [in Greek, *kollybistai*] take their name from the *kollybos*, a coin of small denomination. Those who sell doves are also those who sell the ranks of ordination in the churches, for they are selling the gift of the Holy Spirit, which once appeared in the form of a dove;[4] as a result they are cast out not only from the temple below, but from the one above, for they are unworthy to serve at the altar. But you too, O reader, look and see whether perhaps you have made God's temple, that is, your mind, a den of thieves, that is, the demons' lair. It will be such a den if we have thoughts full of the desire for material things, of buying and selling, and of a love of money that would even compel us to collect these small coins, the *kollyba*. And if we buy and sell the doves, that is, if we should mix spiritual teaching with thoughts of material gain, we have made ourselves a den of thieves.

---

[3] Deut. 18:18

[4] Mt. 3:16

14. And the blind and the lame came to Him in the temple; and He healed them. By healing the infirm He shows that He is God and that rightly does He use His authority to cast out the unworthy from His house. It is also made clear that when the Jews who were attached to the law and to animal slaughter had been cast out, then the blind and the lame of the Gentiles were accepted as His friends and healed by Him.

15-16. And when the chief priests and scribes saw the wondrous things that He did, and the children crying out in the temple, and saying, Hosanna to the Son of David, they were sore displeased, and said unto Him, Hearest Thou what these say? And Jesus saith unto them, Yea; have ye never read, Out of the mouth of babes and sucklings Thou hast perfected praise? When the Pharisees saw the children offering to Christ the hymn of David which the prophet seems to offer to God,[5] they exploded with spite and reviled Him for allowing things of God to be said of Him. But He confirmed this by saying "Yea". For, He says, I am so disinclined to stop the mouths of those who are saying these things to Me, that I will even bring forward the prophet as a witness, and show you up as either ignorant or spiteful. For have you not read, "Out of the mouth of babes and sucklings Thou hast perfected praise?"[6] "Thou hast perfected" means "Thou hast shown a perfect and fitting hymn" even if "the babes and sucklings" seem imperfect, or immature, in age. For it was not they who were speaking what they spoke, but they only gave their mouth to the Spirit and became His instruments. This is why He says, "Out of the mouth of babes", implying that the words were not of their own intellect, but only of their mouth which was moved by divine grace. He also showed that He would be blessed by the childish and foolish Gentiles. This was also a consolation to the apostles, that speech would be granted to them as well though they were simple. And you also, O reader, if you are as a babe innocent of any guile and sucking the milk of the Spirit, the divine words, then you will become worthy to hymn God's praise.

17. And He left them, and went out of the city into Bethany; and

---

[5] Ps. 117:25

[6] Ps. 8:2

He lodged there. He departs from those who were unworthy and goes to Bethany, which means "house of obedience". He goes from those who are disobedient to those who are obedient to Him, and among them He lodges. For He says, "I will dwell and walk among them."[7]

18-20. Now in the morning as He returned into the city, He hungered. And when He saw a fig tree in the way, He came to it, and found nothing thereon, but leaves only, and He said unto it, Let no fruit grow on thee henceforward for ever. And immediately the fig tree withered away. And when the disciples saw it, they marvelled, saying, How soon is the fig tree withered away! Of the many miracles which the Lord performed, all were done to do good, for He performed no miracles of chastisement. Therefore, lest anyone think that He is unable to chastise, here He shows this power as well, not applied to men but to a tree, as He loves mankind. He also did the same on a previous occasion to the swine. He withers the tree, then, in order to chasten men. The disciples marvel, and with good reason. For the fig tree contains a great amount of sap, and so the fact that it withered immediately serves all the more to indicate the miracle. The fig tree means the synagogue of the Jews, which has only leaves, that is, the visible letter of the law, but not the fruit of the Spirit. But also every man who gives himself over to the sweetness of the present life is likened to a fig tree, who has no spiritual fruit to give to Jesus who is hungry for such fruit, but only leaves, that is, temporal appearances which fall away and are gone. This man, then, hears himself cursed. For Christ says, Go, ye accursed, into the fire.[8] But he is also dried up; for as he roasts in the flame, his tongue is parched and withered like that of the rich man of the parable, who in his life had ignored Lazarus.

21-22. Jesus answered and said unto them, Verily I say unto you, If ye have faith, and doubt not, ye shall not only do this which is done to the fig tree, but also if ye shall say unto this mountain, Be thou removed, and be thou cast into the sea; it shall be done. And all things, whatsoever ye shall ask in prayer, believing, ye shall receive.

---

[7] II Cor. 6:16

[8] Mt. 25:41

Great is the promise which Christ makes to His disciples, the ability to move mountains, if only we are not ambiguous in faith, that is, we do not hesitate. Whatever we ask, unhesitantly believing in God's power, we shall receive. One might ask, "And if I ask for something unprofitable, and foolishly believe that God will give me this, will I indeed receive this unprofitable thing? How is it that God is said to love mankind if He would fulfill my unprofitable request?" Listen then. First, when you hear "faith", you should understand that it means not "foolish faith" but "true faith"; and when you hear "prayer", understand it to mean that prayer which asks for things profitable, such as the Lord gave to us when He said, "Lead us not into temptation but deliver us from the evil one," and petitions of similar nature. Then consider the words "doubt not", [literally, "be ye not divided", *mē diakrithēte*]. For how could a man who is united with God as one and not divided or separated from Him, how could that man ask for something unprofitable? So if you are undivided and inseparable from God, then you will ask for and receive things which are profitable for you.

23-27. And when He was come into the temple, the chief priests and the elders of the people came unto Him as He was teaching, and said, By what authority doest Thou these things and who gave Thee this authority? And Jesus answered and said unto them, I also will ask you one thing, which if ye tell Me, I in like wise will tell you by what authority I do these things. The baptism of John, whence was it? From heaven, or of men? And they reasoned with themselves, saying, If we shall say, From heaven; He will say unto us, Why did ye not then believe him? But if we shall say, Of men, we fear the people; for all hold John as a prophet. And they answered Jesus, and said, We do not know. And He said unto them, Neither tell I you by what authority I do these things. Full of spite that He had expelled the peddlers from the temple, the teachers of the law approached and asked Him such things as these: "Who are You to cast out from the temple those who do business there? As a priest do You do this? But You have no priestly office. As a king, then? But neither are You a king, and even if You were, You would not have the authority to do such things. For it is not permitted for kings to do these things in the temple." They were questioning the Lord in this manner so that if He should say, "By My own authority I do them," they could accuse Him of insurrection because

He said that He had His own authority. But if He said, "I do these things by divine authority," they would draw away from Him the multitudes who were praising Him as God, telling them, "Look, He is not God, but He does these things by God's authority, as a servant." How then does Christ, Who is Himself Wisdom, respond? He seizes the sophists in their cunning, and asks them the same questions concerning John; so that if they said the teaching of John was from heaven, their rejection of John's teachings would mark them as enemies of God; but if they said that the teaching of John was of men, they would be in danger from the multitudes, for they all considered John a prophet. The Lord shows us here that we ought not to answer those who ask a question with malicious intent. For He Himself did not reply to those Jews who questioned Him with cunning, although He was not at a loss for an answer. At the same time we learn that it is not Christ's nature to extol Himself. Behold, then, the Lord Who is able to say by what authority He does these things, but does not say, lest He appear to extol Himself.

28-32. But what think ye? A certain man had two sons; and he came to the first, and said, Son, go work today in my vineyard. He answered and said, I will not: but afterward he repented, and went. And he came to the second, and said likewise. And he answered and said, I go, sir: and went not. Which of the two did the will of his father? They say unto Him, The first. Jesus saith unto them, Verily I say unto you, That the publicans and the harlots go into the kingdom of God before you. For John came unto you in the way of righteousness, and ye believed him not: but the publicans and the harlots believed him: and ye, when ye had seen it, repented not afterward, that ye might believe him. He introduces two types of men. One type are those who promised from the beginning: such were the Jews who said, "All which God spoke, we will do and we will obey."[9] The other type are those who disobeyed: such are the publicans and the harlots, but also the people of the Gentiles, who from the beginning were not obedient to the will of God, but later they repented and obeyed. Behold, then, the wisdom of Christ. He did not at once from the start say to them, "The publicans and the harlots are better than you," but first He

[9] Ex. 24:3

got the upper hand over them and they confessed that of the two sons, he who did the will of the father was the obedient one. And when they had so confessed He led them on and said, "John came in the way of righteousness," that is, with a blameless life, and you are not able to say that his life was reprehensible, yet the harlots obeyed him while you did not. Therefore they precede you, that is, enter before you into the kingdom. So you also should struggle to believe, so that you might at least enter in after the harlots, for if you do not believe, you will by no means enter. There are many to this very day who have promised to God their Father to become monks or priests, but afterwards were negligent in their promise. But there are others who did not promise to lead a monastic or priestly life, but now they are monks and priests. So the obedient sons are those who act, although they promised nothing.

33. Hear another parable: There was a certain man, a householder, who planted a vineyard, and hedged it round about, and dug a winepress in it, and built a tower, and let it to husbandmen, and went into a far country. Yet another parable He brings to them, showing that though they were deemed worthy to receive an immeasurable degree of care for their condition, they did not get better. The "man, a householder" is the Lord Who in His love for man calls Himself a man. The vineyard is the Jewish people, planted by God in the land of promise. For He says, "Bring them in and plant them in Thy holy mountain."[10] The hedge is the law which prevented them from mixing with the Gentiles; or, it is the holy angels who guarded Israel. The wine-press is the altar; the tower, the temple. The husbandmen are the teachers of the people, the Pharisees and the scribes. The householder, God, went into a far country when He no longer spoke to them in a pillar of cloud. Or, the departure of God into a far country is His long-suffering; for when He is long-suffering and not in hot pursuit of wrongdoers, demanding an account, He appears to be asleep or absent on a far journey.

34-39. And when the time of the fruit drew near, he sent his servants to the husbandmen, that they might receive the fruits of it. And the husbandmen took his servants, and beat one, and killed

[10] Ex. 15:17

another, and stoned another. Again, he sent other servants more than the first: and they did unto them likewise. But last of all he sent unto them his son, saying, They will reverence my son. But when the husbandmen saw the son, they said among themselves, This is the heir; come, let us kill him, and let us seize his inheritance. And they caught him, and cast him out of the vineyard, and slew him. "The time of the fruit drew near" during the years of the prophets. For the servants who were sent are the prophets who were abused in various ways by the husbandmen, that is, the false prophets and false teachers of those times. One they beat, as they did to Micah when Sedek struck him on the jaw;[11] another they killed, as they did to Zechariah [the father of John the Forerunner] between the temple and the altar;[12] another they stoned, as they did Zechariah, the son of Jodae the high priest.[13] Later the Son of God was sent and He appeared in the flesh. He said, "They will reverence My Son," not unaware that they would kill Him, but signifying what ought to be. For, He says, they ought to honor the dignity of the Son even if they had killed the servants. But the husbandmen saw Him and said, "This is the heir; come, let us kill Him." The Jews, too, said, "This is the Christ," and they crucified Him. They cast Him out of the vineyard, for the Lord was slain outside of the city. But since we would also say that the vineyard is the people, Christ was slain by the Pharisees, the evil husbandmen, outside the vineyard, that is, outside and apart from the will of the guileless people.

40-41. When the lord therefore of the vineyard cometh, what will he do unto those husbandmen? They say unto Him, He will miserably destroy those wicked men, and will let out his vineyard unto other husbandmen, which shall render him the fruits in their seasons. "When He cometh." When? At the second coming? It seems to have this meaning, but a better meaning is this: the lord of the vineyard is God the Father Who sent His Son Who was slain by them. When He comes, that is, when He looks down on the lawlessness which the Jews committed, then He will miserably destroy them by sending the Roman army. And

---

[11] III Kings (I Kings) 22:24

[12] See Bl. Theophylact's comment on Mt. 23:35-36, on p. 202.

[13] II Chron. 24:21

His vineyard, that is, His people, He will give to other husbandmen, that is, to apostles and teachers. Understand the vineyard to mean also the Divine Scriptures, in which the hedge is the letter, and the wine-press that is dug is the depth of the Spirit; the tower is theology, lofty and exalted. These Scriptures, then, were first possessed by bad husbandmen, the Pharisees; but God has let them out to us who cultivate them well. But they slew the Lord outside the vineyard, that is, outside those things of which Scripture spoke.

42-44. Jesus saith unto them, Did ye never read in the Scriptures, The stone which the builders rejected, the same is become the head of the corner: this is the Lord's doing, and it is marvelous in our eyes? Therefore say I unto you, The kingdom of God shall be taken from you, and given to a nation bringing forth the fruits thereof. And whosoever shall fall on this stone shall be broken: and on whomsoever it shall fall, it will crush him to powder to be scattered. The stone means Christ Himself; the builders are the teachers of the Jews who rejected Him as if He were useless, saying, "Thou art a Samaritan and hast a demon." But when He rose from the dead, He was set in place as the head of the corner, that is, He became the head of the Church, joining Jews and Gentiles in one faith. For as the stone which forms the corner of a building makes continuous the walls leading to it and from it, so Christ has bound all together in one faith. This corner is marvelous, and is the Lord's doing.[14] For the Church which connects us and makes us one in faith is the Lord's doing, and is worthy of all wonder, so well is it built. And in another sense is it marvelous, because the Word of Christ has been confirmed and substantiated by marvels, that is, miracles, so that the composition of the Church is marvelous. The kingdom of God, that is, closeness with God, has been taken from the Jews and given to those who believed. Those who stumble against the Rock of Christ and take offence at Him will not only be crushed at the second coming, but already here in this life they have been scattered like powder by Christ. They have been scattered over all the earth, as we now see the pitiable Jews to be. Understand that he who is "crushed to powder to be scattered" is dispersed abroad and scattered in diaspora.

---

[14] See Ps.117:22-23.

45-46. And when the chief priests and Pharisees had heard His parables, they perceived that He spake of them. But when they sought to lay hands on Him, they feared the multitude, because they took Him for a prophet. See once again that the multitude, which is simple and guileless, follows the truth, while the teachers of the law work evil. But even today there are Jews who seek to lay hands on Christ, but they neither grasp nor understand Him. For they shall grasp the Antichrist and shall bow down and worship him, while Christ will not be grasped, that is, understood, by them.

CHAPTER TWENTY-TWO

Concerning those invited to the wedding.
Concerning those who asked about the tribute.
Concerning the Sadducees.
Concerning the lawyer who questioned.
Concerning the questions asked by the Lord.

1-7. And Jesus answered and spake unto them again by parables, and said, The kingdom of heaven is like unto a man who was a king, who made a marriage for his son, and sent forth his servants to call them that were called to the wedding: and they would not come. Again, he sent forth other servants, saying, Tell them who were called, Behold, I have prepared my dinner: my oxen and my fattened calves are killed, and all things are ready: come unto the marriage. But they made light of it, and went their ways, one to his field, another to his merchandise: and the others took his servants, and treated them spitefully, and slew them. But when the king heard thereof, he was wroth: and he sent forth his armies, and destroyed those murderers, and burned up their city. This parable, too, like that of the vineyard, alludes to the disobedience of the Jews. But as that one indicates Christ's death, so this one indicates the nuptial joy, that is, the resurrection. But this parable also shows them to be worse transgressors than the men in the preceding parable. For the husbandmen of the vineyard slew those who demanded fruits of them. But these men vented their murderous rage upon those who had invited them to a wedding. God is likened to a human king, for He does not appear as He is, but as it is fitting for Him to appear to us. When we die as humans, subject to human failings, God appears to us in human form; but when we walk about as gods, then God stands in the congregation of gods.[1] And when we live as wild beasts, then He, too, becomes for us a panther, and a bear, and a lion. He makes a wedding feast for His Son, joining Him to every soul that is beautiful. For the bridegroom is Christ and the bride is

---

[1] Ps. 81:1. "God stood in the congregation of gods, and in the midst He shall stand out among gods." On the godlike nature of the saints when they have been perfected in heaven, see footnote on p. 118.

the Church and the soul. The servants that were sent out first are Moses and those with him, whom the Jews did not obey but provoked God in the wilderness for forty years and did not want to accept the word of God and spiritual joy. Then other servants, the prophets, were sent out; but of these, some they killed, as they did Isaiah; others they treated spitefully, as they did Jeremiah, throwing him into a pit of mire. Those who were less extreme merely declined the invitation: one went his way to his own field, that is, turned towards a life of pleasure and carnal pursuits, for one's "own field" is the body; another, to his merchandise, that is, to a life of acquisition and profit, for merchants are a type of men most greedy for profit. This parable shows that those who fail to attend the wedding feast and the fellowship and feasting with Christ, do so primarily on account of these two things—the pleasures of the flesh, or the passion of greed. In this parable the meal is called a "dinner", although elsewhere the same thing is called a "supper",[2] and not unreasonably. For it is called a supper when this wedding feast appears in perfect form in the latter times, towards evening, that is, at the end of the ages. But it is called a dinner when even in former times the mystery was revealed, although more obscurely. The oxen and the fattened calves [in Greek, *sitista*, grain-fattened calves] are the Old and the New Testaments. For the Old Testament is symbolized by the oxen, for it contained animal sacrifice; the New Testament is symbolized by the grain-fattened calves, for now we offer loaves upon the altar, which could truly be called *sitista* [literally, "formed from wheat"], as the loaves consist of wheat, *sitos*. God therefore calls us to partake of the good things of both the Old Testament Scriptures and the New. But when you see someone clearly interpreting the divine words know that he is giving grain-fattened meat. For when he teaches clearly, it is as if he were feeding the unlearned with rich food. No doubt you will ask why He says here, "Call them that were called." If they were already invited, why are they going to invite them again? Learn, then, that each of us by nature has been called towards the good, for we are being called by the word of the innate teacher within us. But God also sends us external teachers to call us from without, we who were first called by the word in our nature. The king sent his armies, that is, the Roman legions, and destroyed the disobedient Jews and burnt up

---

[2] Lk. 14:16

their city, Jerusalem, as even the truthful Josephus says.[3]

8-10. Then saith he to his servants, The wedding is ready, but they that were called were not worthy. Go ye therefore into the lanes off from the highways, and as many as ye shall find, call to the marriage. So those servants went out into the highways, and gathered together all as many as they found, both bad and good: and the wedding was furnished with guests. Since the previous servants, Moses and those with him, and the prophets, did not persuade them, He sends out other servants, the apostles, and they call the Gentiles who do not walk in the true way but are divided, some here, some there, separated into many ways and doctrines. Indeed, they are to be found along the lanes off from the highways, that is, in great error, delusion, and deviation. They were even at odds among themselves, and were not in the true way, but along the exits, which are the evil doctrines that they taught. For they were not all content with the same doctrines, but some with these and some with those. But perhaps an even better explanation is this: the highway is the life and the manner in which each person lives; the lanes exiting from the highway are doctrines. The pagan Greeks, then, travel along evil highways, that is, they lead reprehensible lives, and from these evil lives they have turned off into godless doctrines, setting up shameful gods as patrons of their own passions. So as the apostles went forth from Jerusalem to the Gentiles, they gathered all together, both evil and good, that is, those filled with every wickedness and also those less wicked whom He calls good by comparison to the others.

11-14. And when the king came in to see the guests, he saw there a man who had not on a wedding garment: and he saith unto him, Friend, how camest thou in hither not having a wedding garment? And he was speechless. Then said the king to the servants, Bind his hands and feet, and take him away, and cast him into outer darkness; there shall be weeping and gnashing of teeth. For many are called, but few are chosen. The entry into the wedding takes place without distinction of persons, for by grace alone we have all been called,

---

[3] Flavius Josephus, born about 37 A.D., was a Jew of aristocratic descent who was captured by the Romans during the Jewish uprising of 66-70 A.D. He later became a Roman citizen and settled in Rome, where he wrote his famous *History of the Jewish Wars*.

good and bad alike; but the life thereafter of those who enter shall not be without examination, for indeed the king makes an exceedingly careful examination of those found to be sullied after entering into the faith. Let us tremble, then, when we understand that if one does not lead a pure life, faith alone benefits him not at all. For not only is he cast out of the wedding feast, but he is sent away into the fire. Who is he that is wearing filthy garments? It is he who is not clothed with compassion, goodness, and brotherly love. For there are many who deceive themselves with vain hopes, thinking that they shall attain the kingdom of heaven, and they include themselves among the assembly of the dinner guests, thinking great things of themselves. Being justified in regard to that unworthy man, the Lord demonstrates these two things to us; first, that He loves mankind, and secondly, that we ought not to pass judgement on anyone, even if they sin openly, unless they have been reproved for their sin. The Lord then says to His servants, the angels of punishment, "Bind his hands and feet," that is, the soul's powers of action. For in this present age is the time to act and to do, but in the age to come all of the soul's powers of action are bound, and a man cannot then do any good thing to outweigh his sins. Gnashing of teeth is the meaningless repentance that will then take place. "Many are called" for God calls many, indeed, all, "but few are chosen." For few are saved and found worthy to be chosen by God. For it is God's part to call, but to become one of the chosen or not, is our part. He shows, then, that this parable was spoken for the Jews who were called but were not chosen, as they did not listen.

15-16. Then went the Pharisees, and took counsel how they might entangle Him in His talk. And they sent out unto Him their disciples with the Herodians. What took place was a plot: therefore Luke also calls them spies,[4] or waylayers, sent secretly to set a trap for Christ. "Herodians" were either soldiers of Herod or those who thought Herod was the Christ. For since the princely line of Judah had failed when Herod, who was not of that line, became king, the Herodians thought that Herod himself was the Christ.[5] So the Pharisees, then, come with these

---

[4] Lk. 20:20

[5] The Herodians misunderstood the prophecy of the Patriarch Jacob spoken to his son Judah (Gen. 49:10): "A ruler shall not fail from Judah, nor a prince from his loins, until there come the things stored up for Him; and He is the Expectation of the Nations." See footnote above on p. 18.

men to set a trap for Him. Hear how they address Him:

16-22. Saying, Master, we know that Thou art true, and teachest the way of God in truth, neither carest Thou for any man: for Thou regardest not the person of men. Tell us therefore, What thinkest Thou? Is it lawful to give tribute unto Caesar, or not? But Jesus, knowing their wickedness, said, Why test ye Me, ye hypocrites? Show Me the tribute money. And they brought unto Him a penny. And He saith unto them, Whose is this image and superscription? They say unto Him, Caesar's. Then saith He unto them, Render therefore unto Caesar the things which are Caesar's; and unto God the things that are God's. When they had heard these words, they marvelled, and left Him, and went their way. Thinking to placate and disarm Him with praise, they flatter Him, so that when He had let down His guard He would say that it was not necessary to pay the tax, and upon that they would seize Him as an insurrectionist who was stirring up the people against Caesar. This is why they also brought along the Herodians, so that they, representing the king, could arrest Him as a rebel. "Thou regardest not the person of men," they say, that is, You would not say anything for the sake of Pilate or Herod. Tell us, then, should we be subject to men's taxation and pay them tribute just as we pay the two-drachma tax to God, or should we pay tribute to God alone, and not to Caesar as well? They said this, as I have explained, so that if He answered that one must not pay tribute to Caesar, they could arrest Him and put Him to death, as they did to the followers of Theudas and Judas[6] who said that one must not make sacrifice in Caesar's name. Jesus persuades them by means of the image of Caesar engraved on the coin, that one must render to Caesar that which is his, namely, that which bears his image, and that in bodily and external things one must submit to the king, but in inner and spiritual things one must submit to God. But one must also understand it in this manner: each one of us must render to Caesar that which is Caesar's, namely, we must throw to the demon who rules below the things which belong to him. As for example when you have anger which comes from Caesar, throw it back to him, get angry against him. Then you will also be able to render to God that which is God's. But since we are of dual

[6] Acts 5:36-37

nature, consisting of both soul and body, to our body, as to Caesar, we owe food and clothing, but to that which is more divine in us, we owe what befits it.

23-28. The same day came to Him the Sadducees, who say that there is no resurrection, and asked Him, saying, Master, Moses said, If a man die, having no children, his brother shall marry his wife, and raise up seed unto his brother. Now there were with us seven brethren: and the first, when he had married a wife, died, and, having no offspring, left his wife unto his brother: likewise the second also, and the third, unto the seventh. And last of all the woman died also. Therefore in the resurrection whose wife shall she be of the seven? For they all had her. When the mouths of the Pharisees and the Herodians had been shut, again the Sadducees put Him to the test. Their heresy was this: they believed neither in a resurrection of the dead, nor in the existence of an immaterial spirit, nor in angels, and in general took a position opposite to that of the Pharisees. Here they contrive an impossible situation. For supposing that two brothers took her and then died, would not the third consider it an omen and refuse the marriage, learning from those who had preceded him? So the Sadducees invent a situation, intending to perplex Christ and so to refute the resurrection. They even draw Moses as an advocate into their invention. They speak of seven brothers so as to ridicule the mystery of the resurrection even more. "Whose wife shall she be?" they ask. One could answer, "O foul Sadducees, she shall be the wife of him who first married her, if we concede that there is marriage in the resurrection; for the others are surrogates and not true and lawful husbands."[7]

29-33. Jesus answered and said unto them, Ye are deluded, knowing neither the Scriptures nor the power of God. For in the resurrection they neither marry, nor are given in marriage, but are as the angels of God in heaven. But as touching the resurrection of the dead, have ye not read that which was spoken unto you by God, saying, I am the God of Abraham, and the God of Isaac, and the God of Jacob? God is not the God of the dead, but of the living. And

---

[7] Deut. 25:5-6

when the multitude heard this, they were astonished at His doctrine. The Saviour shows that there will also be a resurrection, not such a resurrection of the flesh as they mistakenly imagine, but one more divine and more spiritual. Why then are you deluded, not knowing either the Scriptures or the power of God? For if you knew the Scriptures, you would understand that God is not God of the dead but of the living. If you knew the power of God, you would know that for God all things are possible, so that He can even make men to live as angels. See the Lord's wisdom! By using Moses they were intent on overturning the doctrine of the resurrection, but He, also by using Moses, convinces them, quoting, "I am the God of Abraham, Isaac, and Jacob."[8] What Christ means is this: God is not the God of that which is not, but of that which exists and is. For God did not say, "I was," but "I am." Even though they had died, they live in hope of the resurrection. But you may ask, "How is it, then, that he says in another place that He is Lord of both the dead and the living?"[9] Learn, then, that "the dead" means, in that passage, those who have died but who shall live again. Here the Lord says, in opposing the heresy of the Sadducees who teach that there is no immortal soul but that it altogether perishes, that He is not God of the dead, that is, of those who appear to us to have utterly perished, but of the living, that is, of those who have an immortal soul and will be resurrected, though they are dead now.

34-40. But when the Pharisees had heard that He had put the Sadducees to silence, they were gathered together. Then one of them, which was a lawyer, asked Him a question, testing Him, and saying, Master, which is the great commandment in the law? Jesus said unto him, Thou shalt love the Lord thy God with all thy heart, and with all thy soul, and with all thy mind. This is the first and great commandment. And the second is like unto it, Thou shalt love thy neighbour as thyself. On these two commandments hang all the law and the prophets. Out of immeasurable spite this man comes forward to put the Lord to the test. For when they saw the Sadducees put to shame and the Lord praised for His wisdom, they came forward to test Him to

---

[8] Ex. 3:6

[9] Rom. 14:9

see if He would add something to the first commandment, and thus give them the chance to accuse Him of being an innovator who corrects the law. But the Lord discloses their malice, and because they came not to learn, but rather, devoid of love, to show their envy and their spite, He reveals to them the exceedingly great love expressed by the commandments. And He teaches that we ought not to love God partially, but to give all of ourselves to God. For we perceive these three distinctions of the human soul: the vegetative, the animal, and the rational. When the soul grows and is nourished and begets what is like unto it, it resembles the plants; when it experiences anger or desire, it is like the animals; when it understands, it is called rational. See, then, how these three facets are indicated here. "Thou shalt love thy God with all thy heart"—this is the animal part of a man; "and with all thy soul [*or* life]"[10]—this is the vegetative part of a man, for plants are alive and animate; "and with all thy mind"—this is the rational.[11] So one must love God with all one's soul, that is, one must attend to Him with all the parts and powers of one's soul. "This is the first and great commandment," training us in piety. "The second is like unto it," which exhorts us to do to other men what is just and right. For there are two things which lead to perdition, evil doctrines and a corrupt life. Lest we fall into unholy doctrines, we must love God; so that we do not lead a corrupt life, we must love our neighbor.[12] For he who loves his neighbor fulfills all the commandments, and he who fulfills all the commandments, loves God. So by means of each other these two commandments are welded together and united, containing within themselves all the other commandments. For who is it that loves God and his neighbor, but also steals, or bears grudges, or commits adultery, or murders, or fornicates? This lawyer, then, at the onset came to test Him but then, hearing Christ's answer, he amended his ways, and the Lord praised him, as Mark also says that Jesus looked at him with love, and said, "Thou art not far from the kingdom of heaven."[13]

---

[10] On the complex meaning of the Greek word for "soul", *psychē*, see footnote on p. 30.

[11] Deut. 6:5

[12] Levit. 19:18

[13] Mk. 12:34

41-46. While the Pharisees were gathered together, Jesus asked them, saying, What think ye of Christ? Whose son is He? They say unto Him, The son of David. He saith unto them, How then doth David in spirit call Him Lord, saying, the Lord said unto my Lord, Sit Thou on My right hand, till I make Thine enemies the footstool of Thy feet? If David then call Him Lord, how is He his son? And no man was able to answer Him a word, neither dared any man from that day forth ask Him any more questions. Since they thought He was a mere man, He overturns their belief and by means of the prophecy of David[14] teaches the truth, that He is also the Lord, proclaiming His own divinity. For when the Pharisees said that the Christ was the son of David, that is, a mere man, He says, How then does David name Him Lord, and he does not simply name Him Lord, but "in spirit", that is, as revealed to him by the grace of the Spirit? He does not say this to deny that He is the son of David, but to show that He is not a mere man, descended only from the Davidic seed. The Lord asks these questions so that if they would answer, "We do not know," they might ask and learn; or if they would answer the truth, that they might believe; or if they could not answer, that they might be put to shame and leave, no longer daring to interrogate Him.

[14] Ps. 109:1

CHAPTER TWENTY-THREE

Concerning the woe of the Pharisees.

1-3. Then spake Jesus to the multitude, and to His disciples, saying, The scribes and the Pharisees sit in Moses' seat: all therefore whatsoever they bid you observe, that observe and do, but do not ye in the manner of their works: for they say, and do not. When He has shut the mouths of the Pharisees and shown them to be incurably diseased, then He speaks about them. He speaks about their life and manner of living, admonishing His listeners not to despise their teachers even if they have a corrupt life. At the same time He shows that He is not in opposition to the law, but rather desires that the law be practiced even though those who teach it are unworthy. For, He says, whatever the teachers say, you must treat as if it had been spoken by Moses, and indeed by God. Then should everything be done that they say, even if it is bad? We would answer, first, that a true teacher would never even dare to exhort someone to do evil. But then, supposing that there were someone encouraging an evil life, we would say that such a man is not from the seat of Moses, nor does he give utterance from the law. The Lord speaks of those sitting in the seat of Moses, that is, those who teach the law. Therefore, one must listen to those who teach something from the divine law, even if they themselves do not practice it.

4-5. For they bind heavy burdens and grievous to be borne, and lay them on men's shoulders; but they themselves will not move them with one of their fingers. But all their works they do for to be seen by men: they make broad their phylacteries, and enlarge the borders of their garments. The Pharisees laid heavy burdens on men, forcing them to fulfill the commandments of the law which were detailed and difficult to observe. Indeed, they weighed them down with more than the commandments of the law by handing down certain traditions that went beyond the law; these traditions they did not move with even one of their fingers, that is, they themselves did not practice them, nor even dare to undertake such burdens. For whenever a teacher not only teaches but practices what he teaches, then he is seen to carry the burden and to labor along with those who are taught. But when he gives me a load to carry, but himself practices nothing, then indeed he weighs me down, showing by what he himself neglects to do that it is impossible to accomplish what he says. The Lord, therefore, is accusing the Pharisees of themselves not wanting to carry the weight of the commandments and to practice them. Not only do they not do anything good, but they pretend that they do good. Even if they had done something good, because they did it for the sake of appearance, any gain they might have derived from it would have fallen through their fingers. So indeed they are worthy of condemnation now, since they do not do good and yet they wish men to think that they do. What things do they practice? "They make broad their phylacteries and enlarge the borders of their garments." What this means is this: in the law it is said, "Thou shalt bind [the words of the law] to thy hand and they shall be immoveable before thine eyes."[1] So the Pharisees would inscribe on two pieces of leather the ten commandments of the law, and they would attach one to their forehead and suspend the other from their right hand. They would make borders on the ends of their garments, consisting of blood-red threads like a fringe. For this, too, they found a text in the law,[2] so that when they saw these things they would not forget the commandments of God. But God did not desire this; rather, to have the phylactery upon the hand meant that one must labor in the commandments, and the blood-red fringe showed that we must be signed with the blood of Christ. But the Pharisees made large phylacteries and fringes, so that those who saw them would think that they were keepers of the law.

6-7. They love the place of honour at feasts, and the chief seats in the synagogues, and salutations in the markets, and to be called of men, Rabbi, Rabbi. Alas! What is He saying? They are condemned even for loving these things. If he who only loves the place of honor is rebuked, what punishment does that man deserve who does everything to satisfy this love? In the very place where they ought to have taught others to be humble, that is, in "the chief seats in the synagogues", there they themselves were corrupted. For they did everything for the sake of glory, and they were not ashamed of doing these things, but wished all the more

[1] Deut. 6:8

[2] Num. 15:38-40

for men to call out to them, "Rabbi, Rabbi", which means "teacher".

8-12. But be not ye called Rabbi: for one is your Teacher, even Christ; and all ye are brethren. And call no man your father upon the earth: for one is your Father, Who is in heaven. Neither be ye called masters, for one is your Master, the Christ. But he that is greatest among you shall be your servant. And whosoever shall exalt himself shall be humbled; and he that shall humble himself shall be exalted. Christ does not prohibit one from being called "teacher", but rather He prohibits the passionate desire to be so called, and the eager pursuit of every possible means to acquire the name. For the dignity of the office of "teacher" belongs chiefly to God alone. In saying "Call no man your father," He is not prohibiting the honor given to parents, since He desires that we should honor our parents and especially our spiritual fathers; rather He is inducing us to acknowledge the true Father, namely, God, for He is chiefly and essentially our Father. Fathers in the flesh are not the authors of procreation, but rather, servants and accessories. Showing them what is to be gained by humility, He says that he who is great among you should be your servant and the least. For he who exalts himself, presuming to be something, shall be humbled and abandoned by God.

13. Woe unto you, scribes and Pharisees, hypocrites! For ye shut up the kingdom of heaven against men: for ye neither go in yourselves, nor allow ye them that are entering to go in. Not only, He says, are you unbelievers who lead a corrupt life, but you teach others not to believe in Me and you corrupt them by your life and example. For the people are apt to become like their rulers, especially if they see them inclined towards evil. See, therefore, that "woe" is the reward of every teacher and ruler whose evil life obstructs others in progress towards good.

14. Woe unto you, scribes and Pharisees, hypocrites! For ye devour widows' houses, and for a pretence make long prayer: therefore ye shall receive the greater damnation. He calls them hypocrites for professing piety and doing nothing worthy of what they profess, but instead, they would make pretence of long prayer and would devour the widows' means. Indeed they were mockers who deceived the simple and like leeches sucked them dry. "Therefore ye shall receive the greater damnation" because you have devoured everything the widows have, when instead you should have provided for them and relieved their poverty. There is yet another reason why their condemnation will be greater: they prayed pretending to do good while they were in fact doing something evil, that is, devouring the widows' means. For he who lures another into harm by pretending to be good deserves the greatest punishment.

15. Woe unto you, scribes and Pharisees, hypocrites! For ye compass sea and land to make one proselyte, and when he is made, ye make him twofold more the son of gehenna than yourselves. Not only, He says, do you corrupt the Jews, but also those who come to the Jewish religion from idolatry. These were called "proselytes". You are eager to convert someone to the Jewish way of life and to circumcision; but when they Judaize, they perish, corrupted by your wickedness. A "son of gehenna" means he who deserves gehenna and stands so close to it by disposition that he is kindled by its flames.

16-22. Woe unto you, ye blind guides, who say, Whosoever shall swear by the temple, it is nothing; but whosoever shall swear by the gold of the temple, he is a debtor. Ye fools and blind: for which is greater, the gold, or the temple that sanctifieth the gold? And, Whosoever shall swear by the altar, it is nothing; but whosoever sweareth by the gift that is upon it, he is a debtor. Ye fools and blind: for which is greater, the gift, or the altar that sanctifieth the gift? Whoso therefore shall swear by the altar, sweareth by it, and by all things thereon. And whoso shall swear by the temple, sweareth by it, and by Him that dwelleth therein. And he that shall swear by heaven, sweareth by the throne of God, and by Him that sitteth thereon. He calls them blind for not wanting to teach what was right, but instead valuing what was of lesser importance, and giving second place to that which was worthy of honor. For they valued the gold in the temple, the images of the Cherubim and the golden urn, more highly than they did the temple itself. Therefore they taught the people that it was of no consequence to swear by the temple, and instead they taught them to swear by the gold which is in the temple. This gold, however, was precious precisely because it was in the temple. And the Pharisees said that the gifts placed on the altar were more valuable than the altar itself. So the Pharisees even taught that if someone swore by the golden vessel, or the ox, or the sheep brought for sacrifice, and then broke his oath, he was sentenced to pay an equal amount. The Pharisees put a higher value on the gift upon the altar because of the profit they derived from sacrifices. But if some one swore by the temple and then broke his oath, he was absolved [and owed nothing, the Pharisees would say], as it was not possible to build [and pay] anything equal to the temple. And so the oath by the temple was considered to be of lesser consequence because of the Pharisees' love of money. Under the Old Covenant, Christ does not permit the gift to be greater than the altar, but for us it is just the opposite: the altar is sanctified by the gifts, for the loaves are changed by divine grace into the very Body of the Lord Himself. Therefore the altar is sanctified by them.

23-24. Woe unto you, scribes and Pharisees, hypocrites! For ye pay tithe of mint and anise and cumin, and have omitted the weightier matters of the law, discernment, mercy, and faith: these ought ye to have done, without neglecting the others. Ye blind guides, which strain at the gnat, and swallow the camel. Again He reproaches them as foolish for disdaining the greater commandments while demanding strict observance of the lesser; nor do they overlook a tenth part of the cumin, but tithe that as well. And if anyone accused the Pharisees of nitpicking, they would cite the law in their defense. It would have been better and more God-pleasing if they had required discernment and mercy and faith from the people. What is discernment? To do nothing unjust or unreasonable, but rather to do everything with good judgement and with reason. Mercy follows immediately upon discernment. For he who does all things with discernment knows to whom one ought to give alms. And faith follows mercy, for he who is merciful and gives alms, has faith that he will lose nothing but will receive everything. Or, in another sense, one must show mercy but also believe in the true God. For there were many pagan Greeks who gave alms, but did not believe in the living God and did not have that faith that follows mercy. Every teacher, then, must tithe his people, that is, require from the ten senses, five bodily and five spiritual, the one tithe consisting of discernment, mercy, and faith. "These ought ye to have done," the Lord said, not to exhort them to tithe the herbs, but so that He not appear to be in opposition to Moses. He calls them blind guides because by priding themselves in their teaching and extensive knowledge, they were of benefit to no one, but rather, they corrupted every one and cast them into the pit of unbelief. He says that they strain the gnat, meaning that they keep close guard over the slightest sin, while they swallow the camel, that is, disregard the great sins.

25-26. Woe unto you, scribes and Pharisees, hypocrites! For ye make clean the outside of the cup and of the platter, but within they are full of extortion and excess. Thou blind Pharisee, cleanse first that which is within the cup and platter, that the outside of them may be clean also. Preserving the traditions of the elders, the Pharisees would wash the cups and the plates in which their food and drink were to be placed. But they drank wine and ate food gained by extortion, so they were all the more polluted. Therefore Christ says, do not obtain wine from injustice and the inside of the cup will be clean. Or, in another sense, He is speaking not of cups and plates, but of the bodily and external condition in contrast to the inner and spiritual. For, He says, you assume a most comely appearance on the outside of the cup, that is, in your external condition, while you are full of filth within, extorting and practicing injustice. But you must cleanse the inside, that is, the soul. For the radiance of a purified soul illumines the outward appearance of a man.

27-28. Woe unto you, scribes and Pharisees, hypocrites! For ye are like unto whited sepulchres, which indeed appear beautiful outward, but are within full of dead men's bones, and of all uncleanness. Even so ye also outwardly appear righteous unto men, but within ye are full of hypocrisy and iniquity. This analogy, too, has the same meaning as that of the preceding. For they were eager to appear comely in their external condition, just like tombs that are whitened with lime and chalk, but within they are full of every uncleanness, and of dead and rotting works.

29-31. Woe unto you, scribes and Pharisees, hypocrites! because ye build the tombs of the prophets and adorn the sepulchres of the righteous, and say, If we had been in the days of our fathers, we would not have been partakers with them in the blood of the prophets. Wherefore ye be witnesses unto yourselves, that ye are the

children of them which killed the prophets. He deplores them, not for building tombs for the prophets, for that is pleasing to God, but for doing these things in pretence, and for passing judgement on their fathers while doing worse things themselves, and exceeding them by far in malice. They lie brazenly when they say, "If we had been in the days of our fathers, we would not have killed the prophets," for they were rabid with desire to kill the Master of the prophets. Therefore Christ says:

32-33. Fill ye up also the measure of your fathers. Ye serpents, ye brood of vipers, how can ye escape the damnation of gehenna? He neither bids them nor impels them towards their plan to kill Him when He says, "Fill ye up also the measure of your fathers." Rather, this is what He means: since you are serpents and the offspring of such fathers, and have been plunged into such malice that you are incurable, in a short time you will be eager to outdo your fathers when you kill Me. For you shall have attained to the ultimate degree of malice when you fulfill and complete the bloodletting which your fathers omitted. Being such, how shall you escape eternal torments?

34. Wherefore, behold, I send unto you prophets, and wise men, and scribes: and some of them ye shall kill and crucify; and some of them shall ye scourge in your synagogues, and persecute them from city to city. He reproves them for saying falsely, "If we had been in the days of our fathers, we would not have killed the prophets." For "Behold," He says, "I send unto you prophets and wise men, and scribes," but you will kill them. He is speaking of the apostles, for the Holy Spirit adorned the apostles with teachings and made them scribes, that is, teachers of the people, and prophets filled with all wisdom. "I send," He says, thus showing His divine authority.

35-36. That upon you may come all the righteous blood shed upon the earth, from the blood of righteous Abel unto the blood of Zachariah son of Baruch, whom ye slew between the temple and the altar. Verily I say unto you, All these things shall come upon this generation. He says that upon the Jews then alive shall come all the blood shed unrighteously. For they shall be punished more severely than their fathers because they did not amend their lives after receiving such examples. For Lamech too was punished more than Cain, although he had not killed a brother, because he did not learn from the example of Cain.[3] All blood, He says, from Abel to Zachariah shall come upon you. It was appropriate that He mentioned Abel, for as Abel was slain out of envy, so Christ too was envied. Which Zachariah is mentioned here? Some say that it is he who is numbered among the twelve prophets; others say that he is the father of the Forerunner. For there is an account handed down to us, according to which Zachariah, when he was high priest, had Mary the Mother of God stand in the temple in the place of the virgins even after she had given birth to Christ. The Jews were vexed at this and killed him for ranking among the virgins a woman who had given birth. But it is nothing to be wondered at if the father of the Forerunner also had a father named Baruch, as did one of the twelve prophets who was called the son of Baruch. For it is likely that just as they shared the same name, so did their fathers.

37-39. O Jerusalem, Jerusalem, thou that killest the prophets, and stonest them which are sent unto thee, how often would I have gathered thy children together, even as a hen gathereth her chicks under her wings, and ye would not! Behold, your house is left unto you desolate. For I say unto you, Ye shall not see Me henceforth, till ye shall say, Blessed is He that cometh in the name of the Lord. Twice He says the name Jerusalem, pitying and calling out to her with compassion. For as a lover vehemently justifies himself to his beloved, intending to punish her for having spurned him, so Christ accuses Jerusalem of being a murderess. And many times He desired to show mercy to her but she did not want it, but trusted in the devil who scattered her and led her away from the truth which unites, and she did not accept the Lord who gathers together. For there is nothing which disbands and scatters us from God so readily as does sin; just as there is nothing which gathers us back to God as readily as does a good conscience. He gave the example of the hen to show His affection. But as you do not want My affection, I leave the temple empty and abandoned. From this let us learn that God inhabits the temples for our sake, but when we have forsaken God, then the temples are abandoned [by God] as well. Therefore "Ye shall not see Me henceforth" until the

[3] Gen. 4:23-24

second coming. But then, willing or not, you will fall prostrate before Him and say, "Blessed is He that cometh." Understand "henceforth" to mean "after the crucifixion" and not at that time at which He was speaking these things. For they saw Him many times after He said this, but after the crucifixion they did not see Him, nor would they see Him until the moment of His second coming.

CHAPTER TWENTY-FOUR

Concerning the day and the hour of the end of the world.

1-2. And Jesus went out, and departed from the temple: and His disciples came to Him to show Him the buildings of the temple. And Jesus said unto them, See ye not all these things? Verily I say unto you, There shall not be left here one stone upon another, that shall not be thrown down. By going out of the temple, Jesus showed that He was departing from the Jews. And as He had just said, "Your house is left unto you desolate [i.e. abandoned]," so here indeed He accomplishes it. To the disciples He foretells the destruction of the temple, for they were thinking of earthly things and were moved by the beauty of the buildings and so they pointed them out to Christ, as if saying to Him, "Look how beautiful is the house Thou leavest desolate." He draws them away from attachment to earthly things and escorts them towards the heavenly Jerusalem by saying, "There shall not be left here one stone upon another." He said this in vivid language, to portray the utter destruction of the edifice.

3. And as He sat upon the Mount of Olives, the disciples came unto Him privately, saying, Tell us, when shall these things be? And what shall be the sign of Thy coming, and of the end of the world? They come to Him privately to ask Him about matters of great importance. They ask Him two questions. First, "When shall these things be?" that is, the destruction of the temple and the captivity of Jerusalem. Second, "What shall be the sign of Thy coming?"

4-5. And Jesus answered and said unto them, Take heed that no man deceive you. For many shall come in My name, saying, I am Christ; and shall deceive many. Many, He says, will come declaring themselves to be Christs. For Dositheus the Samaritan said, "I am that prophet foretold by Moses;"[1] and Simon the Samaritan called himself

---

[1] Dt. 18:18

the great power of God.[2]

6-8. And ye shall hear of wars and rumours of wars: see that ye be not troubled: for all these things must come to pass, but the end is not yet. For nation shall rise against nation, and kingdom against kingdom: and there shall be famines, and pestilences, and earthquakes, in divers places. All these are the beginning of the pangs of travail. He is speaking of the wars conducted by the Romans in Jerusalem. Not only does He say that there will be wars, but famines and plagues as well, showing that the wrath directed against the Jews is sent by God. For while it can be said that wars are caused by the violence of men, famines and plagues have no other cause than God. Then He says, lest they think that the world will come to an end before they have preached the Gospel, "Be not troubled, the end is not yet." For the destruction of Jerusalem and the end of the whole world will not be at the same time. But "nation shall rise against nation, and kingdom against kingdom," He says, on account of the calamities soon to befall the Jews. And these calamities are the beginning of the pangs of labor; for just as the expectant mother goes into labor but does not give birth yet, so too this present age will first suffer turmoil and wars and then give birth to the things that shall be.

9-13. Then shall they deliver you up to be afflicted, and shall kill you: and ye shall be hated by all nations for My name's sake. And then shall many fall into the snare, and shall betray one another, and shall hate one another. And many false prophets shall rise, and shall deceive many. And because iniquity shall abound, the love of many shall grow cold. But he that shall patiently endure unto the end, the same shall be saved. He foretells the evils that will occur, strengthening His disciples by speaking of these things beforehand. It is often the unexpected that strikes terror and disarray, so He mitigates their fear beforehand by speaking in advance of the terrible events that will be: the spite, the enmity, the snares, and the false prophets who are the forerunners of the Antichrist, deceiving many who will then hurl themselves headlong into every type of iniquity. Because of the burgeoning of

---

[2] Simon Magus. Acts 8:9 ff.

iniquity stemming from the deceit of the Antichrist, men will become so savage that not even towards those closest to them will they preserve the milk of human kindness, but will betray each other. But he that endures patiently until the end, steadfastly withstanding and not giving in to the assaults brought upon him, he it is who will be saved as the proven and tested soldier.

14. And this Gospel of the kingdom shall be preached in all the world for a witness unto all nations; and then shall the end come. Take courage, you will not be hindered from preaching. For the Gospel will be preached to all the nations as a witness, that is, as a reproof, a condemnation of those who do not believe, and then the end will come, not of the world, but of Jerusalem. For prior to the taking of Jerusalem, the Gospel was already preached [as a witness to all the nations], for St. Paul, in writing to the Colossians, speaks of "the Gospel which was preached to every creature under heaven."[3] That Christ is speaking of the end of Jerusalem is clear from what follows, for He says:

15. When ye therefore shall see the abomination of desolation, spoken of by Daniel the prophet, standing in the holy place, (whoso readeth, let him understand.) The "abomination of desolation"[4] means the monument of the city's captor which he set up in the inner sanctuary of the temple. "Of desolation", because the city had been ravaged; "abomination", because statues and images of men were called "abominations" by the Jews, who hated idolatry.

16-18. Then let them which be in Judea flee into the mountains: let him who is on the housetop not come down to take any thing out of his house: neither let him who is in the field return back to take his clothes. To suggest the utter inevitability of the calamities, He says that one must flee without turning back, and without taking any thought for what is in the houses, neither clothing nor any other possessions. Some say that the "abomination of desolation" means the Antichrist who will

---

[3] Col. 1:23

[4] Daniel 9:27, in the Septuagint, reads: "And on the temple shall be the abomination of desolations."

come at the time of the desolation of the world and the destruction of the churches and will sit in the temple. They also interpret these things as follows: he who is on the housetop, that is, he who has attained the heights of the virtues, let him not come down from that height in to order to take with him the things of the body. For the house of the soul is the body. But he must also depart from the field, that is, from earthly things, for the field is earthly life. Neither must we return to take our clothing, which is the former wickedness which we have put off.

19. And woe unto them that are with child, and to them that give suck in those days! Those who are with child will not be able to flee, weighed down as they are by the burden of their womb. Those who give suck, because of their compassion for their children, will not be able to leave them, nor to carry them and survive together, and so they will not escape the wrath that will be. Christ is also implying the eating of children, for Josephus speaks of a woman who, on account of the starvation during the siege, cooked her child and ate it.[5]

20. But pray ye that your flight be not in the winter, neither on the sabbath day. He addressees these words to the Jews in the person of the apostles; for the apostles would have already departed from Jerusalem by the time that flight would be necessary. To the Jews, then, He says to pray that their flight not be in winter when they would not be able to flee on account of the severity of the weather; and that it would not be on the sabbath day when they rested according to the law and would not dare to flee. But you, O reader, understand it also in this manner: we must pray that our flight from this life, that is, our end, not be on the sabbath during idleness from good deeds, nor in winter, when no good fruit is brought forth, but rather in tranquility of soul, free from all disturbance.

21-22. For then shall be great tribulation, such as was not since the beginning of the world to this time, no, nor ever shall be. And except those days should be shortened, there should no flesh be saved: but for the elect's sake those days shall be shortened. There was at that time [of the capture of Jerusalem] unendurable tribulation. For the Roman

---

[5] Josephus, *Jewish Wars*, Bk. VI, Ch. III, 4. cf. Deut. 28:53-57.

soldiers were commanded to spare no one; but God, for the sake of those who would believe or who had already believed, did not allow them to be completely destroyed, but curtailed both the tribulations and the war. For if war had continued any longer, everyone within would have perished of starvation. Some understand these words to refer to the days of the Antichrist; but they are not concerning the Antichrist, but the capture of Jerusalem. That which concerns the Antichrist begins from this point. Listen, then:

23-25. Then if any man shall say unto you, Lo, here is Christ, or there; believe it not. For there shall arise false christs, and false prophets, and shall show great signs and wonders; insomuch that, if it were possible, they shall deceive the very elect. Behold, I have told you beforehand. Since the disciples had brought two questions to Him, one concerning the captivity of Jerusalem, and the other, the Lord's second coming, having already spoken of the captivity of Jerusalem, here He begins to speak of His own coming, and of the end of the world. When He says, "Then if any man shall say unto you," "then" does not mean immediately after the capture of Jerusalem, but rather at that time when this shall occur. So it means, "Then," that is, when the Antichrist is about to come, there will be many false christs and false prophets who, by means of the apparitions of demons who, in order to deceive, will play tricks with the eyes of those who see the apparitions. So that if the righteous were not sober minded, even they would be deceived. But, behold, I have foretold these things to you; you have no excuse, for it is within your power not to be deceived.

26-28. Wherefore if they shall say unto you, Behold, he is in the desert; go not forth: behold, he is in the secret chambers; believe it not. For as the lightning cometh out of the east, and shineth even unto the west; so shall also the coming of the Son of Man be. For wheresoever the corpse is, there will the eagles be gathered together. If the deceivers should come and say, "Christ has come, but He is hiding in the desert, or in a house within its inner chambers," do not be deceived. For the coming of Christ needs no one to point it out, but it will be utterly clear to all, like the lightning. For just as the lightning is sudden and seen by all, so too will the Lord's coming be visible to everyone on earth. It will not be as in the first coming when He went about from place to place, but at the second coming He will appear in a twinkling of an eye. And as the eagles, that is, the vultures, swiftly converge on a corpse, so too all the saints, who soar in the heights, will come where Christ will be and they will be snatched up into the clouds as the eagles. Certainly the corpse is Christ Who died for us and lay as a corpse. As St. Symeon also says, "Behold, this Child is laid out for the fall and resurrection of many in Israel."[6]

29. Immediately after the tribulation of those days shall the sun be darkened, and the moon shall not give her light, and the stars shall fall from heaven, and the powers of the heavens shall be shaken. He says: after the coming of the Antichrist who will be swiftly destroyed, (for this is the meaning of "immediately"), "the sun shall be darkened," instead of being blackened; not disappearing, but being overwhelmed by the light of Christ's appearance, and so too will the stars and the moon. For what need is there for sensory light when the Sun of Righteousness has appeared and night is no more? But the powers of the heavens shall also be shaken, that is, the angelic hosts will be astonished and will tremble seeing creation changed, and all mankind from Adam until now about to give an account.

30. And then shall appear the sign of the Son of Man in heaven: and then shall all the tribes of the earth mourn, and they shall see the Son of Man coming in the clouds of heaven with power and great glory. The Cross will then be seen in heaven shining more brightly than the sun as a reproof to the Jews, for when the Lord comes He will display the Cross as the strongest evidence against the Jews, like one who shows the stone with which he was struck. He calls the Cross a sign, as a trophy and royal ensign. Then all the tribes of the land of Judea will mourn and bewail their own unbelief, and all those who care for earthly things will mourn, though they be Christians. For those who are attached to earthly things might also be called "the tribes of the earth". Although the Lord comes accompanied by the Cross, He also comes "with power and great glory".

---

[6] Lk. 2:34

31. And He shall send His angels with a great sound of a trumpet, and they shall gather together His elect from the four winds, from one end of heaven to the other. He will send the angels to gather together the saints and those risen from the dead, so that they can meet Him in the clouds. He also honors them by calling them with angels. And if Paul says that they will be caught up in the clouds,[7] this is not contradictory. For when they have been gathered together by the angels, the clouds will snatch them up. There will be the trumpet, to cause the greater consternation.

32-33. Now learn a parable of the fig tree; when its branch is yet tender, and putteth forth leaves, ye know that summer is nigh: so likewise ye, when ye shall see all these things, know that it is near, even at the doors. When all these things occur, He says, the time is not far off from the end and My coming. ''Summer'' means the age to come and serenity after the winter storm, but only for the righteous; for sinners, it is instead storm and tumult. For when you see, He says, the branches and leaves of the fig tree, you expect summer; so too, when you see those signs of which I spoke, the sun and the moon being altered, expect My coming.

34-35. Verily I say unto you, This generation shall not pass away, till all these things be fulfilled. Heaven and earth shall pass away, but My words shall not pass away. ''Generation'' here means, not that which was then, but the generation of all believers. It is as if He were saying, ''The generation of believers shall not pass away till all these things have occurred.'' But when you hear of famines and plagues, do not understand that the generation of believers shall perish from these evil things, but it will remain, and no terrible thing will prevail over it. Some have understood ''all these things'' to refer only to the captivity of Jerusalem, and not to the second coming as well, and so they have interpreted it as follows: ''This generation shall not pass away,'' that is, the generation of you apostles shall see the calamities that will befall Jerusalem. Confirming what has been said, He says that it would be easier for heaven and earth, those fixed and immoveable elements, to be

---

[7] I Thess. 4:17

destroyed than for My words to be proven false.

36. But of that day and hour knoweth no man, no, not the angels of the heavens, but My Father only. Here He teaches the disciples not to seek to know things that exceed human knowledge. By saying "not the angels", He restrains them from seeking to learn now that which even the angels do not know. By saying "My Father only", He also prevents them from seeking to learn thereafter. For if He had said, "I know, but I do not wish to tell you," they would have been grieved as though He had disdained them. But now by saying, "Not even the Son knows, but My Father only," He prevents them from asking. It is like a father who will often hold something in his hands and when his children ask for it and he does not want to give it, he hides it and says, "I do not have what you are asking for," and so the children stop crying for it. So too the Lord says, "Even I do not know, but My Father only," in order to put an end to the desire of the apostles to know the day and the hour. That He Himself does know that day and hour is clear from many other things. All that the Father has, belongs to the Son. As the Father has knowledge of the hour, so the Son surely has the same knowledge. It is even more clear from this: how is it possible for the Son to be ignorant of the day, when He knows the things that precede the day, that is, the signs that He has just foretold? For he who has lead another into the vestibule surely knows where the door is as well. But it was for their good that Christ did not open it. For it is never to our benefit to know the time of the end, lest we become lazy. Not knowing, we remain alert.

37-39. But as the days of Noah were, so shall also the coming of the Son of Man be. For as in the days that were before the flood they were eating and drinking, marrying and giving in marriage, until the day that Noah entered into the ark, and they knew not until the flood came and took them all away; so shall also the coming of the Son of Man be. As confirmation of the truth of His words, He draws upon the events that occurred at the time of Noah. Just as then there were those who scoffed at the construction of the ark until the disaster came upon them and destroyed them all; so now there are those who scoff at these words concerning the end. But, Christ says, the destruction will come upon them suddenly. He shows that when the Antichrist comes, men will be giving themselves over to pleasure, reclining at weddings and feasts in a most arrogant manner, just as the giants did in the time of Noah.[8]

40-41. Then shall two be in the field; the one shall be taken, and the other left. Two women shall be grinding at the mill; the one shall be taken, and the other left. Then, He says, when everyone is heedless and engaged in their own work, "the one shall be taken," that is, the righteous man shall be taken to meet the Lord in the air, while the other, that is to say, the sinner, is left behind. Even from among those who are servants and laborers who grind at the mill, the worthy are taken while the unworthy are left. From this we learn that no one, whether servant or woman, is hindered from acquiring virtue.

42-44. Watch therefore: for ye know not what hour your Lord doth come. But know this, that if the master of the house had known in what watch the thief would come, he would have watched, and would not have suffered his house to be broken into. Therefore be ye also ready: for in such an hour as ye think not, the Son of Man cometh. He bids us to keep vigil and to be ready, that is, to have stored up beforehand deeds of virtue so that when the Lord comes asking for the things that He wants, we will have them to give. See how He did not say, "I know not what hour the thief cometh," but "ye know not". A "thief" is what He names the end of the world as well as the death of each person. He also implies here that His coming will be in the night. Just as the thief comes unnoticed, so will My coming be; therefore, be not indolent, but sober and vigilant. For if we knew when our end would be, we would strive to please God only on that day. But since we do not know, we are always vigilant in the deeds of virtue.

45-47. Who then is a faithful and wise servant, whom his lord hath made ruler over his household, to give them food in due season? Blessed is that servant, whom his lord when he cometh shall find so doing. Verily I say unto you, That he shall make him ruler over all his goods. The Lord is doubtful who that wise and faithful servant will be "whom his lord hath made ruler over his household," to show that such a man is rare and hard to find. Two things are required of every

---

[8] Gen. 6:5

steward: faith and wisdom. For if he is faithful and steals nothing, but lacks wisdom and foolishly squanders the household goods, he is of no use; and if he is wise but yet steals, likewise he is of no use. So whoever shall be found then to have been both faithful and wise will also obtain the things that are more excellent, that is, the kingdom of heaven. For the saints will be the inheritors of all of God's possessions. The faithful and wise servant is also every teacher who gives in due season food proper to each one who is taught by him. Such a one was Paul who at times gave milk to drink [to the young in faith] and at other times spoke wisdom [to the more mature], for he was a faithful servant, though before he had been a blasphemer; and he was also a wise servant understanding the thoughts of the enemy. So too everyone who receives anything from God, whether it be money, authority, or dominion, should administer these things faithfully and wisely, since he will give an account.

48-51. But if that evil servant shall say in his heart, My lord delayeth his coming; and shall begin to smite his fellowservants, and to eat and drink with the drunken; the lord of that servant shall come in a day when he looketh not for him, and in an hour that he is not aware of, and shall cut him asunder, and appoint him his portion with the hypocrites: there shall be weeping and gnashing of teeth. Having spoken of how the faithful servant will be honored, now He tells how the wicked servant will be punished. If anyone entrusted with the stewardship of a gift disdains the judgement that will take place and says, "My lord delayeth," that is, God does not impose swift and immediate punishment, the Lord "shall cut him asunder." And if he considers God's long-suffering nature an opportunity for wickedness and strikes his fellowservants by scandalizing them and shaking their conscience, as happens when those who are ruled see their rulers using for evil purposes what has been entrusted to them, the Lord shall likewise "cut him asunder." If a man, then, does such things, he shall be cut asunder, that is, he will be stripped of his gift, and then it will be seen what sort of man he is, and he will be cast into the darkness. Formerly he was able to deceive by means of his appearance, as are many hierarchs who are thought to be holy because of their rank. But then at the Judgement the grace will be taken from them, and they will be punished as hypocrites, being one thing but appearing another.

CHAPTER TWENTY-FIVE

Concerning the ten virgins.
Concerning those who received the talents.
Concerning the coming of Christ.

1-5. Then shall the kingdom of heaven be likened unto ten virgins, who took their lamps, and went forth to meet the bridegroom. And five of them were wise, and five were foolish. They that were foolish took their lamps, and took no oil with them: but the wise took oil in their vessels with their lamps. While the bridegroom tarried, they all slumbered and slept. This parable is on mercy and almsgiving.[1] In telling the parable the Lord uses the person of virgins to teach those who understand the greatness of the virtue of virginity not to strive to accomplish this one virtue alone and neglect the others. But learn that if you do not give alms, though you may be a virgin, you will be cast out with the fornicators. It is only right that he who lacks compassion and mercy is cast out, even if he is a virgin. For a fornicator is overcome by a tyrannical and physical passion, but he who lacks mercy is overcome only by money. Of the two, the foe of the greedy one is the weaker, and therefore he who remains vanquished by the passion of greed does not find forgiveness. Such a man is foolish for the very reason that he has prevailed against a physical fire storm, but has been overcome by the trivial passion for money. ''Slumber'' here means death, and the tarrying of the bridegroom means that the second coming does not occur immediately.

6-13. And at midnight there was a cry made, Behold, the bridegroom cometh; go ye out to meet him. Then all those virgins arose, and trimmed their lamps. And the foolish said unto the wise, Give us of your oil; for our lamps are gone out. But the wise answered, saying, Not so; lest there be not enough for us and you: but go ye

---

[1] That this parable concerns mercy and almsgiving is more immediately apparent in Greek because the word for ''mercy'', *eleos*, and the word for ''olive oil'', *elaion*, though different words, sound nearly the same. Bl. Theophylact has commented in other contexts on this similarity between the two words. See, for example, Mt. 3:16-17 on p. 37 and Mt. 6:17-18 on p. 59.

rather to them that sell, and buy for yourselves. And while they went to buy, the bridegroom came; and they that were ready went in with him to the marriage: and the door was shut. Afterward came also the other virgins, saying, Lord, Lord, open to us. But he answered and said, Verily I say unto you, I know you not. Watch therefore, for ye know neither the day nor the hour wherein the Son of Man cometh. He says that a cry was made in the middle of the night to show that the Lord comes when least expected, as at midnight when we all have fallen into a deep sleep. He also comes with a cry, for a trumpet will sound at the second coming. The lamps are our souls, and each one's mind is also a lamp; the lamp is lit when one has the oil of the virtues and of almsgiving. The virgins were truly foolish in this regard also, that they went to look for oil when it was not the time for work and business. The wise virgins say, "lest there be not enough for us and you." My neighbor's virtue scarcely suffices for his own defense, and certainly not for me as well, for each one will be deemed righteous by his own deeds and not by those of his neighbor. But the foolish virgins went to "them that sell", that is, to the poor. What He is saying is this: the foolish virgins repent of not having given alms and now for the first time they understand that it was from the poor that we should have obtained oil. This is what He means when He says that they went to buy oil from those that sell, that is, their thoughts went to the poor and they pondered how good a thing is almsgiving, but now the door was shut for them. For there is no time for repentance and deeds after our departure from this life. The Lord therefore says to them, "I know you not." For the merciful God Who loves mankind does not know those who lack mercy, for how could He know those who are alien and dissimilar to Him? Understand this, that every soul possesses a lamp and a light from God, and that all arise to meet the Lord, for all desire to meet and have communion with God. But after God has given light and a lamp, the wise, with their good deeds, add the oil. But the foolish, having let their lamps run out of oil, are shut out, having no good deeds with which to fuel the light in their lamps. For if we do not labor and trade with good deeds, we extinguish the light of God that is in us.

14-19. It is as a man travelling into a far country, who called his own servants, and handed over to them his goods. And unto one he gave five talents, to another two, and to another one; to each one

according to his own strength; and straightway took his journey. Then he that had received the five talents went and traded with the same, and made them another five talents. And likewise he that had received two, he also gained another two. But he that had received one went and dug in the earth, and hid his lord's money. After a long time the lord of those servants cometh, and reckoneth with them. Having said above, "You do not know the day when the Lord will come," He adds this parable as well, showing that He will come suddenly. For like a man about to travel into a far country, so too the Lord has called His own servants and distributed His property among them, some to one, some to another. Christ, Who became man for our sake, is the "man travelling into a far country," in reference either to His ascent into the heavens or to the length of time that He is long-suffering and does not summarily demand works from us, but waits. His servants are those who have been entrusted with the ministry of the Word, such as bishops, priests, and deacons, and who have received spiritual gifts, some greater, some lesser, each one according to his own strength, that is, according to the measure of his faith and purity. For into the vessel which I will offer to God, He places His gift to me. If it is a small vessel, a small gift; if it is a large vessel, a large gift. Immediately he who had received the five talents went and traded with them. See the speed with which he acts, not in the least bit negligent, but immediately trading and doubling what he had received. For whether a man be gifted with speech, wealth, the authority of kingship, or any other power or skill, if he desires to benefit not only himself but others as well, he doubles what has been given to him. But he who buries the talent is he who cares only for his own benefit and not for that of others, and he is condemned. But if you should see an intelligent and skilled man misusing his intelligence in various pursuits, in deceitfulness, and in earthly affairs, you may say that such a man has buried his talent in the earth, that is, in earthly matters. But after a long time he who bestowed the silver talent returns. The silver talent may be in the form of a silver tongue, the gift of eloquence, for the eloquence of God is as silver that is tried by fire. Or, the silver talent may be any gift that makes one brilliant and glorious. He comes and demands a reckoning from those who received.

20-30. And so he that had received five talents came and brought another five talents, saying, Lord, thou deliveredst unto me five

talents: behold, I have gained besides them five talents more. His lord said unto him, Well done, thou good and faithful servant: thou hast been faithful over a few things, I will make thee ruler over many things: enter thou into the joy of thy Lord. He also that had received two talents came and said, Lord, thou deliveredst unto me two talents: behold, I have gained two other talents beside them. His lord said unto him, Well done, good and faithful servant; thou hast been faithful over a few things, I will make thee ruler over many things: enter thou into the joy of thy lord. Then he which had received the one talent came and said, Lord, I knew that thou art a hard man, reaping where thou hast not sown, and gathering where thou hast not strewn; and I was afraid, and went and hid thy talent in the earth: lo, there thou hast that is thine. His lord answered and said unto him, Thou wicked and slothful servant, thou knewest that I reap where I sowed not, and gather where I have not strewn: thou oughtest therefore to have put my money with the bankers, and then at my coming I should have received mine own with increase. Take therefore the talent from him, and give it unto him which hath ten talents. For unto every one that hath shall be given, and he shall have in abundance: but from him that hath not shall be taken away even that which he hath. And cast ye the unprofitable servant into outer darkness: there shall be weeping and gnashing of teeth. Both of those who had worked and traded with the talents given to them are praised equally by the master, each one hearing, "Well done, thou good and faithful servant." "Good" we understand here to mean "loving all mankind" and "without spite", he who imparts his own goodness to his neighbors. Those who have shown themselves to be faithful over a few things are made rulers over many things. But even if we are deemed worthy of gifts in this life, that is nothing in comparison to the good things that are to come. "The joy of the Lord" is the unending gladness which God has, rejoicing in His works, as David says.[2] With such a joy do the saints also rejoice in their works, just as the sinners grieve over their own deeds and regret them. The saints have the Lord as their wealth and they rejoice in Him. See that he who received the five talents and he who received two were deemed worthy of the same good things. Though

---

[2] Ps. 103:31

a man may have received but a few things, if he is a good steward even of his small gift, he will enjoy the same honor as he who was deemed worthy of, and accomplished, great things. For each one, according to what he has received, is seen to be perfect to the degree that he accomplishes what he has been given to do. Such are the good servants; but the wicked and slothful servant justifies himself differently, in a manner befitting to him. For he calls his master "hard", as many today call their teachers "hard" or "exacting". It is indeed exacting to look for obedience from men, for God did not create obedience within man, nor did He sow in him an obedient disposition, [but instead God gave man free will]. This is what the unprofitable servant means when he says, "You reap where you have not sown", that is, You require an obedient disposition from all men, although You have implanted in no man an obedient disposition. When the servant says that the master is hard, he condemns himself. For the servant ought all the more to have been diligent knowing that his master was hard and severe. For if the master required this of others, so too would the master require this of him. And you, O unprofitable servant, ought also to have multiplied what you had received and made disciples from whom I, the Master, could demand what is due. Christ calls disciples "bankers", for both exactly account for that which has been delivered to them. What is the increase which He requires of the disciples? The showing of works transacted. For the disciple who receives the word from the teacher, must keep the word and give it back in its entirety; but the disciple also adds to it the interest, which is the doing of good. So God takes the gift away from that wicked and slothful servant. He who has received a gift by which to benefit others, and does not so use it, forfeits the gift itself. Do you see that he who applies the greater diligence draws to himself the greater gift? To him who has the greater diligence, more grace will be given and in abundance. But from him who is not diligent, even the gift which he thinks he has will be taken away. For he who is not diligent and does not work and trade with what he has received, does not have the gift, but only appears to have it. For he has blotted it out by his neglect.

31-33. When the Son of Man shall come in His glory, and all the holy angels with Him, then shall He sit upon the throne of His glory: and before Him shall be gathered all nations: and He shall separate them one from another, as a shepherd divideth his sheep from the

goats: and He shall set the sheep on His right hand, but the goats on the left. Since the first coming of the Lord was not with glory but with dishonor and indignity, He says, ''When He shall come in His glory.'' For at the second coming He will come with glory, escorted by angels. First He will divide the saints from the sinners, delivering them from tribulations, and set them on His right, and then speak to them. He calls the saints ''sheep'' on account of their gentleness, and because they yield fruit and useful things for us, as do sheep, providing wool, which is divine and spiritual protection, and milk, which is the sustenance that is needed. The goats are the sinners, for they walk along the precipices and are unruly and fruitless.

34-40. Then shall the King say unto them on His right hand, Come, ye blessed of My Father, inherit the kingdom prepared for you from the foundation of the world: for I was hungry, and ye fed Me: I was thirsty, and ye gave Me drink: I was a stranger, and ye took Me in: naked, and ye clothed Me: I was sick, and ye visited Me: I was in prison, and ye came unto Me. Then shall the righteous answer Him, saying, Lord, when saw we Thee hungry, and fed thee? or thirsty, and gave Thee drink? When saw we Thee a stranger, and took Thee in? or naked, and clothed Thee? Or when saw we Thee sick, or in prison, and came unto Thee? And the King shall answer and say unto them, Verily I say unto you, Inasmuch as ye have done it unto one of the least of these My brethren, ye have done it unto Me. He does not give honor or punishment until He has first judged. For He loves mankind and teaches us to do the same as well, not to punish until we have made a careful examination. In this way those who are punished after the judgement will have no cause for complaint. He calls the saints ''blessed'' as they have been accepted by the Father. He considers them to be inheritors of the kingdom to show that God makes them participants in His own glory as His sons. For He did not say, ''receive'', but rather ''inherit'' as a man would his father's estate. By ''the least brethren'' He means either His own disciples or, simply, all the poor. For every poor man is Christ's brother for the very reason that Christ, too, spent His life in poverty. See also God's righteousness, how He acclaims the saints; and see the good disposition of their mind, how they deny, with befitting modesty, that they have cared for Him. But the Lord accepts as for Himself the things that were done for the poor.

41-46. Then shall He say also unto them on the left hand, Depart from Me, ye cursed, into everlasting fire, prepared for the devil and his angels: for I was hungry, and ye gave Me nothing to eat: I was thirsty, and ye gave Me no drink: I was a stranger, and ye took Me not in: naked, and ye clothed Me not: sick, or in prison, and ye visited Me not. Then shall they also answer Him, saying, Lord, when saw we Thee hungry, or thirsty, or a stranger, or naked, or sick, or in prison, and did not minister unto Thee? Then shall He answer them, saying, Verily I say unto you, Inasmuch as ye did it not to one of the least of these, ye did it not to Me. And these shall go away into everlasting punishment: but the righteous into life eternal. He sends those on the left into the fire which had been prepared for the devil. For as the demons are without compassion and are cruelly and maliciously disposed towards us, it is fitting that they who are of like mind with them, and who have been cursed by their own deeds, should merit the same punishment. See that God did not prepare the fire for men, nor did He make hell for us, but for the devil; but I make myself liable to hell. Tremble, then, O man, and understand from this that these men were not punished as fornicators, or robbers, or perpetrators of any other vice, but for not having done good. For indeed, if you consider things well, the robber is he who has much and does not give alms, even if he does no obvious injury. For whatever he has in excess of his needs, he has stolen from those who are in need and who have not received anything from him. For if he had shared these things with them, they would not be in need. Now that he has locked these things up and kept them for himself, for this very reason they are in need. So he who does not give alms is a robber, doing injustice to all those whom he could have helped but did not, and for this reason he and those like him shall go away into eternal punishment which never ends; but the righteous shall enter into eternal life. For just as the saints have unceasing joy, so too the unjust have unceasing punishment, despite the gibberish of Origen who says that there is an end to hell and that sinners will not be punished for ever, but that there will be a time when they enter the place of the righteous because they have been purified by suffering in hell.[3] Origen is clearly refuted

[3] Origen's false teaching of *apokatastasis*, the restoration of all things, was condemned as a heresy at the Fifth Ecumenical Council held at Constantinople in 553 A.D.

here, both when the Lord speaks of "everlasting punishment", that is, never ending, and when He likens the righteous to sheep and the sinners to goats. For just as a goat can never become a sheep, neither can a sinner ever be cleansed and become righteous after the Judgement. "Outer darkness" [mentioned in the preceding parable of the talents] is that which is furthest from the light of God and for that reason renders the punishment more harsh. There is another reason that could be mentioned, and that is that the sinner is in darkness even in this life, as he has fallen away from the Sun of Righteousness, but as there is still hope of conversion, this is not yet the "outer" darkness. But when he has died and an examination has been made of the things he has done, then the outer darkness in its turn receives him. For there is no longer any hope of conversion, but he undergoes a complete deprivation of the good things of God. While he is here in this life he enjoys to some degree the good things of God, I mean, the tangible things of creation, and he believes that he is in some manner a servant of God, living out his life in God's house, which is this creation, being fed by Him and provided with the necessities of life. But then he will be altogether cut off from God, having no share at all in the good things of God. This is that darkness which is called "outer" by comparison to the darkness here, which is not "outer" because the sinner is not yet completely cut off from this time onward. You, then, O reader, flee from this absence of compassion, and practice almsgiving, both tangible and spiritual. Feed Christ Who hungers for our salvation. If you give food and drink to him who hungers and thirsts for teaching, you have given food and drink to Christ. For within the Christian there is Christ, and faith is nourished and increased by teaching. If you should see someone who has become a stranger to his heavenly fatherland, take him in with you. While you yourself are entering into the heavens, lead him in as well, lest while you preach to others, you yourself be rejected. If a man should cast off the garment of incorruption which he had at his baptism, so that he is naked, clothe him; and if one should be infirm in faith, as Paul says, help him; and visit him who is shut up in the dark prison of this body and give him counsel which is as a light to him. Perform, then, all of these six types of love, both bodily and also spiritually, for we consist of both soul and body, and these acts of love are to be accomplished by both.

CHAPTER TWENTY-SIX

Concerning the Lord's anointing with myrrh.
Concerning the Pascha.
Concerning the Mystical Supper.
Concerning the betrayal of Christ.
Concerning Peter's denial.

1-2. And it came to pass, when Jesus had finished all these sayings, He said unto His disciples, Ye know that after two days it is the Pascha,[1] and the Son of Man is betrayed to be crucified. After speaking of the kingdom and of retribution, it was opportune that He should then speak also concerning His own Passion, all but saying, "And those who crucify Me shall merit the fire."

3-5. Then assembled together the high priests, and the scribes, and the elders of the people, at the palace of the high priest, who was called Caiaphas, and took counsel together that they might take Jesus by guile, and kill Him. But they said, Not on the feast, lest there be an uproar among the people. The law commanded that there be one high priest for life, but they, contrary to the law, had then the practice of making a new high priest each year, so that there were many.[2] So they approached the high priest of that year to deliberate a murder with him whose duty it was to punish murderers. "The high priests" are those who had already fulfilled their year of service. Intending to commit this unholy murder, they were fearful, not of God, but of the multitude. For the high priests were afraid that if they murdered Jesus on the feast, the multitude would rise up in His defense, or that the people would refrain from offering the prescribed sacrifices on account of the murder, and so

[1] "Pascha" is the Greek transliteration of the Hebrew word *Pesach* meaning "Passover". It denotes not only the passage of the children of Israel through the Red Sea, and the feast commemorating this event, but also the slain lamb and the accompanying meal ordained by God to be eaten at this feast. Many church fathers have noted the providential similarity between the word *pascha* and the Greek word *paschein*, meaning "to suffer", drawing attention to the intimate connection between "Pascha" and the Lord's Passion.

[2] See Eusebius, *The History of the Church*, Bk. 1, 10.

the high priests would lose the profit they gained from the sacrifices. Perhaps the high priests also feared that if He were murdered on the feast, His death would become all the more renowned and noteworthy; for they wished to erase all memory of Him. So in this manner they plotted before the feast to murder Him immediately after the feast. But He allows them to arrest Him at the time of Pascha, thus showing that He goes to His Passion not when they wished, but rather when He so desired. So that when the figurative Pascha took place, then it was that the true Pascha occurred.[3] We can also understand from this the degree of their bloodthirstiness. For though they had not wished to slay Jesus on the feast, when they found the betrayer they did slay Jesus at that very time, forgetting even the multitude in their eagerness to accomplish their will.

6-7. Now when Jesus was in Bethany, in the house of Simon the leper, there came unto Him a woman having an alabaster box of very precious myrrh, and poured it on His head, as He sat at table. Some say that there are three women who anointed the Lord, of whom the four evangelists make mention.[4] Others say that there are two, the one mentioned by John, who is Mary the sister of Lazarus, and the one mentioned here by Matthew, who is the same one mentioned by Luke and Mark. Some say that this Simon the leper is the father of Lazarus, and that Christ cleansed him of leprosy and then ate dinner with him. Some also say that when the Lord told His disciples to go to a certain man who would show them an upper room furnished,[5] that He sent them to this man. And of course the man welcomed the Lord to celebrate the Pascha there. So when the woman saw the leper who had been cleansed, she dared to believe that she too would obtain remission of sins and cleansing of spiritual leprosy. She confessed great faith by unstintingly pouring out such precious myrrh. She poured it out on His head, honoring the chiefest

---

[3] The *Pascha*, or Passover, celebrated by the Jews of old Israel is described in Exodus 12. It was a foreshadowing of the true Pascha now celebrated by Christians, the new Israel, with words like these:

"It is the Day of Resurrection, let us be radiant, O ye people; Pascha, the Lord's Pascha: for from death to life, and from earth to heaven, Christ God hath brought us, as we sing the hymn of victory." (Irmos of the First Ode of the Paschal Canon)

[4] Mk. 14:3-9, Jn. 12:1-8, Lk. 7:36-38.

[5] See Lk. 22:10-12.

part. And you also, O reader, if you suffer from the spiritual and pharisaical leprosy of arrogance which cuts us off from God, accept Jesus into your house and anoint Him with the myrrh of the virtues. For you are able to procure myrrh for Jesus Who has cleansed you of your leprosy, and to pour it over His head. What is the head of Christ if not His divinity to which we offer the fragrance of the virtues? For David says, "Let my prayer be set forth as incense before Thee, O Lord."[6] Offer, then, fragrance of myrrh, intricately blended of many virtues, to Christ's divinity. For if you teach that Christ is not merely a man, but also God, then you have made fragrant His head, that is, His divinity, with your words of theology.

8-11. But when His disciples saw it, they were indignant, saying, To what purpose is this waste? For this myrrh might have been sold for much, and given to the poor. When Jesus understood it, He said unto them, Why trouble ye the woman? For she hath wrought a good work upon Me. For ye have the poor always with you; but Me ye have not always. Since the disciples had heard much about almsgiving and had given it much consideration, they found fault with the woman, thinking that God desired mercy towards others more than honor for Himself. But He rebukes the disciples for their unwarranted criticism of the woman. For one should not expect exalted things from those who have only recently approached Christ, and especially from those whose emotions are unrestrained, but one should accept even their measure of faith. For whenever someone wants to offer a gift to God, do not scorn him, or cut him off in his eagerness by sending him away to give to the poor, but let him fulfill his offering. But if he should ask your advice as to whether he should give to the poor or make an offering to God, advise him to give to the poor. However, if he has already made the offering to God, there is no reason to scorn him, for one should prefer honor rendered to God above everything else, even almsgiving itself. Nor should you think that because Christ in His love for mankind accepts mercy shown to others as something offered to Himself, that we should overlook God and only practice almsgiving. For if this were so, we ought then to steal from the temples and use what is stolen for almsgiving. But

---

[6] Ps. 140:2

it is not so; and that you may understand that it is not the same thing to show mercy to the poor and to honor Christ Himself and to serve Him, listen: "For ye have the poor always with you; but Me ye have not always." Do you see, then, that it is one thing to serve Christ and another thing to show mercy to the poor, even though Christ in His love for mankind accepts for Himself the things that are done for the poor?

12-13. For in that she hath poured this myrrh on My Body, she did it for My burial. Verily I say unto you, Wheresoever this Gospel shall be preached in the whole world, there shall also this, that this woman hath done, be told for a memorial of her. He teaches us that the woman did this by some divine inspiration, prefiguring His death and the burial of His Body. For the Lord would not have allowed Himself to be anointed with myrrh if it did not reveal a mystery. Being God, He foretold what would be, that the deed which the woman did would be told everywhere in praise of her. Behold God's love for mankind, how He rewards the woman with a great gift; for He causes her memorial to be kept universally, for as long as His Gospel endures. How did the myrrh symbolize His burial? It was the practice among the Jews to prepare bodies for burial by anointing them with myrrh, as the Egyptians did, to prevent decay and foul odor. He is saying, "By pouring the myrrh the woman shows that My Body will be buried." He said all these things to shame and reprove Judas by whom He would be betrayed and handed over for burial. Understand it also in a spiritual sense: the leper is the Gentile people, the sinful woman is the congregation and the Church from among the Gentiles, who poured out myrrh, that is, faith, on the head of Christ, which is His divinity. For everyone who believes that Christ is God pours out myrrh on the head of Christ. But Judas, who rebuked the woman, as John says,[7] is a symbol of the Jews who still to this day murmur against the Church.

14-16. Then went one of the twelve, called Judas Iscariot, unto the high priests, and said unto them, What will ye give me, and I will hand Him over to you? And they covenanted with him for thirty pieces of silver. And from that time he sought an opportunity to

---

[7] Jn. 12:4-6

betray Him. When the woman who was a stranger and a harlot had shown Jesus such honor, then it was that His own disciple departed to betray Him. For it was not without meaning that the evangelist says, "Then went...," but in order to show the shamelessness of Judas. He adds the name "Iscariot" to better identify him. For there was another Judas who was also called Lebbaeus.[8] The betrayer, however, was from a certain village named Iscara. "They covenanted with him for thirty pieces of silver," that is, they agreed, they determined an amount to give, and not as many think, that they weighed out and paid the money. "He sought an opportunity" to betray Him to them when He was alone, for they feared the multitude, and for this reason they paid Judas to inform them when Jesus would be alone.

17-19. Now the first day of the feast of unleavened bread the disciples came to Jesus, saying unto Him, Where wilt Thou that we prepare for Thee to eat the Pascha? And He said, Go into the city to such a man, and say unto him, The Master saith, My time is at hand; I will keep the Pascha at thy house with My disciples. And the disciples did as Jesus had appointed them; and they made ready the Pascha. He says, "The first day of the feast of the unleavened bread," meaning "the day before the feast of the unleavened bread", as we would say it. They intended to eat the Pascha on Friday evening, which was called "the feast of the unleavened bread". The Lord, therefore, sends the disciples on Thursday, which the evangelist calls "the first day of the feast of the unleavened bread", being the day before the Friday on the evening of which they would eat the unleavened bread. The disciples then approach and ask, "Where wilt Thou that we prepare for Thee to eat the Pascha?" For neither they, nor He, had their own house. He sends them to a man whom they did not know and who did not know them, just as He had done before entering Jerusalem when He sent them to find the ass, showing them that He is able by His words alone to persuade even those who do not know Him at all to accept Him. He wanted to keep the Pascha, lest He appear opposed to the law. He calls His slaying His "time", so that we may learn that He was not slain unknowingly or unwillingly. And to the words, "I will keep the Pascha at thy house", He

[8] See Mt. 10:3 and Lk. 6:16.

adds "with My disciples", so that there would be sufficient preparation for the large number of those who intended to eat.

20-22. Now when the even was come, He sat down with the twelve. And as they did eat, He said, Verily I say unto you, that one of you shall betray Me. And they were exceeding sorrowful, and began every one of them to say unto Him, Lord, is it I? From this some believe that the Lord did not eat the Pascha that year. For they say that only while standing was the Paschal lamb to be eaten. Yet Christ sat down; hence it could not have been the Pascha which He ate. But we might say that first He ate the Pascha standing, and then He sat down and gave them His own Mystery and Sacrament.[9] For having first kept the Pascha in type, He then kept it in truth. He foretells the things that Judas would do, in order to correct him by making him ashamed of what he planned to do while they ate together, and by filling him with dread and awe as he realized that he was about to betray God Who knows the hearts of men. The other disciples were agonized, for though the conscience of each was clear, they put more trust in Christ than in themselves since He knew their hearts better than they did.

23-25. And He answered and said, He that dippeth his hand with Me in the dish, the same shall betray Me. The Son of Man goeth as it is written of Him: but woe unto that man by whom the Son of Man is betrayed! It had been good for that man if he had not been born. Then Judas, who betrayed Him, answered and said, Master, is it I? He said unto him, Thou hast said. Jesus openly reproves the betrayer since he did not amend his ways when he was reproved secretly. This is why He reveals him by saying, "He that dippeth his hand with Me," so that even now he might amend his ways. But Judas was shameless and dipped his hand into Christ's dish. Then Christ said, "The Son of Man goeth as it is written of Him," that is, even though it is preordained that Christ suffer for the salvation of the world, Judas of course is not to be honored for the part he played, but rather, woe to him! For he did not do

[9] As Bl. Theophylact himself acknowledges, other Orthodox fathers and writers are not in agreement with him as to when, or indeed whether, the Lord ate the old Pascha, that is, the Passover meal, that year. For an account of the different viewpoints, see *Eustratios Argenti*, Timothy [now, Bishop Kallistos] Ware, Clarendon Press, Oxford, 1964, pp. 112-121.

this deed in cooperation with God's will; instead he did it out of his own malice. For if you consider well, Christ [in His human nature] did not desire beforehand to be crucified; He shows this when He prays that the cup might be taken from Him. But since Christ [in His divine nature] knew from before all ages that because of the malice of the enemy there was no other way for man to be saved, what He had not willed beforehand became His will. By saying that it would have been better if that man had not been born, He shows that it is better not to exist than to exist in sins. Observe also the word "goeth". It shows that His dying will not be death, but instead a departure to another place.

26. And as they were eating, Jesus took bread, and gave thanks, and broke it, and gave it to the disciples, and said, Take, eat; this is My Body. Matthew added the words "as they were eating", to reveal the cruelty of Judas. For worse than a beast, Judas did not become more meek when he partook of the common meal. Not even when reproved did he listen, but he went so far as to taste of the Lord's Body, and still did not repent. But some say that Christ did not give the Mysteries to the other disciples until Judas had left. So we too should do the same and withhold the Mysteries from those who are evil. When He is about to break the bread He gives thanks, teaching us also to offer the Bread with thanksgiving. At the same time He also shows by this that He gladly accepts as if it were a gift the breaking of His own Body, that is, His death, and that He is not displeased as if it were something that He is unwilling to accept, so that we too, in the same manner, might gladly accept martyrdom as a gift.[10] By saying, "This is My Body," He shows that the bread which is sanctified on the altar is the Lord's Body Itself, and not a symbolic type. For He did not say, "This is a type," but "This is My Body." By an ineffable action it is changed, although it may appear to us as bread. Since we are weak and could not endure to eat raw meat, much less human flesh, it appears as bread to us although it is indeed flesh.

---

[10] The Greek words *eucharisteō* and *eucharistōs* (one a verb and the other an adverb) from which we derive "eucharist", in a rich and profound manner express both God's good pleasure to give and man's good will to receive. In this passage of Theophylact's commentary they have been rendered variously as "giving thanks" and "gladly [accepting] as a gift", although neither phrase captures the perspective of the gracious Giver.

27-28. And He took the cup, and gave thanks, and gave it to them, saying, Drink of it, all of you; for this is My Blood of the New Testament, which is shed for many for the remission of sins. Just as the Old Testament had sacrificial slaughter and blood, so too the New Testament has Blood and slaying. He said, "shed for many", meaning "shed for all", for "all" are also "many". Why did He not say above, "Take, eat, all of you," but here, "Drink of it, all of you?" Some say that He said this because of Judas; for Judas took the bread and did not eat it, but hid it to show to the Jews that Jesus called bread His own Body. But Judas drank the cup, albeit unwillingly, not able to hide that at all. For this reason, then, Christ said, "Drink of it, all of you." In a more spiritual sense, some say that not all are able to approach the solid food, but only those who are more mature, while all can drink. For this reason, then, He said, "Drink of it, all of you." For all can receive the simpler teachings.

29. But I say unto you, I will not drink henceforth of this fruit of the vine, until that day when I drink it new with you in My Father's kingdom. Having tasted of the cup, He forgoes bodily drink from that time on. But He promises some new manner of tasting in the kingdom, that is, after the Resurrection. For when He rose He ate and drank in some new manner, not in need of the food of bodily taste, but rather to confirm the true and real nature of His Body.[11] He appropriately calls His own Resurrection the "kingdom", for when He abolished death, He truly appeared as King. Or, you might understand it in this way: the new drink is the revelation of the mysteries of God, which will be revealed in the kingdom of God, that is, at the second coming. They are new, that is, of such a nature as we have not heard before. Christ is said to drink these things with us, in that He considers our benefit to be His food and drink.

30. And when they had sung a hymn, they went out to the Mount of Olives. They sang a hymn of praise when they had eaten, so that we might learn to do the same as well. Jesus went to the Mount of Olives and not to any other place, lest He appear to be fleeing. For it was not to some unknown place that He went, but to a place very well known to the Jews. At the same time, He departed from that bloodthirsty city,

---

[11] i.e. that it was not an apparition.

abandoning it so that He might be pursued, and might later reprove them for coming after Him even as He was retreating from them.

31-32. Then saith Jesus unto them, All ye shall stumble and fall because of Me this night: for it is written, I will smite the shepherd, and the sheep of the flock shall be scattered abroad. But after I am risen again, I will go before you into Galilee. As God He foretells what will be. To avoid offending them by seeming to accuse them, He says, "It is written, I will smite the shepherd, and the sheep shall be scattered abroad,"[12] thus implying, It is I Who have held you together and My departure from you will scatter you. The Father is said to "smite" the Son, in that the Jews crucified the Lord in accordance with the Father's plan of salvation, hence, with His consent. It is said that the Father smote, because He was able to prevent it, yet did not. Then Jesus takes away their grief by announcing to them the good tidings, saying, "I shall rise and go before you, that is, precede you, into Galilee." By this He shows that He will leave Jerusalem and go to the Gentiles, for Gentiles dwelt in Galilee.[13]

33-34. Peter answered and said unto Him, Though all shall stumble and fall because of Thee, yet will I never stumble and fall. Jesus said unto him, Verily I say unto thee, That this night, before the cock crows, thou shalt deny Me thrice. With great audacity Peter alone promises not to stumble. Therefore Christ permitted him to fall in order to convince him not to be confident in himself but in God, and also to value Christ's words as more trustworthy than his own knowledge of himself. Because Peter's words "though all men shall stumble and fall" were full of arrogance, Christ shows him to be a braggart who did not know his own weakness. The Lord then foretells to him both the hour, that it will be "this night" and "before the cock crows", and also the number of the denials, that he will deny Him three times.

35-36. Peter said unto Him, Even if I must die with Thee, yet will I not deny Thee. Likewise also said all the disciples. Then cometh

---

[12] Zechariah 13:7

[13] See note on Mt. 4:12-13 on p. 41.

Jesus with them unto a place called Gethsemane, and saith unto the disciples, Sit ye here, while I go away and pray yonder. Wanting to show that he had genuine love, Peter contradicted the Saviour. He had earlier been freed of the fear that he himself might be the betrayer, and now Peter, with great love but also out of a desire for honor, began to rise up against the others and even to oppose Christ. But equally the other disciples, before they had experienced the trials, in ignorance made promises that they would not be able to keep. Jesus went away to pray in private, for prayer requires quiet and solitude.

37-39. And He took with Him Peter and the two sons of Zebedee, and began to be sorrowful and very heavy. Then saith He unto them, My soul is exceeding sorrowful, even unto death: tarry ye here, and watch with Me. And He went a little farther, and fell on His face, and prayed, saying, O My Father, if it be possible, let this cup pass from Me: nevertheless not as I will, but as Thou wilt. He does not take all the disciples with Him, but only the three to whom He showed His glory on Mt. Tabor, lest the others see Him very heavy of heart while He was praying, and be scandalized. But He leaves even these three and goes away to a place to pray that was yet more private. He was sorrowful and heavy in accord with the divine plan, so as to confirm that He was truly man. For it is human nature to fear death; it was against our nature that death entered, and for this reason our nature flees from it. At the same time, Christ was sorrowful so that the devil would unknowingly leap upon Him, the God-man, and bear Him down to death as though He were mere man, and thus the devil himself would be crushed. Moreover, if the Lord had rushed towards death it would have given the Jews the excuse that they did not sin in killing one who was so eager to suffer. From this we learn not to throw ourselves into trials and temptations, but to pray that we may be delivered from them. For this reason, too, He did not move away a great distance, but was near the three disciples, that they might hear Him and remember when they themselves fell into temptations, and pray in the same manner. He calls His Passion a cup [as of wine], either because of the sleep which it brought, or because it became the cause of gladness and salvation for us. He wants the cup to be removed either to show that as a man subject to nature He pleads to escape death, as was said above, or because He did not wish the Jews to commit a sin so grave that on account of it the temple would be destroyed and the people perish. Yet He desires that His Father's will be done, that we also may learn that it is precisely when our nature draws us away from obedience that we must obey God and fulfill His will.

40-41. And He cometh unto the disciples, and findeth them asleep, and saith unto Peter, What, could ye not watch with Me one hour? Watch and pray, that ye enter not into temptation: the spirit indeed is willing, but the flesh is weak. Because Peter and the other disciples had been brash and made reckless promises, Jesus now rebukes them for their weakness, and in particular addresses Peter. Could you not keep vigil one hour with Me? How then will you lay down your life for Me? But again, after wounding them with His rebuke, He heals them by saying that the spirit is willing, but the weakness of the flesh resists. That is to say, I consider you deserving of forgiveness, because you fell asleep not out of disdain, but out of weakness. But since you are weak, do not be overly bold; rather pray that you not enter into temptation at all. Others understand "that ye enter not into temptation" to mean "that you not be defeated by temptation". For, they say, He did not bid us to be without temptations, for temptations are our crowns. Rather He bids us to pray that we not be swallowed up by temptation and enter into its belly, as into the belly of a wild beast. For he who is overcome by temptation enters into it, that is, is swallowed up by it.

42-43. He went away again the second time, and prayed, saying, O My Father, if this cup can not pass away from Me, except I drink it, Thy will be done. And He came and found them asleep again: for their eyes were heavy. And He left them, and went away again, and prayed the third time, saying the same words. When you hear that the Lord Himself prayed many times, learn, O man, that you ought to pray continuously when beset by temptations. When Jesus found them sleeping again, He did not rebuke them lest He grieve them, but He let them be. And He left them and prayed for the third time, thus confirming His human nature. For the number three signifies both truth and confirmation.

45-46. Then cometh He to His disciples, and saith unto them, Sleep on now, and take your rest: behold, the hour is at hand, and the Son of Man is betrayed into the hands of sinners. Rise, let us be going: behold, he is at hand that doth betray Me. Showing that He has no need of their help, even when He is about to be betrayed, He says to them, "Sleep on now." Or, He is speaking with irony, as if to say, "Behold, the betrayer is at hand—sleep, if you so desire and time allows." Then He rouses them from that place where He was praying and approaches those who are about to arrest Him, and goes forward to meet them as if they were about to present Him with some delightful gift. Thus we see that Christ God prayed as a man in Gethsemane to confirm the divine economy, the plan of salvation. His prayer in Gethsemane also showed His desire to avoid His suffering, knowing that as a consequence of the Crucifixion the Jews would be destroyed for their sin against Him.

47-50. And while He yet spake, lo, Judas, one of the twelve, came, and with him a great multitude with swords and staves, from the chief priests and elders of the people. Now he that betrayed Him gave them a sign, saying, Whomsoever I shall kiss, that same is He: hold Him fast. And forthwith he came to Jesus, and said, Hail, Master; and kissed Him. And Jesus said unto him, Friend, wherefore art thou come? Then came they, and laid hands on Jesus, and took him. Do you see the weapons of the chief priests? Staves and swords! So peaceful were they, and possessed of such a spirit of meekness! The evangelist says, "one of the twelve," marveling that though Judas had been chosen and ranked among the first, yet he gave himself to the devil. So you, too, O man, be fearful though you may be among the most intimate of the Lord's friends, lest you become careless and lazy and fall away. Judas gave a sign because it was night and they were not able to identify Jesus. For those who came to arrest Him were not from the multitude, but were servants of the high priest, who perhaps did not know Jesus at all. But the disciple reveals the Master to them with a kiss. For Judas knew the Lord's love for mankind, and hence was emboldened to kiss Him. The Lord was patient even to the last moment, eager to win Judas by His long-suffering. Even so Judas was not brought to reason, whereupon the Lord caused the servants of the high priest to fall, as John says,[14] so that in falling down they would recognize His power. But even so they did not desist from their brazenness, whereupon Jesus gives Himself over to them. He calls Judas "friend", deriding and disparaging him for

[14] Jn. 18:5-6

supposedly giving Him a friend's kiss. "Wherefore art thou come?" means "For what reason have you come here? As a friend? Then there was no need to come with swords. As an enemy? Then why do you kiss Me?" Thus He rebukes him as a treacherous deceiver.

51-54. And, behold, one of them which were with Jesus stretched out his hand, and drew his sword, and struck a servant of the high priest, and smote off his ear. Then said Jesus unto him, Put up again thy sword into its place: for all they that take the sword shall perish with the sword. Thinkest thou that I cannot now pray to My Father, and He shall immediately set beside Me more than twelve legions of angels? But how then shall the Scriptures be fulfilled, that thus it must be? Peter was the one who drew the sword, as John says.[15] For he had a sword, having just recently sacrificed the lamb which they ate. But let us not condemn Peter, for it was not on his own behalf, but for his Master, that he acted so zealously. But the Lord converts Peter to the evangelic life lived according to the Gospel, teaching man not to use the sword, not even when presuming to avenge God. Peter cuts off the ear, signifying that the Jews suffered from the infirmity of deafness in that they would neither hear nor heed. Then Christ gives the dictum of the law, that he who slays will himself be slain. For the law says that "they who take the sword shall perish with the sword."[16] He implies that the Jews who take up the sword against Him will be destroyed by the sword of the Romans. He did not say, "I can bring to My side twelve legions of angels," but "[I can] pray to My Father," speaking by divine dispensation as a man, out of consideration for their weakness. By sweat, by fear, and in many ways did He show His human nature. For His words would not have seemed plausible if He had said, "I Myself can bring angels to My side." Instead of twelve disciples, He says, "Twelve contingents of angels would stand beside Me if I so desired." The legion is the largest military contingent, consisting of six thousand horsemen.[17] All these things must be, He says, in order to fulfill the Scriptures which

---

[15] Jn. 18:10

[16] See Gen. 9:6 and Jer. 15:2

[17] The Roman legion at the time of Christ consisted primarily of footsoldiers. Bl. Theophylact's statement here reflects the later Byzantine armies.

had foretold them. The Jews were not wicked because the Scriptures had foretold that they would be; rather, these events were described in the Scriptures beforehand by the inspiration of the Holy Spirit because the Jews would do these things of their own evil will.

55-56. In that same hour said Jesus to the multitudes, Are ye come out as against a thief with swords and staves for to take Me? I sat daily with you teaching in the temple, and ye laid no hold on Me. But all this was done, that the Scriptures of the prophets might be fulfilled. He shows the absurdity of their efforts, and that they did not seize Him by their own strength. "For when I was in the temple," He says, "you wanted to take Me but you could not because I did not permit you; but now I voluntarily give Myself over to you. For I know that it is impossible that the Scriptures which foretold your wickedness should be proved false."

56-58. Then all the disciples forsook Him, and fled. And they that had laid hold on Jesus led Him away to Caiaphas the high priest, where the scribes and the elders were assembled. But Peter followed Him afar off unto the high priest's court, and went in, and sat with the servants, to see the end. The other disciples fled, but Peter, who was more fervently devoted to the Master, followed at a distance. If John also followed, it was not as a disciple but as an acquaintance of the high priest.[18]

59-60. Now the chief priests, and elders, and all the council, sought false witness against Jesus, to put Him to death; but found none: yea, though many false witnesses came forward, yet found they none. They brought Jesus to Caiaphas who was the high priest for that year. There Caiaphas spent the night along with the others, not keeping the Pascha at that time, but waiting so that they might kill the Lord, and thus transgressing the law.[19] For the Lord kept the Pascha in keeping with the law, but they despised the law that they might slay the Lord.

---

[18] Jn. 18:15

[19] Jn. 18:28

60-64. At the last came two false witnesses, and said, This fellow said, I am able to destroy the temple of God, and to build it in three days. And the high priest arose, and said unto Him, Answerest Thou nothing? What is it which these witness against Thee? But Jesus was silent. And the high priest answered and said unto Him, I adjure Thee by the living God, that Thou tell us whether Thou be the Christ, the Son of the living God. Jesus saith unto him, Thou hast said. Truly these were false witnesses. For Christ had not said, "I am able to destroy," but "You shall destroy." And He had not said, "the temple of God," but "this temple," that is, "My Body". And again, He had not said, "I shall build," but "I shall raise."[20] So they were clearly false witnesses, the Lord having said one thing while they reported that He had said another. Jesus therefore kept silent, knowing that their tribunal was unlawful. For how would a verbal defense persuade those whom signs had not persuaded? The high priest asks the question, wanting to induce Him to blaspheme; so that if He should say, "I am the Son of God," He might be condemned as a blasphemer, but if He should deny it, the High priest would have Him as a witness against Himself. But the Lord caught those sophists in their own cunning, and answers, "Thou hast said," meaning, "Your mouth has confessed that I am the Son of God."

64. Nevertheless I say unto you, Hereafter shall ye see the Son of Man sitting on the right hand of power, and coming upon the clouds of heaven. He is speaking to them from the prophecy of Daniel who said, "I saw one coming as the Son of Man upon the clouds."[21] For since they thought that He was deluded, as He appeared to them in humble form, He said, "You shall see Me then coming in power and seated with the Father." "Power" here means that of the Father, and the Son of Man will be coming not from earth but from heaven.

65-66. Then the high priest rent his clothes, saying, He hath spoken blasphemy! What further need have we of witnesses? Behold, now ye have heard His blasphemy. What think ye? They answered and said,

---

[20] Jn. 2:19. "Jesus answered and said unto them, Destroy this temple, and in three days I will raise it up."

[21] Daniel 7:13

He is guilty unto death. It was the practice of the Jews to tear their garments whenever something insufferable would befall them. In order to deceive the crowd, Caiaphas tears his clothes as if he were faced with manifest blasphemy, meaning to create the impression that Christ had greatly blasphemed, and thus to impel the crowd to say that He was guilty unto death. Nevertheless, learn that when Caiaphas rent his clothes, it was a symbol that the high priesthood of the Old Testament had been rent.

67-68. Then did they spit in His face, and buffeted Him; and others smote Him with the palms of their hands, saying, Prophesy unto us, Thou Christ, Who is he that smote Thee? When they had condemned Him, then they abused Him and mocked Him, wrapping His face in a cloth, as another evangelist says.[22] They mocked Him in this manner because the people considered Him a prophet. To "buffet" is to strike with the hands with the fingers clenched, or, to put it more plainly, to punch with the fist.

69-75. Now Peter sat without in the courtyard: and a servant girl came unto him, saying, Thou also wast with Jesus of Galilee. But he denied before them all, saying, I know not what thou sayest. And when he was gone out into the porch, another maid saw him, and said unto them that were there, This fellow was also with Jesus of Nazareth. And again he denied with an oath, I do not know the man. And after a while came unto him they that stood by, and said to Peter, Surely thou also art one of them; for thy speech discloseth thee. Then began he to curse and to swear, saying, I know not the man. And immediately the cock crowed. And Peter remembered the word of Jesus, which said unto him, Before the cock crows, thou shalt deny Me thrice. And he went out, and wept bitterly. Overcome with immense fear, Peter forgot his promises and became enslaved to human weakness, as if he were lifeless with fear, not knowing what he was saying. Understand it also in the spiritual sense, that Peter was rebuked by the servant girl, that is, by human weakness which is lowly and meant to be governed, until the cock crowed and brought him to his senses. The

[22] Lk. 22:64, Mk. 14:65

rooster is the Word which does not permit us to be lazy and to sleep, but says, "Wake up and rise, O sleeper!" Peter, therefore, was wakened by the Word as if by a rooster. Going out of the palace of the high priest, that is, the confines of a hardened mind, and leaving behind senselessness, he wept bitterly. While he was in the courtyard of the hardened mind, he could not weep, for he had lost his sense; but as soon as he went out, he came to his senses.

CHAPTER TWENTY-SEVEN

Concerning Pilate the governor.
Concerning Judas' regret.
Concerning the scourging, the punishments,
and the crucifixion of Christ.
Concerning the request for the Lord's Body,
and those who guarded the tomb.

1-2. When the morning was come, all the chief priests and elders of the people took counsel against Jesus to put Him to death: and when they had bound Him, they led Him away, and delivered Him to Pontius Pilate the governor. Behold how the devil held them all in his grasp, convincing them to commit murder on such high days when they ought to have been making many sacrifices and offerings for their other sins, and for their purification and cleansing. But instead they bound Him and led Him away to Pilate the governor, who was from Pontus[1] but was subject to the Romans who had sent him to be the governor of Judea. The chief priests and elders handed the Lord over to Pilate on the grounds that He had fomented sedition and had plotted against the emperor.

3-5. Then Judas, who had betrayed Him, when he saw that Jesus had been condemned, repented, and returned the thirty pieces of silver to the chief priests and elders, saying, I have sinned in that I have betrayed innocent blood. And they said, What is that to us? see thou to that. And he cast down the pieces of silver in the temple, and departed, and went and hanged himself. Judas began to have second thoughts and he repented, but it was not a good repentance. To pass judgement against oneself is good, but to hang oneself is of the devil; for Judas was not able to endure the thought of the reproaches that would later be heaped upon him and so he fled from this life, when he ought instead to have wept and reconciled himself to Him Whom he had betrayed. Some say that Judas in his greed believed that he himself could

[1] a region now in northern Turkey, along the southern coast of the Black Sea.

gain the silver by betraying Christ, without Christ actually being slain, as He would escape from the Jews as He had done on many occasions. But when Judas saw that Jesus had been condemned and already sentenced to die, he repented that the affair had not turned out as he had planned. Whereupon he hanged himself thinking to precede Jesus into hades and there to plead for his own salvation. Nevertheless, know that while he did put his neck into the noose and hanged himself from a tree, the tree bent and he survived, as God wanted to save his life, either so that he could repent, or to make an example of him and to shame him. They say that Judas later became so bloated from dropsy that he could not pass through an opening that a wagon could easily pass through; and then falling face forward he burst asunder, or ruptured, as Luke says in the Acts of the Apostles.[2]

6-10. And the chief priests took the silver pieces, and said, It is not lawful to put them into the corban, because it is the price of blood. And they took counsel, and bought with them the potter's field, to bury strangers in. Wherefore that field was called, The field of blood, unto this day. Then was fulfilled that which was spoken by Jeremiah the prophet, saying, And they took the thirty pieces of silver, the price of Him that was valued, Whom they of the sons of Israel did value, and gave them for the potter's field, as the Lord appointed me. The corban was the treasury in the temple in which they put the gifts offered to God. See how God brings to naught their schemes by exposing their bloodstained minds. For to this day, it says, that field is called "The field of blood", as a reminder to all that they murdered the Lord. Learn this as well, that the Jews were so diligent in providing hospitality that they purchased a plot where even strangers could be buried. Let us be ashamed, then, we who think we live a more perfect life while disregarding strangers. "The price of Him that was valued," it says, that is to say, the price of Christ. He was beyond price, yet the sons of Israel set a price on Him, having agreed to give Judas thirty pieces of silver.

11-14. And Jesus stood before the governor: and the governor asked Him, saying, Art Thou the King of the Jews? And Jesus said

---

[2] Acts 1:18

unto him, Thou sayest. And when He was accused by the chief priests and elders, He answered nothing. Then said Pilate unto Him, Hearest Thou not how many things they witness against Thee? And He answered him never a word; insomuch that the governor marvelled greatly. He was brought to Pilate accused of crimes against the state, which is why Pilate asked Him if He had fomented an insurrection or attempted to make Himself king of the Jews. But Jesus said to him, "Thou sayest," giving a most wise answer. For He neither said that He was nor that He was not, but He said, somewhere between the two, "Thou sayest." For this could be interpreted either as "I am what you say", or, "I do not say it, but you do." He gave no other answer, however, for He knew that the tribunal was an unjust proceeding. Pilate marveled at the Lord because He scorned death, and because, though He was eloquent and could have said a myriad of things in His own defense, He made no answer and disregarded His accusers. May we also learn from this to say nothing when we are brought before a corrupt court lest we cause a greater stir and provoke those who refuse to hear our defense to condemn us all the more.

15-18. Now on that feast there was the custom that the governor would release unto the people a prisoner whom they wanted. And they had then a notorious prisoner whom they called Barabbas. Therefore when they were gathered together, Pilate said unto them, Whom will ye that I release unto you? Barabbas, or Jesus Who is called Christ? For he knew that out of envy they had delivered Him. Pilate was eager to release Christ, though even that would have been cowardly; for he ought to have stood up for the truth. First Pilate asked the Lord, "Do You not hear what they are testifying against You?" He asked this so that if Christ had given a defense, he would have had a reason to release Him. But the Lord did not defend Himself, since, all-knowing, He knew that even if He made a defense He would not be freed. Pilate then turned to another course of action. He appealed to the custom at the feast, all but saying, "Even if you do not release Him as innocent, pardon Him on the feast as one who has been condemned." For how could Pilate have suspected that the people would demand the crucifixion of Jesus, Who was innocent, and the release of the guilty thief? Pilate knew, then, that Jesus was not guilty but was the object of spite, and it was for this reason that he asked them to choose which prisoner they wanted released. This shows that he was cowardly; for he ought to have disdained all danger to champion the good. Therefore he merits condemnation for having covered up the truth. "Barabbas" means "son of the father", "bar" meaning "son", and "abbas", "father". These Jews, therefore, demanded the son of their spiritual father, the devil,[3] but Jesus they crucified. And to this day, there are those like them who have chosen Antichrist, the substitute messiah, the son of their father, and have rejected Christ, the true Messiah.

19-26. When he was seated upon the judgement seat, his wife sent unto him, saying, Have thou nothing to do with that righteous man: for I have suffered many things this day in a dream because of Him. But the chief priests and elders persuaded the multitude that they should ask for Barabbas, and kill Jesus. The governor answered and said unto them, Which of the two will ye that I release unto you? They said, Barabbas. Pilate saith unto them, What then shall I do with Jesus Who is called Christ? They all say unto him, Let Him be crucified. And the governor said, Why, what evil hath He done? But they cried out the more, saying, Let Him be crucified. When Pilate saw that he could prevail nothing, but that rather a tumult was made, he took water, and washed his hands before the multitude, saying, I am innocent of the blood of this righteous man: see ye to it yourselves. Then answered all the people, and said, His blood be on us, and on our children. Then released he Barabbas unto them: and when he had scourged Jesus, he delivered Him to be crucified. O, how miraculous! While being judged by Pilate, Christ caused his wife to suffer a fright. It was not Pilate who saw the dream, but his wife; either because he was unworthy, or because the people would not have believed that he had seen such a dream and would think that he said this only with a view towards granting a pardon. And perhaps he would have kept silent if he had seen the dream, as he was the judge. The dream was a work of providence, not occurring so that Christ would be released, but so that the woman would be saved. Why, then, did Pilate not release Him? Because it was not politic to do so as Jesus had been charged with accusations

---

[3] In John 8:44, Jesus speaking to the Pharisees said, "Ye are of your father the devil, and the lusts of your father ye will do."

concerning kingship. But Pilate should have asked for evidence either that Jesus had enlisted soldiers or that He had forged weapons. Instead, Pilate let himself be drawn to their side, like one who is mute and cowardly, and because of this he is not without blame. For when they demanded the man who was notorious for wickedness, he handed Barabbas over; but when it came to Christ, he asked them, "What then shall I do with Jesus?" thus making them masters of the decision. Yet he was the governor and could have snatched Christ away from them, as the chief captain did with Paul.[4] They said, "Let Him be crucified," desiring not only to kill Him but to mark Him as a criminal, for the cross was reserved as a punishment for criminals. Pilate washed his hands as if to show that he was clean of defilement, but his thoughts were evil. For he called Jesus a righteous man and yet handed Him over to murderers. The people took upon themselves the punishment for His murder, and this punishment indeed overtook them when the Romans destroyed them and their children. But even to this day, the Jews, who are children of those who slew the Lord, have His blood upon them.[5] Because of their disbelief in the Lord they have been persecuted by all, and they have had no boldness before their persecutors on account of those words spoken to Pilate. Pilate scourged Jesus, that is, he had Him whipped, either to gratify the people, or else to show that it was he himself who had condemned Christ, and to make it appear that they were not about to crucify an innocent man, but rather one who was dishonorable. Thus was fulfilled this prophecy of Isaiah as well, "I gave My back to scourges."[6]

27-30. Then the soldiers of the governor took Jesus into the praetorium, and gathered unto Him the whole company of soldiers. And they stripped Him, and put on Him a scarlet cloak. And when they

---

[4] Acts 21:31-33

[5] St. John Chrysostom says in his homily on this passage:

"Even though the Jews acted with so much madness against both themselves and their children, the Lord, the Lover of man, so far from pronouncing this sentence upon their children, did not even pronounce it upon them. But from both them and their children He has received those who repented, and He counts them worthy of good things beyond number. For indeed even Paul was one of them, and also the thousands of Jerusalem that believed; for it is said, "Thou seest, brother, how many thousands of Jews there are which believe" (Acts 21:20). But if some continued in their sin, let them blame their punishment on themselves." Homily 86 on the Gospel of St. Matthew, section 3.

[6] Is. 50:6

had plaited a crown of thorns, they put it upon His head, and a reed in His right hand: and they bowed the knee before Him, and mocked Him, saying, Hail, King of the Jews! And they spit upon Him, and took the reed, and smote Him on the head. Here was fulfilled the word of David, "Thou hast made Me a reproach to the foolish."[7] For the soldiers were foolish, and did things that befitted their foolishness: they clothed Him with a cloak as if it were the imperial purple; they gave Him a reed for a scepter and a crown of thorns for a diadem; they paid Him homage, in mockery, for this is the meaning of "bowed the knee". See how they performed every sort of insult and abuse: His face they reviled with spit, His head with a crown, His hand with a reed, the rest of His Body with a cloak, and His ears with words of mockery. But if they did these things in derision, you, O reader, must understand them also in a more spiritual manner, as something not merely done to, but accomplished by, Jesus. The scarlet cloak reveals our nature, bloody and murderous, which He assumed and sanctified by wearing it. The crown is made of thorns which are the sins resulting from our cares for this life; these Christ consumes with His own divinity, for His head represents His divinity. The reed is a symbol of our weak and crumbling nature which the Lord assumed, as David also says, "The right hand of the Lord hath exalted me."[8] By receiving insults in His ears, He healed Eve of the whispering of the serpent which had entered her ears.

31-32. And after they had mocked Him, they took the cloak off from Him, and put His own raiment on Him, and led Him away to crucify Him. And as they came out, they found a man of Cyrene, Simon by name: him they compelled to bear His cross. The three evangelists say that Simon carried the cross of Jesus, while John says that the Lord carried it Himself. It is likely that both events occurred. At first Jesus carried the cross as no one else was willing to carry it; but along the way they found Simon and placed the cross on him. You, O reader, learn this as well, that "Simon" means "obedience"; therefore he who possesses obedience is he who carries the cross of Christ. And Cyrene

---

[7] Ps. 38:11

[8] Ps. 117:16

was one of the five cities of Pentapolis,[9] signifying the five senses that are compelled to bear the cross.

33-37. And when they were come unto a place called Golgotha, which means, a place of a skull, they gave Him vinegar to drink mingled with gall: and when He had tasted thereof, He would not drink. And they crucified Him, and parted His garments, casting lots: that it might be fulfilled which was spoken by the prophet, They parted My garments among them, and upon My vesture did they cast lots. And sitting down they watched Him there; and set up over His head His accusation written, THIS IS JESUS KING OF THE JEWS. It was called "a place of a skull", because those who have learned from the tradition of the fathers say that Adam was buried there; it was necessary that all we who had died in Adam were thus made alive in Christ.[10] Do not be troubled when you hear Matthew say that vinegar with gall was offered to the Lord, Mark, wine flavored with myrrh,[11] and John, vinegar with gall on hyssop.[12] For many things were done by many people, as there was a disorderly crowd present, some doing one thing, others another. It is likely that one offered wine and another vinegar mixed with gall. There were many ways to be put to death, but Christ was put to death on the cross so that He might sanctify the wood of the tree by which we were cursed, and bless the whole universe: the heavens, which were signified by the upper portion of the cross; the underworld, signified by the "footstool";[13] and the ends of the earth, the east and the west, signified by the transverse portions of the cross. But He was also put to death on the cross so that He might stretch out His arms to embrace and gather together the children of God who had been dispersed. The soldiers divided even His clothing, as He was poor

---

[9] The district of Pentapolis, named for its five cities, was a Greek colony on the North African coast west of Egypt.

[10] I Cor.15:22

[11] Mark 15:23.

[12] Jn. 19:29. [In actuality, St. John makes no mention here of gall.]

[13] This is the lowest transverse bar of the three-barred cross, to which our Lord's feet were attached, and it takes its name "footstool" from the prophetic words of David: "Exalt ye the Lord our God, and worship the footstool of His feet." Ps. 98:5. See also Ps. 131:7.

and had nothing else. That which the evangelist John calls His ''title'',[14] Matthew calls His ''accusation''. For they wrote down an indictment giving the reason for His crucifixion, namely, that He was accused of claiming to be ''King of the Jews'' and of leading an insurrection. They indicted Him as ''King'' meaning to slander Him, but in truth their indictment was unimpeachable evidence admitted by His adversaries. For indeed the Lord is King, and came for this very reason, to save the Jews. But since those who were Jews in the flesh did not want Him to reign over them, He became King of the spiritual Jews, that is, of those who confess Him. For ''Jew'' means ''he who confesses''.

38-44. Then were there two thieves crucified with Him, one on the right hand, and the other on the left. And they that passed by reviled Him, shaking their heads, and saying, Thou that destroyest the temple, and buildest it in three days, save Thyself. If Thou be the Son of God, come down from the cross. Likewise also the chief priests mocking Him, with the scribes and elders, said, He saved others; Himself He cannot save. If He be the King of Israel, let Him now come down from the cross, and we will believe in Him. He trusted in God; let Him deliver Him now, if He will have Him: for He said, I am the Son of God. The thieves also, which were crucified with Him, likewise reproached Him. As a slander against Christ the two thieves were crucified with Him, so that people would think that He, too, was such a transgressor of the law as they were. The two thieves were symbolic of the two races, the Jewish and the Gentile, for both races had transgressed the law and reviled Christ, just as both these thieves at first reviled Him. But later the one thief understood Who He was and confessed Him as King; whereupon he also said, ''Remember me, Lord, in Thy kingdom.''[15] So, too, did the Gentile race confess Christ, while the other thief, the Jewish race, blasphemed. The devil prompted them to say, ''If Thou be the Son of God, come down from the cross,'' in order to provoke Him to come down and thus overturn the salvation of all being accomplished on the cross. But Christ, Who is indeed the Son of God, was not persuaded by the enemy, so that you, O reader, might learn

---

[14] Jn. 19:19

[15] See Lk. 23:42.

that we ought not to be persuaded by the ploys of the devil, but do what is good even if men think ill of us.

45-49. Now from the sixth hour there was darkness over all the land unto the ninth hour. And about the ninth hour Jesus cried out with a loud voice, saying, Eli, Eli, lama sabachthani? that is to say, My God, My God, why hast Thou forsaken Me? Some of them that stood there, when they heard that, said, This man calleth for Elijah. And straightway one of them ran, and took a sponge, and filled it with vinegar, and put it on a reed, and gave Him to drink. The rest said, Let be, let us see whether Elijah will come to save Him. The darkness which occurred was not according to the natural order of events, as when a solar eclipse occurs in nature. For there is never a solar eclipse on the fourteenth day of the lunar cycle; rather, solar eclipses occur when there is a so-called "new moon". The day of the crucifixion was certainly the fourteenth day of the lunar cycle, as that is when the Jews celebrate the Passover. Therefore the incident was beyond nature. The darkness was universal, not partial as was the darkness in Egypt, to show that the whole of creation mourned the Passion of the Creator, and that the light had been taken from the Jews. Let those Jews who were asking for a sign from heaven now see the sun darkened. On the sixth day, when man had been created, and at the sixth hour, when he had eaten of the tree (for that is the hour of eating), the Lord, refashioning man and healing his sin, on the sixth day and at the sixth hour was stretched out on the tree. Jesus speaks prophetically in the Hebrew tongue to show that He does not contend with the Old Testament. He said, "Why hast Thou forsaken Me?"[16] to show that He was truly man, and not just in appearance. For man avidly desires life and has a physical appetite for it. Just as Christ agonized and was sorely troubled before the cross, showing the fear that is ours by nature, so now He says, "Why hast Thou forsaken Me?" displaying our natural thirst for life. For He was truly man and like us in all respects, but without sins. Some have understood it in this manner: the Saviour spoke on behalf of the Jews and said, "Why hast Thou forsaken the Jewish race, O Father, that it should commit such a sin and be handed over to destruction?" For as Christ was one of the Jews,

[16] Ps. 21:1

He said "forsaken Me," meaning, "Why hast Thou forsaken My kinsmen, My people, that they should bring such a great evil upon themselves?" The multitude did not understand His cry, being uncouth and ignorant of the prophets, and thought that He was calling upon Elijah. For not all the Jews knew the prophets, just as now not all Christians, perhaps, know the Gospel. They gave Him vinegar to drink so that He might die more quickly, before Elijah could come to help Him. This is why the others say, "Let be, let us see whether Elijah will come to save Him;" that is, "Do not make Him die, for we want to know if Elijah will help Him."

50-53. Jesus, when He had cried out again with a loud voice, yielded up the spirit. And, behold, the veil of the temple was rent in twain from the top to the bottom; and the earth did quake, and the rocks rent; and the graves were opened, and many bodies of the saints which slept arose, and came out of the graves after His resurrection, and went into the Holy City, and appeared unto many. Jesus cries with a loud voice so that we may know that it was true when He said, "I have authority to lay down My life."[17] For He released His soul by His own authority. What was it that He cried with a loud voice? "Into Thy hands I commit My spirit."[18] Not under compulsion, but by His own will He released His spirit. For this is what is meant by "I commit". He also shows that He will take it back again. For what is committed or deposited can be returned. Thanks be to the Lord, that when He died and committed His spirit into the hands of the Father, from that time forward the souls of the saints are also committed into the hands of the Father, and not as before into the recesses of hades. So the death of Christ became our sanctification. For this reason He summons death with a loud voice, for death did not dare to approach until it had been summoned. The veil of the temple was a cloth of fine linen hanging in the middle of the temple, separating the inner sanctuary from the outer like a partition wall. This veil was rent, and God thereby showed that the inaccessible and unseen temple, whose innermost part, the Holy of Holies, had been secluded by the veil, would be made common and

---

[17] Jn. 10:18

[18] Lk. 23:46

profane so as to be visible and accessible to all. Some give further explanations. The veil being rent, they say, indicated that the letter of the law had been stripped away to reveal the entirety of the law which formerly had been concealed by the letter as if by a veil; and what before had been obscure and enigmatic in the law would now be made clear by its fulfillment in Christ.[19] One might also mention that it was the custom of Jews to rend their clothing when they heard blasphemies against God. So now the divine temple rent its own clothing, the veil, as if abhorring the death of Christ.[20] There is more that one could say, but this suffices. The elements quaked, showing at one and the same time that it was the Creator Who suffered and that all things would be changed. For earthquakes are mentioned in Scripture to mark a change in the course of affairs.[21] And there did occur a change in the scope of God's supervision of mankind, namely, from the Jews to the Gentiles. Even the stones, which are the stony hearts of the Gentiles, were split open to accept the seed of Truth. And those who were dead in sins arose and entered the Holy City, the heavenly Jerusalem, and appeared to the many who were walking the broad road [leading to perdition]. By appearing to them, they became an exemplary model of a good life and of repentance. For if one sees a man who was formerly deadened by many passions now changed and ascending to the holy heavenly City, he imitates that man in every way, and himself repents. These things have been explained in a rather elaborate manner; but you, O reader, understand that the raising of the dead which occurred at the Lord's crucifixion, also revealed the freeing of the souls in hades. Those who arose at that time were seen by many, lest the event appear to have been only an apparition. They arose as a sign from God, and it is evident that they again died. Some say that after Christ's resurrection, these arose and have not yet died; but I do not know if this should be accepted.

54-56. Now when the centurion, and they that were with him keeping watch over Jesus, saw the earthquake, and those things that

---

[19] See II Cor. 3:14-16.

[20] See Mt. 26:65 and commentary on p. 237.

[21] See Mt. 24:7, Mt. 28:2, Joel 2:10, Amos 1:1, III Kings (I Kings) 19:11, Is. 29:6, Jer. 23:19, among others.

were done, they feared greatly, saying, Truly this was the Son of God. And many women were there beholding afar off, who had followed Jesus from Galilee, ministering unto Him: among which was Mary Magdalene, and Mary the mother of James and Joses, and the mother of the sons of Zebedee. The Gentile centurion and those with him believed because of these great signs, but the Jews, who had clearly heard the prophets and the law, remained unbelieving—such an evil thing is malice! And this centurion later bore witness to Christ.[22] The women who beheld these events, who were the most tender of all in their compassion [and so ought to have been less able to endure the sight of the Lord's suffering], and were of the gender that was condemned [because of the sin of Eve], were the first to enjoy this vision of good things. The disciples fled while the women were stalwart. "Mary the mother of James and Joses" means the Theotokos, the Virgin Mother of God, for James and Joses were the sons of Joseph by his first wife. And since the Theotokos was called the "wife" of Joseph, she is rightly called the "mother" of his children, meaning "stepmother". The mother of the sons of Zebedee was named Salome. They say that she also was a daughter of Joseph.

57-61. When the even was come, there came a rich man of Arimathea, named Joseph, who also himself was Jesus' disciple: he went to Pilate, and begged the Body of Jesus. Then Pilate commanded the Body to be delivered. And when Joseph had taken the Body, he wrapped It in pure linen, and laid It in his own new tomb, which he had hewn out in the rock: and he rolled a great stone to the door of the tomb, and departed. And there was Mary Magdalene, and the other Mary, sitting over against the sepulchre. Joseph of Arimathea before had hidden himself, but now he dares to do a great deed, risking his life for his Teacher's Body, and taking upon himself the enmity of all the Jews. Pilate gives him the Body as a great favor. As Christ had been put to death as a rebel, it is likely that they were going to throw His Body aside unburied. But Joseph was rich and probably gave gold to Pilate; then he took the Body and honored It by placing It in a new tomb in which no one else had ever been placed. This was by God's provi-

[22] The centurion is St. Longinus, commemorated by the Church on October 16.

dence, so that when the Lord had risen, no one could say that it was another dead man who had previously been buried there that had risen. For this reason the tomb was new. Mary Magdalene and "the other Mary", that is, the Theotokos, who above was called the mother of James and Joses, were sitting opposite the tomb and waiting for the frenzy of the Jews to subside, so that they could go and embrace the Body and anoint It with myrrh. Isaiah spoke concerning these women, "Ye women coming from the sight, come hither; for this is a people without understanding."[23] He is clearly saying that the Jewish people who crucified the Lord lacked understanding.[24] He is calling upon the women, then, to forsake the mindless people and to go to the apostles and bring them the good tidings of the Resurrection.

62-66. Now the next day, that followed the day of preparation, the chief priests and Pharisees came together unto Pilate, saying, Sir, we remember that that deceiver said, while He was yet alive, After three days I will rise. Command therefore that the tomb be made secure until the third day, lest His disciples come by night, and steal Him away, and say unto the people, He is risen from the dead: so the last fraud shall be worse than the first. Pilate said unto them, Ye have a guard: go your way, make it as secure as ye know how. So they went, and made the tomb secure, sealing the stone, and setting a guard. The evangelist did not call the sabbath "the sabbath", for it was not the sabbath as far as the Jews in their malice were concerned. For though the law forbade anyone on the sabbath day to wander about, these Jewish transgressors of the law assembled at the place of the foreigner, Pilate, instead of at the place of assembly ordained by the law. They were moved by their own evil to approach Pilate and then to secure the tomb. This was God's providence, that the Resurrection might occur with them, His enemies, as witnesses guarding the sealed tomb. It is worth asking where the Jews learned that He had said that on the third day He would rise; for undoubtedly the Lord never said this clearly and openly. We can say that they surmised this from the example of Jonah. For Christ had said that "just as Jonah was in the belly of the whale for three days, so

---

[23] Is. 27:11

[24] Lk. 23:34

too will I be in the belly of the earth;''[25] and also, ''Ye shall destroy this temple.''[26] Before they had not understood these sayings, but had thought that He was speaking of the Jewish temple. On this charge they had borne witness against Him. But now they understood that by ''temple'' He meant His own Body, and they were afraid and denounced Him as ''a deceiver'', not ceasing from their malice even after His death.[27]

---

[25] Mt. 12:40

[26] Jn. 2:19. See Mt. 26:60-64 and commentary above on p. 236.

[27] Here follows Bl. Theophylact's explanation of the Greek word in the text of St. Matthew for ''guard'', *koustodia*: ''*koustodia*'' is the word the Romans used for ''guard''; the soldiers assigned to stand guard were called the *koustodia*.'' (cf. ''custody'' in English)

CHAPTER TWENTY-EIGHT

Concerning the Lord's Resurrection.
Concerning the guards at the tomb,
witnesses of the Resurrection.
Concerning Christ's appearance
to the apostles and women in Galilee.

1-8. After the sabbath, as it began to dawn toward the first day of the week, came Mary Magdalene and the other Mary to see the tomb. And, behold, there was a great earthquake: for the angel of the Lord descended from heaven, and came and rolled back the stone from the door, and sat upon it. His countenance was like lightning, and his raiment white as snow: and for fear of him the guards did shake, and became as dead men. And the angel answered and said unto the women, Fear not ye: for I know that ye seek Jesus Who was crucified. He is not here: for He is risen, as He said. Come, see the place where the Lord lay. And go quickly, and tell His disciples that He is risen from the dead; and, behold, He goeth before you into Galilee; there shall ye see Him: lo, I have told you. And they departed quickly from the tomb with fear and great joy; and did run to bring His disciples word. "After the sabbath" means the same thing that Luke said, "at deep dawn", and that Mark said, "very early in the morning at the rising of the sun."[1] By "sun" we should understand here "the first dawning rays of the sun". For by the eighth hour of the night it is the beginning of the next day, and it already feels like morning. So it was then, after the sabbath, at the beginning of Sunday which the evangelist calls "the first day of the sabbath". As "sabbath" is the name they gave also to the seven days of the week when considered together, so Sunday, the Lord's day, [in Greek, *kyriakē*] is "the first day of the sabbath", that is, the first day of the week. Following the first day are the Second, the Third, the Fourth and the Fifth.[2] When the Lord rose, the

[1] Lk. 24:1, Mk.16:2

[2] In Greek, these are the actual names of the days Monday through Thursday. Friday is called "the [day] of Preparation", Saturday, "the Sabbath", and Sunday, as mentioned above, "the Lord's [Day]".

stone was still in place against the tomb. Therefore, after the Lord had risen, the angel came to roll away the stone and give the women entrance into the tomb. There was an earthquake so that the guards would wake up and learn of this new and wondrous occurrence. The Lord rose on the third day; but how are the three days reckoned? He was crucified at the sixth hour on Friday; from then until the ninth hour, there was darkness: to me, this means "night". Again, from the ninth hour, there was light: this means "day". Lo, one day and night. Again, the night of Friday and the day of Saturday, the second day and night. And again, the night of Saturday and the dawn of Sunday, as Matthew says, "as it began to dawn towards the first day of the week;" the dawn is figured as one whole day. Lo, the third day and night. But three days can also be reckoned in another way: on Friday He gave up His spirit; this is the first day. On Saturday He was in the tomb; this is the second day. He rose during the morning hour of Sunday; from the part, Sunday is figured as another day. Behold, three days. So it is with those who have reposed; if one should die about the tenth hour of the day [i.e. 4 p.m.] and another about the first hour of the same day [i.e. 7 a.m.], they are both said to have died on the same day. But I have yet another explanation to give you of how three days and three nights can be reckoned. Attend closely. On Thursday evening the Lord had the supper and said to His disciples, "Take, eat, this is My Body." As He had authority to dispose of His own life, it is clear that from that moment He sacrificed Himself, in that He imparted His Body to His own disciples. For no one eats any meat which has not first been slaughtered. Therefore, reckon the three days as follows: on Thursday evening He imparted to them His own Body; that night and the day of Friday until the sixth hour—lo, the first day and night. Again, from the sixth hour until the ninth hour there was darkness, and from the ninth hour there was light until evening—lo, the second day and night. Again, the night following Friday, and the day of Saturday—lo, the third day and night. After the sabbath, He arose. These are three entire days and nights. Matthew says that the angel sat upon the stone, while Mark says that, having rolled away the stone, the angel sat inside the tomb, on the right side. Do they contradict each other? Not at all. It is likely that the angel first appeared seated upon the stone; then when the women entered, the angel preceded them and again appeared inside the tomb seated on the right side. The angel said to the women, "Fear not ye," that is, the guards indeed have reason to be afraid, but you, the women disciples of the Lord, need not fear. After taking away their fear, he announces to them the good tidings of the Resurrection. For it was necessary that he first cast out fear, and then bring the good tidings. He is not ashamed to call the Lord "He Who was crucified"; for the angel boasts in the cross as in a trophy of victory, the source of every good thing for us.

9-10. And as they went to tell His disciples, behold, Jesus met them, saying, Rejoice! And they came and grasped His feet and worshipped Him. Then said Jesus unto them, Be not afraid: go tell My brethren that they should go into Galilee and there shall they see Me. Jesus says to the women, "Rejoice!"[3] As womankind had been sentenced to sorrow, so the Lord procured joy for womankind by His Resurrection, and blessed them. With extreme reverence and honor for Him they grasped His feet, in their piety not daring to touch any other part of His Body. Some say that they grasped His feet purposely to ascertain if He had truly risen, and was not only an apparition or a spirit. For they suspected that He was a spirit. These two Mary's, therefore, touched His feet; but according to John, Mary Magdalene attempted to touch Him but was not permitted to do so, because she wanted to continue to be with Him as she had before.[4] Or perhaps she was not permitted to touch Jesus, in John's account, because she was being too curious. For since she had already touched His feet, as Matthew says, what need was there for her to touch Him again? So He kept her at arm's length.

11-15. Now when they were going, behold, some of the guard came into the city, and told the chief priests all that had taken place. And when they had assembled with the elders and taken counsel, they gave a large sum of money to the soldiers, saying, Say ye, His

---

[3] The Greek word for this greeting and salutation is simply the present imperative of the verb *chairein*, meaning "to rejoice". When Judas betrays his Master (Mt. 26:49) and when the soldiers mock Jesus as King (Mt. 27:29), it seems more appropriate to render it in English as "Hail!" But here, as well as in Lk. 1:28 where the Archangel greets the Virgin Mary, it has been translated as "Rejoice!" for in these instances the fathers and hymnographers of the Church are unable to comment upon the salutation without mentioning the fundamental element of joy.

[4] Jn. 20:17

disciples came by night, and stole Him away while we were sleeping. And if the governor should hear of this, we will persuade him, and secure you from trouble. So they took the money and did as they had been directed: and this story is commonly told among the Jews until this day. The guards reported everything: that there had been an earthquake, that the stone had been lifted away of a sudden, and that they themselves had been terrified and had become as ones dead. But the Jews were shamed neither by the miracles which had occurred at His Passion nor by the things which the soldiers had witnessed at the tomb; instead they corrupted the soldiers by their own favorite passion, the love of money, inducing the soldiers to utter the most impious and ridiculous thing of all: that He had been stolen. How, you foolish ones, could the disciples have stolen Him when in fear they had secluded themselves and did not even dare to go out at all? How, if they had stolen Him, would they later die for Him, preaching that He had risen, and be hacked to pieces for a lie?

16-20. Then the eleven disciples went away into Galilee, to the mountain which Jesus had appointed for them. And when they saw Him, they worshipped Him: but some doubted. And Jesus came and spake unto them, saying, All authority has been given unto Me in heaven and on earth. Go ye therefore, and make disciples of all nations, baptizing them in the name of the Father, and of the Son, and of the Holy Spirit, teaching them to observe all things whatsoever I have commanded you: and, lo, I am with you always, even unto the end of the world. Amen. According to John, Jesus was first seen by His disciples on the same day of the Resurrection, when the doors were closed; then eight days later when Thomas also believed. Then, since He intended to meet them in Galilee, they no longer assembled all together, but He next appeared only to those seven who were fishing on the sea of Tiberias. So the events Matthew described here occurred later, while the events in John's account occurred earlier. For forty days Jesus appeared to the disciples many times, coming to them and then withdrawing, but not remaining continually with them. Therefore the eleven foremost disciples, together with all the others who followed Christ, worshipped Him; "but some doubted." In all likelihood this should be understood in the following sense: the eleven disciples went to Galilee and the eleven worshipped Him. "But some" of the seventy, perhaps, had doubts concerning Christ; but later they also were assured. Some understand it in this manner: Matthew omitted to say who it was that doubted; but John mentioned what Matthew omitted, saying that it was Thomas who doubted.[5] Yet perhaps they all doubted, as Luke says.[6] You ought therefore to understand it in this manner, that when they came to Galilee they worshipped Him. But they who worshipped in Galilee had previously doubted in Jerusalem, as Luke says. Jesus said to them, "All authority has been given unto Me in heaven and on earth." This means, "As God and Creator I have always had authority over all things." "For all things are Thy servants," as David says to God.[7] "But I did not yet have man's voluntary submission. Now I shall have this as well. For all things shall be subjected unto Me, since by means of the cross I have conquered him who had the power of death." Submission is of two kinds: the one is involuntary, inasmuch as we are all the servants of God even unwillingly, as are the demons themselves. The other is voluntary, as seen in Paul who voluntarily became a servant of Christ. Formerly it was as if the Saviour had authority over all things in half measure only, that is, He received only the involuntary submission of all. But after the cross, when the knowledge of God has been divulged to all, and all who submitted to Him did so freely of their own will, Christ rightly says, "Now have I received all authority. Previously My authority was in part, as they served Me only involuntarily in that I was their Creator. But now that men serve Me with knowledge as well, total and complete authority has been given unto Me." By whom was it given to Him? By Himself alone and by His own humility. For if He had not humbled Himself and engaged the adversary by means of the cross, He would not have saved us. So the words "Authority has been given unto Me" you must understand as follows: "By My own struggles and fierce contests I have saved mankind who have become My lot and a special people." The Lord, therefore, has authority on earth because all the earth has acknowledged Him; and He has authority in heaven because the reward of those who believe in Him, as well as the place where they shall live, is in the heavens. In yet another sense does He have authority in heaven: since human nature

---

[5] Jn. 20:24-25

[6] Lk. 24:41

[7] Ps. 118:91

which formerly had been condemned is now fundamentally joined to God the Word, human nature itself sits in heaven and is worshipped by the angels. He rightly says that "All authority has been given unto Me in heaven," for human nature which had formerly been servile, now in Christ rules over all things. Considering both interpretations, then, you may understand Christ's words "All authority has been given unto Me" as follows: taking the words to have been spoken by God the Word, "All authority has been given unto Me in that those who formerly served Me with involuntary submission now also voluntarily acknowledge Me as God." But taking the words to have been spoken by human nature, understand them thus: "I, the human nature that was formerly condemned, am now God because of the unconfused union with the Son of God, and therefore I have received authority over all things, so that I am worshipped by the angels in heaven, and glorified in all the ends of the earth." He no longer sends His disciples to the Jews alone, but since He has received authority over all, and has sanctified all human nature in Himself, it is right that He sends them to all the nations, commanding the disciples to baptize them in the name of the Father, and of the Son, and of the Holy Spirit. Let Arius then be put to shame[8] because Christ did not say to baptize "in the names", but "in the name", for the name of the Three is one, the Godhead, and the Three are one God. And let Sabellius be put to shame[9] because the Lord spoke of Three Persons, and not, as that man prattles, of one person having three names, at times called the Father, at times, the Son, and at times, the Holy Spirit. But the Three Persons have one Name, which is God. Because it is not sufficient only to be baptized, but one must also labor to do good after his baptism, Christ then says, "Teaching them to observe all things whatsoever I have commanded you; not just two or three, but all My commandments." Let us tremble then, brethren, when we realize that if even one thing is lacking in us, we are not perfect servants of Christ, for we are required to keep all the commandments. See that the Lord's words contain those two essentials of Christianity: theology and active virtue. For by saying

---

[8] The false teaching of Arius, that Jesus Christ is not of one Divine Essence with the Father and the Holy Spirit in the Triune Godhead, was condemned as heresy at the First Ecumenical Council at Nicaea in 325 A.D.

[9] The false teaching of Sabellius was condemned as heresy at Church councils in Alexandria in 261 and in Rome in 262.

that it is necessary to baptize in the name of the Trinity, He handed down to us theology. And by saying that it is also necessary to teach the keeping of the commandments, He guides us in the way of active virtue. Since He is sending them out among the Gentiles to face death and danger, He gives them courage by saying, "Fear not, for I will be with you until the end of the age." See also how He mentioned the end so as to arouse in them disdain for these calamities. Do not be downcast, He says, for all things will have an end, both worldly sorrows and worldly joys. Do not be oppressed by sorrows for they will pass, and do not be deceived by good things, for they, too, will come to an end. His promise to be with them was not made only to the apostles, but to all His disciples. For of course the apostles would not live unto the end. He makes this promise even to us, and to those after us, not that He would be with us until the end, and then after the end He would depart from us—far from it! For it is rather from that moment on that He will be with us ever more clearly and distinctly. For the word "until", wherever it occurs in Scripture, does not exclude the things that come after.[10] Giving thanks, therefore, to the Lord Who is with us here, and provides us with every good thing, and again will be with us more perfectly after the end, here let us end the explanation. For to Him is due all thanksgiving, glory, and honor unto the ages of ages. Amen.

THE END OF THE HOLY GOSPEL OF ST. MATTHEW

---

[10] See commentary on Mt. 1:25, above, on p.22.

Index of Hebrew Names

The following names, the majority of them Hebrew, are interpreted by Bl. Theophylact in the *Explanation*, and their meaning is incorporated into the commentary. It is probable that Bl. Theophylact did not himself have first-hand knowledge of Hebrew, but learned what he knew of Hebrew from Greek sources such as commentaries and aids for the Old Testament. In any case Bl. Theophylact's etymologies are fairly accurate, which was not always the case in the ancient and medieval world.

Each name is followed by the interpretation given by Bl. Theophylact. Numerals refer to page number in the text of the *Explanation*.

Saint Herman of Alaska Brotherhood

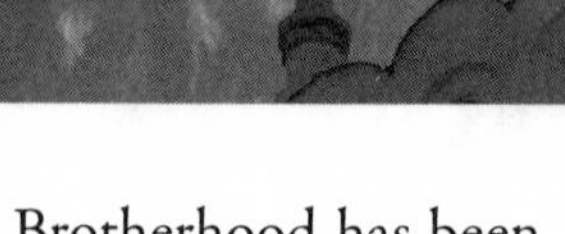

Since 1965, the St. Herman of Alaska Brotherhood has been publishing Orthodox Christian books and magazines.

View our catalog, featuring over fifty titles,
and order online, at
www.sainthermanmonastery.com

You can also write us for a free printout of our catalog:

St. Herman of Alaska Brotherhood
P. O. Box 70
Platina, CA 96076
U.S.A.